CITIES AND THE GLOBAL ENVIRONMENT

Proceedings of a European Workshop
The Hague 5-7 December 1990

CITIES AND THE GLOBAL ENVIRONMENT

Proceedings of a European Workshop
The Hague 5-7 December 1990

European Foundation
for the Improvement of Living and Working Conditions
Loughlinstown House, Shankill, Co. Dublin, Ireland.
Tel: (01) 2826888   Telex: 30726 EURF EI   Fax: 2826456

Text:
Edited by Tjeerd Deelstra
Original language: English

Production:
Foundation's Publications Officer: Susan Ryan-Sheridan
Typesetting and Design: Printset & Design Ltd, Dublin
Printing: European Foundation, Dublin, Ireland

Luxembourg: Office for Official Publications of the European Communities

Cities and the Global Environment

ISBN 92-826-3247-4

© Copyright: THE EUROPEAN FOUNDATION FOR THE IMPROVEMENT OF LIVING AND WORKING CONDITIONS, 1992 For rights of translation or reproduction, application should be made to the Director, European Foundation for the Improvement of Living and Working Conditions, Loughlinstown House, Shankill, Co. Dublin, Ireland.

PROCEEDINGS OF EUROPEAN WORKSHOP ON CITIES AND THE GLOBAL ENVIRONMENT

organised by

The European Foundation for the

Improvement of Living and Working Conditions

in co-operation with

The Municipality of The Hague

edited by

Tjeerd Deelstra

1991

The revision of the papers presented by non-English native speakers was done by **Philip Potter**, Klaus Novy Institut, Köln.

CONTENTS

Foreword
by Dr. Clive Purkiss, Director of the European Foundation
for the Improvement of Living and Working Conditions.   **11**

The editor's introduction to the proceedings
by Mr. Tjeerd Deelstra, Director of the International
Institute for the Urban Environment.   **12**

PROCEEDINGS OF PLENARY SESSION   **19**

Welcome and opening of the Workshop
by Mr. J.G.M. Alders, Minister for the Environment,
The Netherlands.   **21**

Opening address
by Mr. Sandro Giulianelli, Cabinet of Mr. Carlo Ripa di Meana,
Commission of the European Communities.   **24**

Welcome
by Mr. René Vlaanderen, Alderman for the Environment, Quality of
Life and Public Relations, The Hague.   **28**

Background, objectives and structure of the Workshop
by Dr. Clive Purkiss, Director of the European Foundation
for the Improvement of Living and Working Conditions.   **31**

Cities and the Global Environment
Introduction to the Workshop
by Mr. Tjeerd Deelstra, Director of the International
Institute for the Urban Environment.   **33**

Themes of the Workshop
Introduction by Dr. Voula Mega, the European Foundation
for the Improvement of Living and Working Conditions.   **38**

PROCEEDINGS OF WORKING GROUPS	45
Group 1: URBAN TRANSPORTATION AND INFRASTRUCTURE	47
Cities, Transport and Health by Claude A. Lamure - INRETS, Paris.	49
Transport, Urban Form and Town Size by Stephen Plowden - London.	83
Summary of discussion, recommendations.	88
Group 2: URBAN PRODUCTION AND CONSUMPTION SYSTEMS	91
Urban Resource Management in the Greenhouse Age by David Morris - Institute for Self-Reliance, Minnesota, U.S.A.	93
The Potential of European Cities for Sustainable Environmental/Energy Policy by Peter Nijkamp and Adriaan Perrels - Free University, Amsterdam.	107
Summary of discussion, recommendations.	125
Group 3: URBAN RESOURCES AND WASTE MANAGEMENT	127
The Management of Household Wastes by Daniel Beguin - ANRED, France.	131
The New Waste System of Aarhus, Denmark by Michael R. Jacobsen - Aarhus Municipality.	141
Summary of discussion, recommendations.	151
Group 4: ATTITUDES, BEHAVIOUR AND ENVIRONMENTAL CHANGES	155
The Healthy Cities Project by Heather MacDonald - WHO Regional Office for Europe.	157
The Healthy Cities Programme in the Basque Autonomous Community by Ricardo Garcia Herrera - Department of Public Health, Basque Government.	161
Urban Environment Improvement and Economic Development by Emilio Gerelli - University of Pavia, Italy.	175
Urban Planning and the Environment: A Global Approach in Search of a New Urban Balance for French Towns by N. Sougareva - Ministère de l'Environnement, Paris, France.	181

The Deterioration of the Environment:
Key Factors for a Social Contract
by Jose Quintero - Huelva, Spain. 185

Summary of discussion, recommendations. 195

Group 5: URBAN PLANNING FOR THE 21ST CENTURY 199

Athens: A Mediterranean Metropolis undergoing Radical Change
Characteristics and Future Role
by Yannis Polyzos - Ecole d'Architecture d'Athenes, Greece. 201

Technology, Cities and Planning for the 21st Century
by Sten Engelstoft - University of Copenhagen,
Denmark/Directorate General for Science, Research and
Development, Commission of the European Communities. 211

Activities of the World Meteorological Organisation in the Area of
Urban Climatology
by Jon Wieringa - World Meteorological Organisation, Geneva,
Switzerland. 225

Related Work of the Council of Europe
by Richard Hartley - Council of Europe, Strasbourg, France. 235

Man and City Environment in Developing Countries
by K. Khosh-Chashm - World Health Organisation/EMRO. 242

Summary of discussion, recommendations. 259

CONCLUSIONS AND SUGGESTIONS EMERGING FROM THE WORKSHOP
by Tjeerd Deelstra, International Institute for the Urban
Environment, Delft, The Netherlands. 265

APPENDIX 269

LIST OF PARTICIPANTS 271

FOREWORD

Until 1989, Foundation work on urban areas had focused on their social and economic aspects. When defining its four-year programme 1989-1992, the scope of the programme was widened to include urban environmental issues, and a more integrated and coordinated approach was adopted. A working group, set up to discuss priority areas recommended that the Foundation's work be centred around the organisation of three international workshops on:

- the impact of cities on the global environment;

- the improvement of the built environment and social integration in cities;

- land use management and the improvement of the built environment.

These proceedings are the outcome of the first workshops being held, annually, which was jointly organised with the Municipality of The Hague. Berlin and Lisbon will host the remaining two workshops.

The Hague workshop focused on the global environment. It looked especially at:

- urban transportation and infrastructure;

- urban production and consumption systems;

- urban resources and waste management;

- attitudes, behaviour and environmental change;

- urban planning for the 21st century.

Political leaders, policy-makers and representatives of the Governments, the Commission, the Economic and Social Committee, the social partners, international organisations and a range of other experts, all worked together in order to synthesise their collective knowledge and available information and developed ideas for innovative policy and action.

We hope that these proceedings will provide policy- and decision-makers at many levels (international, European, national, local) with information and with ideas which will be useful in a common effort to contribute to a better global environment through an improved urban environment.

Clive Purkiss
Director

Eric Verborgh
Deputy Director

**THE EDITOR'S INTRODUCTION TO THE PROCEEDINGS
BY TJEERD DEELSTRA
DIRECTOR OF THE INTERNATIONAL INSTITUTE FOR THE URBAN ENVIRONMENT**

The Proceedings of the European Workshop on CITIES AND THE GLOBAL ENVIRONMENT which was held in The Hague on 5th - 7th December 1990, are structured according to the programme of the workshop.

As can be observed from the programme on the following page, most of the time allotted to the workshop was dedicated to discussion (organised in parallel working groups).

Immediately after the plenary opening session on the morning of 6th December, participants separated into five parallel working groups for the purpose of reacting to a specified number of presentations, and for discussions relating their individual expertise to the subject themes.

The working groups continued during the afternoon of 6th December and the morning of 7th December.

The groups reconvened in plenary, where they summarised and recommended, which led to a general debate. The workshop was then concluded by a general report by the editor of these proceedings and comments from the Foundation.

Not all speakers wrote a text, but papers that were available have been reproduced here.

PROGRAMME OF WORKSHOP

Wednesday, 5 December 1990

18.30-20.30   Arrival, registration and informal getting together of participants from abroad

Thursday, 6 December 1990

MORNING SESSION

08.30-09.45   Registration of participants

10.00-10.50   **First plenary session**

  Chairman: Mr. Jørn PEDERSEN, Head of Environmental Programme, European Foundation for the Improvement of Living and Working Conditions

  Welcome and opening of the Workshop by:

  Mr. J. G. M. ALDERS, Minister for the Environment, The Netherlands

  Mr. Sandro GIULIANELLI, Cabinet of Mr. Carlo Ripa di Meana, Commission of the European Communities

  Mr. René VLAANDEREN, Alderman in charge of the Environment and Urban Management, The Hague

  Dr. Clive PURKISS, Director of the European Foundation for the Improvement of Living and Working Conditions

10.50-11.25   Introduction to the workshop by Mr. Tjeerd DEELSTRA, Director of the International Institute for the Urban Environment, and Dr. Voula MEGA, European Foundation for the Improvement of Living and Working Conditions

  Aims and organization, by the Chairman

11.25-11.50   Coffee/tea break

11.50-12.50   **Working Groups - presentation of issue papers, innovative experiments and case studies**

  The participants worked in five groups. Based notably on practical experience and examples, each group discussed and analysed the major issues within their area in the light of likely developments and trends in society and the measures taken and planned to improve the situation.

They are expected to adopt a comprehensive and integrated approach and to develop, in particular, innovative ideas about further strategies and actions for improving the urban environment in the light of the need for meeting the threat which urban concentrations pose to the global environment.

GROUP 1: URBAN TRANSPORTATION AND INFRASTRUCTURE

Chairman: Mr. Ariel ALEXANDRE, OECD

Rapporteur: Prof. Enrique CALDERÓN, ETSI Caminos, Madrid

Presentation of papers by:
- Mr. Claude LAMURE, Institut National de Recherche sur les Transports et leur Sécurité (INRETS), Paris
- Mr. Stephen PLOWDEN, London
- Mr. Laurent SELLES, DRIVE Programme, Commission of the European Communities
- Mr. Jack SHORT, European Conference of Ministers of Transport (7 December a.m.)

GROUP 2: URBAN PRODUCTION AND CONSUMPTION SYSTEMS

Chairman: Dr. Michael J. BANNON, Director of the Service Industries Research Centre, Dept. of Urban and Regional Planning, University College Dublin

Rapporteur: Mr. Hugh WILLIAMS, Joint Managing Director, ECOTEC Research and Consulting Ltd., Birmingham

Presentation of papers by:
- Prof. Peter NIJKAMP, Free University of Amsterdam
- Representative of the COMPASS Programme, OECD
  (the paper prepared by Dr. David Morris and presented in group 3 should also be considered as a background paper for the discussion in group 2)

GROUP 3: URBAN RESOURCES AND WASTE MANAGEMENT

Chairman: Mr. D.W. PURCHON, Director of Health and Consumer Services, Sheffield

Rapporteur: Mr. Serge KEMPENEERS, Institut Bruxellois pour la Gestion de l'Environnement

Presentation of papers by:
- Dr. David MORRIS, Institute for Local Self-Reliance, Washington D.C.

- Mr. Daniel BEGUIN, Head of Consumption Department, Agence Nationale pour la Récupération et l'Elimination des Déchets (ANRED) - Le Transformeur, Angers
- Mr. Michael R. JACOBSEN, City Chief Engineer, Municipality of Aarhus

GROUP 4: ATTITUDES, BEHAVIOUR AND ENVIRONMENTAL CHANGES

Chairperson: Ms. Jacqueline MILLER, Free University of Brussels

Rapporteur: Dr. Edith BRICKWELL, Senate of Berlin

Presentation of papers by:
- Ms. Heather MACDONALD, Consultant, Healthy Cities Project, WHO Regional Office for Europe
- Mr. Ricardo GARCIA, Department of Public Health, Basque Government
- Prof. Emilio GERELLI, University of Pavia
- Ms. N. SOUGAREVA, Ministère de l'Environnement, Paris
- Mr. Jose QUINTERO, Huelva, Spain

GROUP 5: URBAN PLANNING FOR THE 21ST CENTURY

Chairperson: Ms. Wendy O'CONGHAILE, European Foundation for the Improvement of Living and Working Conditions

Rapporteur: Prof. Kai LEMBERG, Roskilde University

Presentation of papers by:
- Mr. Yannis POLYZOS, Assistant Professor at the School of Architecture, Technical University of Athens
- Dr. Sten ENGELSTOFT, FAST-Programme, Commission of the European Communities
- Prof. John WIERINGA, World Meteorological Organisation
- Mr. Richard HARTLEY, Council of Europe
- Mr. Kawmers KOSH-CHASHM, World Health Organisation, EMRO, Alexandria

13.00-14.30   Lunch

Thursday, 6 December 1990

AFTERNOON SESSION

14.30-16.00   Presentation of papers (cont.) and working groups discussion. The groups considered the following issues within their specific theme:

- the policies and actions required in the short, medium and long term at the global, European, national and local levels and the likely implications for key activities in society;

- the mechanisms through which goals can be achieved and the role of the various actors in this process (international organizations, European Community institutions and bodies, governments, cities, industry, social partners and citizens);

- examples of good practice, particularly innovative and successful responses at the various levels;

- the implications for the work of the European Community institutions, notably the Commission, in the light of the Green Paper on the Urban Environment of 27 June 1990 (the groups are expected to discuss and put forward ideas regarding the areas covered by and the proposals made in this paper, insofar as they relate to the global environment); the implications for the work of Community agencies and bodies (including the Foundation) as well as international organisations.

16.00-16.30   Coffee/tea break

16.30-18.00   Working groups discussion (cont.)

18.30-22.00   Reception and dinner hosted by the Dutch Ministry of Housing, Physical Planning and Environment and the City of The Hague

Friday, 7 December 1990

MORNING SESSION

09.00-11.00   Working groups discussion (conclusion); preparation of reports and recommendations

11.00-11.30   Coffee/tea break

11.30-12.45   **Second plenary session**

                 Chairman : Mr. Eric VERBORGH, Deputy Director of the
                            European Foundation for the Improvement of
                            Living and Working Conditions

                 Presentation of reports and recommendations from working
                 groups

12.55-14.15   Lunch

Friday, 7 December 1990

AFTERNOON SESSION

14.15-16.00   **Third plenary session**

                 Chairman : Mr. Eric VERBORGH

14.15-15.00   Discussion on the reports and recommendations from the
                 working groups

15.00-15.50   General questions and discussions on conclusions and
                 suggestions emerging from the workshop

                 General Rapporteur: Mr. Tjeerd DEELSTRA

15.50-16.00   Concluding comments and closure of the Workshop by the
                 Chairman

PROCEEDINGS OF PLENARY SESSION

**WELCOME AND OPENING OF THE WORKSHOP
BY MR. J.G.M. ALDERS
MINISTER FOR THE ENVIRONMENT, THE NETHERLANDS**

Ladies and gentlemen,

By the year 2000 half of the world's population will be living in urban areas. This is one of the points made by the Brundtland Commission in its report entitled "Our Common Future". The same conclusion has been reached by the United Nations Commission on Human Settlements (UNCHS).

The reports draw attention to the serious crisis affecting cities in developing countries. I shall confine myself to discussing the problems confronting conurbations in industrialised countries.

"Our Common Future" concludes that we are faced with a deteriorating situation. The infrastructure in these conurbations is in decline, the environment will be further damaged and the inhabitants will be caught up in a downward spiral of poverty and environmental degradation.

The intergovernmental conference on Human Settlements and Sustainable Development, held last month in The Hague, confirmed the emerging pattern of deteriorating living and working conditions. The principal victims will be the poorer sections of the population. Moreover, developments of this kind in urban areas will also contribute to the deterioration of the environment and the exhaustion of sources of aid.

A recent report by the World Health Organisation's regional office for Europe underlines yet again the adverse effects of air pollution on health and life expectancy, specifically in these urban areas. Alarming reports on the dire environmental situation in central and eastern Europe only confirm this picture.

Fortunately, not all European cities are affected in this way. Many of them have made great efforts to reverse the downward trend. Improvement and renewal of the urban milieu is already an important component of the policies of a number of national governments. This also applies to the Netherlands, and at this point I should like to give a brief outline of our policy.

When it comes to urban renewal, proper care for the environment is regarded as an important starting-point. This involves understanding - and intervening in - the city's metabolism (the relationship between production and ecology) and conscious control of the interaction between more artificial and more natural structures as a point of application for differentiating the urban environment (the relationship between structure and ecology).

A factor of major importance here is the relationship between the quality of the physical environment and the sustainability of that quality. There is no sense in maintaining quality by repeatedly intervening in a situation which is itself steadily declining. The quality of the physical environment requires structural conditions which make it easy to maintain by normal, careful management methods.

What aspects do such structural conditions involve?

- first of all, reducing and preventing environmental pollution;
- then, organising land use;
- then, integrated management;
- and finally, integrating ecological functions into and with the city;

I will use an example to illustrate these aspects more fully.

The first point involves reducing and controlling environmental pollution to such an extent that vulnerable activities can continue to exist. In practice, this aim will not always be fully realisable, certainly in an intensively urbanised area such as the Randstad. Examples are zones around airports, sites with heavy industrial and distribution activities and locations adjoining busy main roads. This problem is obviously crucial in connection with the Schiphol and Rijnmond Action Plans.

Organising land use involves limiting energy consumption and environmental pollution by stepping up the intensity of urban land use - for example by building compactly and durably - and by coordinating living and working activities at district level. The principal means of achieving the latter aim must be an improved policy for locating industry and commerce - putting the right factory or office in the right place.

Integrated management can ensure the sensible use of supplies of energy, water and materials in and around the urban area. The most important aspect of water management will be the way in which rainwater drainage is dealt with.

As regards integration, areas that are crucial for the ecological (infra)structure must be spared from urbanisation. Where this is not possible, there must be concrete plans for integrating ecological functions into and with the city. This involves integration on three levels:

- connection with the rural area around the city, for example by creating areas of woodland and wetland on the urban fringes;

- as regards the structure of green spaces, connection between landscape green space and urban green space, for example by maintaining and strengthening a "lobe" pattern (Amsterdam);

- establishment, zoning and management of urban parks to connect up with the "green lungs" and in combination with the creation of low-density traffic routes.

The problems of conurbations have not reached the same stage everywhere in Europe. Owing to political, social and economic differences, less attention is devoted to such problems in some European countries. Possibly the account of Dutch policy I have sketched out here may suggest some starting-points for these countries.

So far I have not mentioned the global environment which features in the name of this workshop. Since the Second World Climate Conference held in Geneva in early November, climatic change has been recognised as a world problem requiring immediate action at world level.

Scientific studies have already highlighted the consequences of climatic change for urban areas and in particular for the giant conurbations of the developing countries. Among the aspects that come to mind are changes in groundwater levels, deterioration of drinking-water supplies, changed patterns of agricultural production and the consequences of a rising sea level.

We ourselves have created this common external threat by our own actions. It is up to us, therefore, to ensure that sustainable development can take place in our cities.

Ladies and gentlemen, today is the second time I have spoken on the theme of cities and the global environment. The first time was in the Japanese city of Osaka in June this year (Osaka International Forum on Global Environment and the City). There I tried briefly to explain how we in the Netherlands have learnt to handle urbanisation and de-urbanisation and how we take account of the needs of the global environment at city level.

But at this workshop we are dealing with a subject on which the last word has certainly not yet been spoken. The initiative taken by the European Foundation for the Improvement of Living and Working Conditions in organising the workshop therefore deserves the highest praise. I hope that your conclusions, when you come to formulate them tomorrow, will contribute to further debate on this important subject. I wish you every success.

**OPENING ADDRESS
BY MR. SANDRO GIULANELLI
CABINET OF MR. CARLO RIPA DI MEANA
COMMISSION OF THE EUROPEAN COMMUNITIES**

The Green Paper on the urban environment, as published by the Commission of the European Communities in 1990, was conceived as a useful means of establishing the framework for effective Community action to be taken in close co-operation with the municipal authorities and national governments.

Although the aim was not to prepare a treatise on the ills of our cities and their remedies nor to cover the whole subject in every detail, preparation of the Green Paper proved to be a somewhat complex operation. First there was widespread consultation, which took the form of a series of international conferences. These were held last year and gave people the opportunity, in person, to contribute information and ideas, proposals and suggestions.

This Green Paper breaks new ground in that, for the first time, the Commission of the European Communities is taking a general approach to the problems facing our cities, rather than the usual piecemeal sectoral approach.

There is ample justification for the Commission's interest in the urban environment, and the commitment it has shown, since more than 80% of Europe's population (i.e. some 250 million people) lives in urban areas. Although city-dwellers enjoy all the advantages of city life, they also have to put up with all the disadvantages of the "urban condition", in other words, the heavy environmental burdens under which our cities suffer.

Moreover, because they are so highly developed and because of the density of population and activities concentrated within them, urban areas are sources of pollution. Hence measures to improve environmental conditions in cities will have major repercussions on the environment as a whole, particularly with regard to the greenhouse effect and acid rain.

Obviously the urban environment is first and foremost a local or national problem. The Commission of the European Communities does certainly not want to set itself up as some kind of "super-body" making plans and presenting solutions in a centralised manner. We are fully aware of all the ramifications of urban problems and of the profound differences between the cities of Europe, each of which requires specific solutions and specific plans.

However, urban environmental problems often have a major impact outside the confines of the municipal area and affect much larger areas (I am thinking here, for example, of the pollution of the major rivers of Europe which cross national boundaries and have pollutants discharged into them by many different cities). Because of the scale of these problems they need to be tackled jointly, and to this end it is useful to exchange notes on as wide a scale as possible and to encourage more specific Community commitment.

The first task is to identify and quantify the environmental problems affecting urban areas. Our international conferences made it quite clear that there is a shortage of general and easily comparable data.

Very few cities have reliable quantitative data on specific environmental problems like noise, atmospheric pollution and waste treatment. This means that general assessment of the urban environment problems facing the Community tends to be qualitative and subjective. In most cases we know the nature of the problem but not its scale. I feel that it is a priority to use methods of measuring and controlling environmental conditions on a systematic and comparable basis and, to this end, the proposed European Environment Agency could be of tremendous help.

We then need to open up the debate and identify the causes behind urban environment problems. To this end I feel that it would be extremely useful to engage in general discussions on the effects which the single market in 1992 will have on our cities by, in many cases, emphasising the impact of market forces. In fact, the probable increase in competition between European cities to attract economic activities and investment will be a double-edged sword.

In one respect, competition will force cities to offer a better and more "competitive" environmental quality and standard of living. However, cities will also be more disposed to accommodate companies or conglomerates wishing to set up premises or develop activities which are not always compatible with the size and structure of those cities. There is thus a risk that some patterns of deterioration already taking place in the urban areas of Europe will be speeded up, like the building of office blocks in old city centres, which drives out the residents who then move out to individual houses in increasingly far-flung and low-quality outlying areas, thus increasing traffic congestion.

I therefore feel that we should all pool our thoughts on these problems in order to provide local authorities with the best methods of tackling the problems ahead. This should be done precisely by improving cities because it is the cities which are fighting the biggest battles on the environment.

Some consider cities to be the root cause of the pollution which is gradually undermining our quality of life. The city is then portrayed as an environmental catastrophe from which it is necessary to escape.

The Green Paper takes an opposing view, based on these anti-urban principles, that the city is rather the context in which the problems facing our society are expressed and concentrated, often in their most acute form. Would it not therefore make more sense to see cities as the key to solving these problems? To this end we feel that it is necessary to rethink the way in which today's cities are organised and developed.

Town planners are aware that the mechanical application of the principles of functionalism has resulted in people being forced to travel, and to travel alone, producing noise, atmospheric pollution and congestion of public areas. If, instead of keeping each function separate, cities are planned so that the whole range of activities and functions are combined and grouped together in each part of the city, the problem of mobility becomes less acute because the various urban functions are all easily accessible in the vicinity.

Traffic is in fact one of the most serious problems. Europe now has 379 cars for every 1000 inhabitants, which adds up to some 120 million cars in all. It has been estimated that, if the trend continues, this number will increase by 35% over the next 20 years, which will mean another 45 million cars, and consequently more jams, congestion and pollution.

What can be done about this? Clearly the answer is not to increase the capacity of towns for absorbing traffic by building viaducts and urban motorways.

The example of Paris is significant. It has shelved grandiose plans for high-speed road tunnels because it has been shown that to increase capacity by building new infrastructure attracts more traffic and thus causes further environmental deterioration, often destroying the historical features of the cities in which these major infrastructure projects are carried out.

In Brussels, a city which symbolises Europe, whole areas have been destroyed, and unfortunately are still being destroyed, to make way for huge office blocks and various infrastructure. There the opposite problem arises: the need to seriously restrict private car access to the centre (which is one of the main thrusts of the Green Paper) and, obviously, to improve public transport instead.

Each specific case requires a different solution depending on the nature of the city and its geography. In Oslo, for example, anyone wishing to drive into the old centre has to buy an entrance ticket.

Clearly, if the city is to play its proper environmental and social role, it must maintain its specific character as a place of diversity and concentration.

"The right to cities" is the title of a well known book by Henry Lefèvre which appeared in March 1968. What does this right entail today? I think that basically the right to cities is the right to variety, because it is in cities that this variety is concentrated: past and present, young and old, rich and poor, locals and immigrants.

The town planner who adopts the functionalist approach, on the other hand, divides up the city into a number of separate areas which have the same social make-up and the same activities, so that each individual is to some extent isolated and perceives the world only within the small confines of his television screen or the larger confines of the hypermarket.

The city is the exact antithesis of all this. It is the place where people meet and the unlikely happens, where there are all kinds of changing social relationships and infinite possibilities. This is the meaning behind the famous phrase "Stadtluft macht frei" ("City air lets you breathe").

I believe that the next few years will provide the cities of Europe with a real opportunity to revert to this vital role, which the intensification of the environmental crisis is threatening to take away. Although their situations vary, Europe's cities are now going through a transitional stage. The abandonment of industrial areas, for example, is perhaps the clearest sign that we are finally shaking off the methods of planning the physical, functional, economic and social aspects of cities which we inherited from the nineteenth century.

The decline of industrial areas also highlights the fact that we are also gradually abandoning major technological infrastructure like gasometers, marshalling yards, bridges, canals, port infrastructure, wharfs and quays, and major social infrastructure like hospitals, prisons, schools and markets, and vast military areas.

Because more and more areas are becoming vacant or suddenly no longer serve a specific purpose, we face the problem of trying to decide how to reuse this land in such a way as to revive the city and to change the way it is organised. In this awkward transitional stage, it is my view that attention to environmental problems is of fundamental importance and essential if cities are to become once again focal points for social intercourse and a sense of community.

In this connection, the Green Paper lists a number of possible areas of action, including town planning, transport, protection and enhancement of the cultural heritage of the cities of Europe, water management, management of the city's energy supply, protection of the natural environment in cities and urban waste.

As I said at the beginning, courses of action are still to be discussed and investigated. After that, the operational stage will consist, on the one hand, of preparation of specific Community directives or recommendations and, on the other, of the launching of pilot schemes to be carried out in conjunction with the municipal authorities on the various aspects of the urban environment problem.

From this meeting, and from all the others which have been organised in other cities of Europe, we are hoping for suggestions and criticism which will help us to devise more effective ways of bringing about a substantial improvement in the urban environment. In this connection, I would like to thank all of you present for the contribution I know you will make to our efforts.

**WELCOME BY MR. RENÉ VLAANDEREN
ALDERMAN FOR THE ENVIRONMENT, QUALITY OF LIFE AND PUBLIC RELATIONS
THE HAGUE**

Mr. Chairman, Mr. Minister, Ladies and Gentlemen,

Our cities, on the one hand, are splendid and radiant, marvels of technical innovation in the field of architecture, traffic and information technology.

But on the other hand in those same cities we see a tremendous consumption and waste of raw materials and an ever-growing need for energy resources, an increasing impairment of the environment through the pollution of soil, water and air and as a result of this the depletion and destruction of ecosystems leading, among other things, to less biological diversity.

This being so no one can deny that cities are important sources of global change. Cities change the quality of the air, the temperature, the rain and the earth not only locally but on a world scale.

Human behaviour has consequences for the environment, for the way we live together, for the quality of life here and elsewhere in the world. We now know that our natural resources are not inexhaustible. The regenerative capacity of water, soil, air has its limits.

If we want to keep the earth a place worth living in we will have to put an end to the way we are exploiting our environment - and fast, right now in fact.

We should increasingly allow ourselves to be guided in our behaviour by our environmental awareness and knowledge.

If we revert to the subject of this conference: "Cities and the Global Environment" the points of departure for urban policy will have to be checked against certain criteria, a number of which I should like to mention:

- refraining from using limited or non-renewable natural raw materials (for example, tropical hard woods);

- combating pollution of air, water, soil contamination and destruction of ecosystems as well as climate change through other forms of urban building and town planning;

- promotion of other production methods and other consumer behaviour (refraining from using environmentally harmful materials);

- reduction in car traffic and promotion of public transport;

- economical energy consumption;

- paying more attention to the physical and psychological health of city dwellers. Ideas which have led notably to the Healthy City Movement;

- developing and implementing environmental education and information programmes thus giving substance to the slogan **"Think Globally, Act Locally"**.

As an alderman of the city of The Hague I am responsible among other things for the environment and the quality of life in our city. Together with the city management service, work is being done to improve the urban environment in our city in various ways.

I should like to give you a number of examples:

- In the Hague traffic plan the general objective is that no more car kilometres should be travelled in The Hague region in 1995 than in 1990. For this purpose public transport has to be considerably improved and the situation made more attractive to cyclists.

- The use of hard wood in The Hague is being abolished.

- 100 bottle banks were placed in The Hague in 1980. Nowadays every neighbourhood has its own bottle bank. 5500 tonnes of glass per annum are offered for recycling in more than 250 bottle banks.

- In four districts in The Hague vegetable, fruit and garden waste is collected separately on a voluntary basis. This produces 922 tonnes per year which is subsequently composted. This form of separate collection of waste will be considerably extended in the next few years.

- In 1985 a modest start was made on the separate collection of small chemical waste. At the moment two chemical waste collectors travel through the city to collect such waste at about 310 collection points. This produces an annual 250 tonnes.

- Ecological corridors are currently being taken into account in the lay-out and organisation of the city: these are green corridors between areas linking nature areas, parks, the urban peripheries and country estates so as to promote the mobility of plants, birds and insects.

- The Hague was the first city in the Netherlands to appoint an urban ecologist in 1988 to take stock of the natural assets and to address the issue of ecological corridors as part of the arrangements for the lay-out of the city. An attempt is being made, under the guidance of the urban ecologist, to reintroduce wild flowers in roadside verges and along the water banks with the aim of bridging the gap between the urban and rural environment.

- A lot of attention is paid in our city to environmental education programmes. Every year has a theme. This year the theme is waste. Schools are involved as well as all kinds of organisations working with and for adults. The programme draws attention to the immense amount of waste which we produce unnecessarily, the depletion of natural resources and looks at concepts such as recycling and patterns of consumption.

- You will find twelve city farms in The Hague often combined with educational gardens and environmental education centres. A guiding principle is that environmental education can only be successful if we take as a point of departure peoples' own social structures, their own living environment and world of experience. You have to begin close to home with familiar examples and then proceed in ever-increasing circles via the local surroundings, the city, the region, the country to the world.

The provision of educational facilities in the middle of residential districts has the big advantage that locals can be immediately involved in city management. The result is that local residents then tend to keep a closer eye on what is going on around them and there is less vandalism. Furthermore youngsters meet older people and a mixture of contacts arise among the ethnic groups. Social interaction and integration can lead to better mutual understanding. For environmental education this is a prerequisite. After all environmental education leads to environmental awareness, to willingness to carry responsibility, wanting to be involved in what is happening around one but also to interest in the wider world and to a multiracial community which is prepared to give form and content to a harmonious and healthy environment.

For me this means a reversal in our thinking, a breaking point in our behaviour. It requires responsibility, daring and creativity in the approach to short-term problems and to longer-term thinking. It also requires exchange of information and cooperation to feed that different way of thinking.

It will be in this spirit that you will be preoccupied during this conference. I should like to wish you every success and would like to close by observing that the Burgomaster and Aldermen of the city of The Hague are very glad that you have chosen to hold your conference in our city. As the alderman who is also responsible for Tourism and Public Relations I cannot refrain from pointing out to you that The Hague has a lot to offer in the field of culture, history and modern architecture, urban renewal, parks and other gardens. I hope that you will have pleasant memories of your visit to The Hague.

BACKGROUND, OBJECTIVES AND STRUCTURE OF THE WORKSHOP
BY DR. CLIVE PURKISS
DIRECTOR OF THE EUROPEAN FOUNDATION FOR THE IMPROVEMENT
OF LIVING AND WORKING CONDITIONS

BACKGROUND OF THE WORKSHOP

The Foundation's work in urban areas focused, until 1989, on the social and economic aspects, as the projects on environmental aspects in the four-year programme 1985-1988 had to be abandoned owing to lack of resources. When defining its four-year programme 1989-1992, the Foundation decided, however, to re-introduce urban environmental issues so as to enable it to adopt an integrated and co-ordinated approach as reflected, inter alia, in the Single European Act, combining the environmental, social and economic problems which affect a number of urban areas in the Community. A working group was set up to discuss the priority areas to be included in the work programmes 1990-1992 and the ways in which this effort would be the most effective in view of the considerable number of studies already undertaken at the national and international level.

The group recommended that the Foundation's work be centred around the organization of three international workshops (one to be held each year) focusing on the following three key issues:

- the role of cities in relation to the global environment;

- social polarisation and the urban environment;

- land use management and environmental improvements.

The group also suggested that the workshops be held in different European cities, which would be invited to act as hosts, and that they be attended by representatives of the governments, the European Parliament, the Commission of the European Communities, the Economic and Social Committee, the social partners and international organisations as well as political leaders and other policy-makers of European cities and independent and internationally acknowledged experts.

OBJECTIVES OF THE WORKSHOPS ON THE URBAN ENVIRONMENT

The three workshops together will cover most of the major existing and foreseeable environmental issues in urban areas and their social and economic context. They are expected to highlight, in particular, recent developments and trends as well as innovations and to indicate possible solutions. They will therefore constitute a valuable source of information for the parties involved, notably local and central government, the European Community institutions and international organizations, as well as a unique opportunity for exchange of ideas. Moreover, the workshop in The Hague will provide the Commission with a first European-wide and representative response to its proposals in the Green Paper on the Urban Environment.

In view of these considerations, the principal objectives of the workshop are the following:

- to pull together and synthesise information on existing and planned research and actions and to analyse this information in a wider environmental and socio-economic policy context;

- to develop ideas on innovative policies and actions;

- in doing so, to support the Commission's work on the urban environment;

- to disseminate the above-mentioned information, analyses and innovative ideas in a way which make them useful for policy- and decision-makers at the various levels (international, European, national, local).

STRUCTURE AND CONTENT OF WORKSHOP ON CITIES AND THE GLOBAL ENVIRONMENT

The workshop will consist of two relatively short plenary sessions, one at the beginning and one at the end, and of longer sessions in the five working groups, so as to allow in-depth discussions and analyses of specific issues based, inter alia, on a number of papers presented in or made available to the groups.

The workshop will focus on the following key areas in relation to the **global environment**:

- urban transportation and infrastructure;

- urban production and consumption systems;

- urban resources and waste management;

- attitudes, behaviour and environmental change;

- urban planning for the 21st century.

In each of these areas, the working groups are expected to consider, in particular:

- the policies and actions needed at the various levels in the short, medium and long term and the likely implications for key activities in society;

- the mechanisms required and the role of the actors involved;

- examples of good practice, notably innovative and successful responses at the various levels;

- the implications for the work of the European Community institutions, notably the Commission, in the light of the Green Paper on the Urban Environment of 27 June 1990, and for the work of Community agencies and bodies (including the Foundation) as well as international organizations.

I wish you a very successful meeting.

CITIES AND THE GLOBAL ENVIRONMENT

Introduction to the Workshop
by Tjeerd Deelstra
Director of the International Institute for the Urban Environment
Delft, The Netherlands

INTRODUCTION

1. Environmental impacts of cities

Cities are centres of economic and cultural activities. In order to make cities places that are productive and creative, cities extract resources from the natural environment, with risks of exhaustion, extinction, damage and disruption of natural species and ecosystems.

Cities attract people and import materials, half-products and marketable products from elsewhere; they also export services and products to other cities and rural areas.

While the city attracts resources, people and goods from nearby and remote hinterlands, and exports to markets outside the city, a considerable flow of traffic and transport is required which seriously affects the environment.

Cities are also centres of locally produced pollution. The conventional way to minimise the negative health impacts of pollution in the city is to remove pollutants to outside. This can be done by building higher chimneys and longer pipelines, or by dumping wastes downstream or in rural areas.

2. Scale of environmental problems related to urban activities

Although the conventional policy to solve threats to the urban environment is by the removal of pollutants and wastes, it is difficult to solve all kinds of problems by these means. For this reason cities suffer from insufficient cleaning and removal of waste water and solid wastes, from polluted soils at (former) industrial sites, from polluted and unhealthy buildings, urban smog and air pollution in streets, from noise and accidents. Problems of this kind require forceful environmental policies at the local level.

As a consequence of conventional policies to remove pollutants and wastes from cities to outside areas, pollution is mounting up at the regional level. Depositions in lakes and seas (this includes the accumulation of non-degradable waste and chemicals in soils under water), and leakages from solid waste dumps are disrupting water-related natural systems. There are also negative effects on regional terrestrial ecosystems, caused by waste incineration in cities, mining for urban industry and extraction of ground water for city use.

Cities are not only a threat to air, water and soils in regions. The uncontrolled urban sprawl has unnecessary negative impacts on natural areas such as forests, and also limits agricultural use of the land. As cities are mostly located in fertile areas the latter is frequently the case. Important impacts also stem from recreational activities of urban dwellers, who seek compensation for the stresses of modern life in cities and move in weekly or seasonal rhythms to rural, mountainous, or coastal areas.

In connection with local policies, concentrated action at regional levels is now needed in order to restore disrupted environments and to structure developments towards making urbanised regions attractive again.

There are also local pollutants that affect the environment at the scale of Europe as a whole. The air above Europe is heavily polluted. Acid rain has impacts on all urban areas causing damage to monuments, thus endangering the rich architectural heritage of Europe. Acid rain also affects green spaces in cities and urban forests, and has a negative impact on the productivity of agricultural systems and on the biological diversity of the European landscapes (forest die-out).

Next to air pollution in Europe, water pollution is a serious problem. The hydrological infrastructure of Europe, determined by the Atlantic, the North Sea, the Irish Sea, the Baltic, the Mediterranean and the Black Sea, polar seas and major rivers such as the Rhine, Rhone, Volga and Danube (as well as more local and regional river-systems such as Dnjestr, Dnjepr, Don and Dwina, Seine, Loire, Garonne, Visla, Ebro and Po) are intensively affected by waste streams from industry and households in cities. Apart from the negative impact on coastal and rural ecosystems, the latter reduces possibilities for commercial fisheries and recreation, and limits the possibilities of cities to extract clean healthy water for industries and households. In some cases water is polluted by nuclear waste. Calamities caused by the chemical industry occasionally endanger urban water resources. Causes of the environmental threats described here are again local and action to prevent pollution is necessary at the local level, but complimentary coordinated policies at European level are required too.

In addition to environmental problems, recognised at the scale of the European continent and its related areas, environmental effects can now be observed on a global scale. These effects and how to prevent them are the subject of this particular workshop.

It is internationally admitted that cities all over the world play a key role in developments that lead to the greenhouse effect and the depletion of the ozone layer, and to irreversible reduction of global and biological diversity (which is determining the sustainability of the Earth's human life-support system). Cities cause irreparable damage to the global environment by contributing largely and in a particularly concentrated way to these effects.

The climate system of the world is, in particular, influenced by the rather intense level of energy consumption of cities in the Northern Hemisphere, and the related amount of emission of carbon dioxide. The production in cities of methane (CH_4), nitrous oxide (N_2O), tropospheric ozone (O_3) and chlorofluorocarbons (CFC's) also contribute to climate change.

Among the effects of the increased earthly greenhouse are: a general rise of temperature, causing sea level rise and changes in oceanic movements (of cold and hot water). This will occasionally lead to local storms and increased rainfall, or local draughts and heatwaves. In general the water cycle in Europe will change fundamentally with consequences for available water needed for consumption and industry in cities, and transport over waterways.

Changes in the water cycle will affect green spaces and trees in cities. Changes in temperature and the water cycle may also affect human health in cities; heatwaves may lead to the death of vulnerable groups within the urban population; changes in insect populations (including pests) may lead to the outburst of infectious diseases in cities and towns.

The changes in urban living and working conditions might result in migration from cities that face degrading environments, towards cities which profit from climatic changes (in particular the Northern parts of Europe). Areas of tourism, such as the Alps, might lose their attractiveness because skiing is no longer possible (no snowfall). The Mediterranean might become too hot and dry for recreation.

The depletion of the ozone layer of the stratosphere will reduce the earth's capacity to absorb solar ultraviolet (UV) radiation, which may increase skin cancer, eye disorder and immune suppression, and influence bioproductivity and green spaces in cities.

Apart from changes in climatic conditions and the depletion of ozone, the rapid reduction of biodiversity is equally important, endangering the human and urban life support system of the Earth. Cities contribute heavily to this environmental threat. Species will become extinct as a result of changes in temperature, hydrological conditions and UV radiation, but acidification is also a serious contributor to the reduction in the number of species. The Earth's aquatic and terrestrial ecosystems are heavily affected by acid depositions.

Acidification is caused by the production of nitrogen oxides (NO) and sulfur dioxide (SO_2). Once produced in cities they are transformed in the atmosphere by catalytic and photochemical reactions. After travelling a few hundred kilometres the chemicals are precipitated. In aquatic ecosystems, fish and other organisms die; terrestrial systems are influenced by changes in soil and vegetation, leading to slow growth or "forest die-back" in coniferous as well as deciduous trees.

Due to the growing international relations in trade and commerce, the hinterlands and markets of European cities can be found in developing and less developed countries, which export timber, raw materials and agricultural products to the North; thus reducing the diversity of the biosphere.

At present the greatest loss of species and genetic diversity takes place as a result of deforestation in tropical rain forests, which contain over half of the Earth's species. As a consequence subterranean organisms conditioning soil fertility are becoming extinct, thus reducing the capacity of the Earth's species to reproduce and continue to maintain food chains in natural communities. Cities in Europe play a key-role in deforestation of the tropics. The Netherlands now uses approximately 13 million hectares in developing countries for the food industry in and around Dutch cities. These 13 million hectares can be found in Thailand (for export of cassave and tapioca), in Malaysia (for export of soya and palm oil) and in Brazil (for export of soya; all contributing to the Dutch food industry, in addition to the 2.4 million hectares of agricultural areas in the Netherlands itself. Other European countries demonstrate comparable figures.

Urbanised regions in Europe effect ecosystems in tropical zones in similar ways by importing steel, other minerals and oil from vulnerable areas in developing countries.

In addition to the attack on ecosystems and pillaging of the tropical forests for export to the North European cities, vulnerable ecosystems in developing countries are affected by the import of dangerous waste products (such as nuclear and chemical waste) from the richer countries, which are dumped or stored in the Third World.

Natural habitats in Europe itself rapidly become extinct as result of the continuing process of changes in land-use and uncontrolled urban growth, in combination with acidification. This also reduces global biological diversity.

3. Urban policies

Our society is more and more an urban one and our economic system is increasingly urban.

The European Community of Twelve contains 229 cities with more than 330,000 inhabitants; 122 of them have a core population exceeding 200,000 inhabitants (definition for cities in EP's Session Document, A2-0294-88) many more medium sized and small towns and cities can be found in Europe. The communality of environmental problems caused by cities and towns and the recognition of its European dimension, calls for a wide range of joint actions, as expressed in the Green Paper.

This workshop concentrates on the global issues related to urban structures and processes. Questions are:

What can be done on various scales or administrative/political levels to reduce impacts of cities on the global environment?

What are, in particular, opportunities for and within the European Community?

The conventional approach to urban environmental problems (as characterised in the first section of this introduction) is working towards the mitigation of dangerous effects, but would it not be better to prevent environmental problems, and develop a policy concentrating on the sources of pollution, rather than on the effects?

Concentrating policies on the sources of pollution will certainly lead to new systems of transport and production, and of consumption in cities. This is not only a matter of technology or physical urban planning, but the subject of economic and cultural change.

New policies would lead to forms of urban management that seek to reduce the level of urban consumption of energy, water, food and raw materials, that are selective in the kind of resources that are used, that look for opportunities for recycling and recovery, amongst others, in order to reduce waste streams from cities. Less transport of people and goods by energy-intensive traffic between, and in cities would be another target for a new policy for sustainable development. New urban policies also include more careful site-specific urban planning, more compact urban design and better management of green spaces and urban landscapes.

Each city or town is unique. This implies that in order to improve environmental conditions it is important that cities can learn from each other and that local experiences and approaches can be exchanged.

However, when all is said and done, we all live and work in a local situation, most of us in cities or towns. Learning from experiences at the city level seems to be the most productive approach. The development of a wider European urban policy at supranational level is strongly dependent on local experiences. The European Community is in fact able to facilitate learning and exchange of experience. Local approaches can be supported but in addition they can be completed by policies at higher levels. The European Community could develop such complementary policies on a European scale for urban areas.

THEMES OF THE WORKSHOP

Introduction by Dr. Voula Mega
European Foundation for the
Improvement of Living and Working Conditions

EUROPEAN WORKSHOP ON CITIES AND THE GLOBAL ENVIRONMENT

The workshop is structured into 5 working groups, which discuss local projects, programmes and approaches.

The working groups of this workshop will have the task of examining the relationships of major urban components, activities and sectors with global environmental issues, and the policies needed for achieving the least polluting (and most livable) city. Dividing the meeting into groups is due to practical and methodological reasons. In every working group it should be recognised that there is a need for a holistic approach and comprehensive policy.

In general: The international implications of pollution originating from

European dimension are the main factors relating the urban environment to the global environment.

I) GROUP 1: URBAN TRANSPORTATION AND INFRASTRUCTURE

Urban transport is a major contributor in NO_x emissions and an important contributor in CO and CO_2 emissions. In many cities, the transport sector is responsible for almost 90% of carbon monoxide emissions, while, for CO_2, almost half of transport combustion is estimated to be due to urban traffic. Urban traffic is, therefore, a major contributor to acid rain and the greenhouse effect. The major actions, concerning urban transportation and targeting the improvement of the global environment, which should be discussed, are:

1.1 Balance between modes of transport; favouring public transport and bicycle over private car; giving priority to the pedestrian

Traffic structure and traffic capacity in the European cities. Experiences in shifting the balance to public transport. Urban transportation expenditure and effectiveness. Supply and demand for public transport. Compromise between the desired trips of separate users and the features (particularly speed and cost) of the modes available. Urban growth patterns favouring the use of the private car and promotion of the mass transportation or the non-motorised vehicle. Transportation economic and social costs in the European cities.

- Infrastructure for the use of bicycles and public transport and restraints for the use of the private car. Tariff and Taxes policies in the city transportation systems. Subsidisation of urban public transport.

- Public investments in roads, parking spaces and public transport infrastructure. The evolution of the investments, as a direct reflection of policies and attitudes. Effectiveness of the investments.

1.2 Development of environment friendly vehicles and environmentally compatible transport structures

- Encouragement of the use of bicycles, creation of the appropriate infrastructure, combined with mass-transportation schemes, economic incentives and legislative measures,

- Electric vehicles, electricity generation pollution versus car emissions, advantages and constraints,

- Improvement of the current technology of motor vehicles, current achievements in vehicle design, important instrument of urban environment policy.

1.3 Traffic management for the improvement of environmental conditions

- Reducing the accumulated unhealthy traffic distance,
- Prediction of traffic flows and the management of change,
- Communication technologies and traffic management,
- The EC's DRIVE Research Programme.

1.4 Multifunctional environment created by the pedestrian, cyclist and public transport

Pedestrians and cyclists should be the priority target groups in urban transport planning. They are the least polluting and most vulnerable groups, most exposed to the in-city pollution. Promoting footpaths and cycleways, and protecting their flows is a basis principle for the multifunctional transport planning. Experiences inventoried in European cities. Perspectives.

1.5 Urban Transport Planning and Allocation of Economic Activities

- Urban Transport cost as an added economic cost for the economic activities,
- Present transport networks and location of the activities,
- Transport Planning as an instrument of orienting new activities location.

II) GROUP 2: URBAN PRODUCTION AND CONSUMPTION SYSTEMS

The ecological networks of the biosphere are highly influenced by the urban metabolism, done through production and consumption processes. It depends on the relationships between the urban cores and their resource hinterland and therefore on the dynamics of the human settlements network.

Industry, main component of the urban economy, is an important source of air pollution (CO_2 and SO_2). On the other hand, many industries installed near rivers (ways of transportation of raw materials, fuels and products) have proved disastrous to the quality of the water.

Cities are places where energy consumption is very high, even if with the steady tertiarisation of urban economies less energy and materials are required. Progress has been made in reducing air pollution from the by-products of coal burning, but with its replacement by electricity other pollutants have been created. Let's remind ourselves here that 75% of the world energy consumption is in the form of fossil fuels, while the remainder is supplied by biomass, hydropower and nuclear power. The regenerative capacity of energy reservoirs is decisive for the cities and for the biosphere.

The quality of the urban environment, which highly influences the quality of the global environment, seems a main factor for the economic sustainability of the cities, and their power of attracting people and capital.

The main issues suggested for discussion in this group should be:

2.1 Industrial Production and Consumption:

- Experiences in non-polluting production plants, "Clean Technologies" in industry;
- Distribution actions with less polluting effects.

2.2 Energy Production and Consumption:

- Renewable energy sources for urban consumption;
- Experiences in non-polluting production plants and space heating;
- Nuclear energy, radioactivity and urban protection.

2.3 The creation of Industrial Technological Parks:

- Location factors and environmental control;
- Industrial technological production and environmental infrastructure;
- Increasing productivity and environmental quality.

2.4 Sustainable economic development and urban environment
- Short, medium and long-term economic effectiveness due to environmental quality;
- "Clean Environment" as a factor of economic growth.

III) GROUP 3: URBAN RESOURCES AND WASTE MANAGEMENT

Cities import raw materials and export waste. They are the places where most resources are consumed and most waste produced. The management of the resources is essential for the self-efficiency of the cities. On the other hand, the management of domestic and industrial waste is a common problem for local authorities in Europe, landfill and incineration seem to provoke soil and air pollution respectively, while prevention of industrial waste and avoidance, reuse and recycling of domestic wastes seem the major solutions. The main issues to be discussed in this group should be:

3.1 Management of the flows of supplies and waste

- Supplying capacity on the hinterland and irreversible resource depletion;
- Absorptive capacity of the surrounding ecosystems;
- Coping with cities' vulnerability to shortages of food and water.

3.2 Management of water resources and sanitation systems

- The quality of the metropolitan water, ground and surface in Europe;
- Sewage treatment works and quality of the drinking and bathing waters;
- Industrial liquid waste and pollution of the wider aquatic environment;
- State of degradation of marine resources, wetlands and coastal areas.

3.3 Innovative action concerning hazardous waste

- Management of nuclear waste;
- Waste treatment methods and energy production;
- Preventive and avoidance experiences;
- Potential dangers of all kinds of waste.

IV) GROUP 4: ATTITUDES, BEHAVIOUR AND ENVIRONMENTAL CHANGE

The sensitisation of all urban population is the first step for the environmental change. Environmental education and training is one of the most effective, fundamental and powerful measures available to governments. Public education through schools, organisations and the media has low financial and social costs and it can be the most effective long-term investment.

The awareness on environmental quality is a civic value. The broad understanding of the deeper causes of the environmental problems forms the basis for a consensus which allows local, national and European action to be efficient.

The urban space is vulnerable, if it is not the expression of a society realising a minimum of unanimous consensus. How the multiplicity of wills, that constitute our contemporary democratic process, can coalesce into positive unified actions for the common cause of environmental upgrading?

The economic measures to change attitudes and behaviour can be very varied, prices, taxes and trade policies can provide economic and financial incentives for reducing resources over-exploitation, waste and pollution. At last, "the polluter pays" can be a principle for social policy concerning pollution.

In this group, recommendations for discussion:

4.1 Education and training for environmental change

- Guidelines and modules for environmental education from preschool through university;
- Training programmes for adults;
- The role of media in environmental education;
- Feeling responsibility for the global environment.

4.2 Behaviour patterns of the different actors and change of environmental practices

- The households as actors, the inhabitants as consumers and citizens;
- The industrial sector as an actor and the dynamics of the industrial behaviour;
- The government as an actor.

4.3 Public awareness and political will for environmental change

- Direct democracy in choices for the environment;
- Direct participation in integrated planning;
- Political mobilisation actions.

4.4 Economic measures for changing environmental attitudes

- Market imperfections as causes of environmental degradation;
- Tariff policies for energy and industrial inputs;
- Pricing regulations for depletion of resources and waste production;
- Car taxation systems;
- The "polluter pays" principle to control emissions.

V) GROUP 5: URBAN PLANNING FOR THE 21st CENTURY

The environmental crisis of the cities is a fact; it can be a mortgage for their future. The whole urban culture (system of assets, norms and social relations, with an historic specificity and proper logic of organisation and of transportation) is in danger, as well as the global environment.

All indicators show that, as we move towards the 21st century, European cities will continue to be the main centres of economic, social and cultural activity. What the ecological planning scenarios aimed at intervention are in search of the multifunctional, creative city:

The main actions for discussion in this group should be:

5.1 The components of the integrated ecological planning

- Land use planning and environmental protection, especially in urban fringe areas;
- Greening the cities, making more of nature;
- Exploiting climatic conditions in planning;
- Energy planning aiming at reducing energy requirements and pollution;
- Ecological changes in urban structure and spatial distribution of economic activities;
- Environmentally compatible communication networks;
- Industrial relocation and environmental constraints on trade.

5.2 European co-operation for the urban regeneration and the upgrading of the global environment

- The uniqueness of the cities and the promotion and implementation of international strategies;
- European standards for measuring and respecting the carrying capacity of urban and ecological support systems;
- Financial and technological means to improve the urban and global environment;
- The North-South dialectics.

5.3 Assuring the cultural identity and continuation of the cities

- Action for the urban historical and natural heritage, threatened by the high level of air pollution;
- The enhancement of the cultural heritage, as a factor of economic sustainability.

5.4 The cities of the 21st century: Spaces of freedom?

- The complexity of the 21st urban organism;
- Creating the antropoupolis, biological habitat for mankind.

PROCEEDINGS OF WORKING GROUPS

GROUP 1

URBAN TRANSPORTATION AND INFRASTRUCTURE

Chairperson: Mr. Ariel ALEXANDRE, OECD

Rapporteur: Professor Enrique CALDERON, ETSI Caminos

Participants :

Ms. Inés AYALA, Union General de Trabajadores de España (UGT)

Mr. Jan GOEDMAN, National Physical Planning Agency, The Hague

Mr. Wigand KAHL, Stadtdirektor, Landeshauptstadt München

Mr. Claude LAMURE, INRETS

Mr. Michel MILLER, ETUC

Mr. Christiaan J. NYQVIST, Streekvervoer Nederland

Mr. Stephen PLOWDEN, London

Mr. Laurent SELLES, DG XIII, DRIVE Programme, Commission of the EC

Mr. Jacques SHORT, European Conference of Ministers of Transport

Mr. H.W. STRUBEN, International Society of City and Regional Planners

Mr. Wolfgang ZUCKERMANN, EcoPlan International

CITIES, TRANSPORT AND HEALTH

Claude A. Lamure
INRETS
Consultant to PNUE

1. INTRODUCTION: THE URBAN CONTEXT

How much sleep, I ask you, can one get in lodgings here?
Unbroken nights - and this is the root of the trouble -
Are a rich man's privilege, The waggons thundering past
Through those narrow twisting streets, the oaths of draymen
Caught in a traffic-jam - these alone would suffice
To jolt the doziest sea-cow of an Emperor into
Permanent wakefulness. If a business appointment
Summons the tycoon, **he** gets there fast, by litter,
Tacking above the crowd. There's plenty of room inside:
he can read, or take notes, or snooze as he jogs along -
Those drawn blinds are most soporific. Even so
He outstrips us: however fast we pedestrians hurry
We're blocked by the crowds ahead, while those behind us
Tread on our heels. Sharp elbows buffet by ribs,
Poles poke into me...

Juvenal, Satire III, 239-246, translated by Peter Green (Penguin)

Rome had undoubtedly already reached more than 1,200,000 inhabitants in the second century B.C.: when Jérôme Carcopino analysed this question, he examined the densities of habitation and concluded that there must certainly have been over-population, trouble in moving around, and noise from carts during the night. However, despite the rustic nature of transport and the low levels of hygiene, the city of Rome was already attracting citizens and freed-men from all over the Empire, just as Constantinople and Baghdad did later on.

The problems raised by transport are not purely contemporary; they have, however, taken on new forms and we shall examine in particular the nuisances most frequently cited by people living in large cities.

The rise in urban population in all countries of the world is striking; only China still seems to hesitate. 550 cities will have upwards of a million inhabitants by the year 2000; the urban population of India has been multiplied by 15 during the 20th century, although it will still only be 35% of the total population of India in the year 2000, as against 70% to 85% elsewhere; in the world in 2000 we will have more than 20 megalopolises with upwards of ten million inhabitants, growing rapidly. The human settlements constituted in this way are difficult to define: Is Los Angeles a city? A city of 16 million or 2 million inhabitants? What is its surface area? Will the idea of labour pools have any meaning in the era of telecommunications?

For the last 25 years, economic development has brought a continuous increase in the traffic of travellers and goods, which have been multiplied respectively by 2.2 as measured by passengers per km, and by 1.75 in tonnes per km, in 15 European countries. These levels of traffic bring nuisance factors which are more and more difficult for populations to accept.

2. THE EFFECTS ON THE ENVIRONMENT

The negative effects of transport are strongly influenced by individual cases, but they can be grouped into three main areas (a description by mode of transport appears in an annexe):

The physical environment, nuisances:

* noises and vibrations (most frequently cited by residents)
* air pollution: gas and dust
* water pollution (hydrology - quality)
* soil pollution (geomorphology, pedology)
* hazards (fire, explosion, asphyxiation).

The man-made or socio-economic environment:

* rehousing, compulsory purchase
* trouble with local movement and safety.

Destruction of heritage:

* fauna and vegetables
* sensitive sites - parks - leisure zones - forests
* archaeological, geological, literary heritage
* landscapes and architecture: visual intrusion.

We will give details later on of some of the most significant effects.

2.1 Urban Noise

The sound environment in our cities has undergone, for the last thirty years, the consequences of motorisation and the extraordinary expansion of the car. On the other hand, forms of architecture have developed, the "open" town planning used since the 1950s is very susceptible to noise, while the old style of continuous alignment of buildings along streets used to ensure a certain tranquillity in those rooms which did not face the street. It ought to be possible, all the same, to enjoy light, sunshine and quiet when one wants it.

Surveys show that motor traffic is the nuisance which is cited far more than any other by the inhabitants of developed countries, but among decision-makers the problems of pollution and consumption have, for the last 15 years, taken precedence over the preoccupation with noise reduction. The extension of noise represents a phenomenon of great inertia, the negative consequences of which are well established. A very large proportion of European housing is exposed to more than 55 dBA in front, a level which constitutes a well-established comfort threshold (cf. figure 1).

Figure 1: **Exposures of national populations to traffic noise. Beginning of the 1980s (Source: OECD). Percentages of populations exposed to external LeqA levels higher than 75, 65 and 55.**

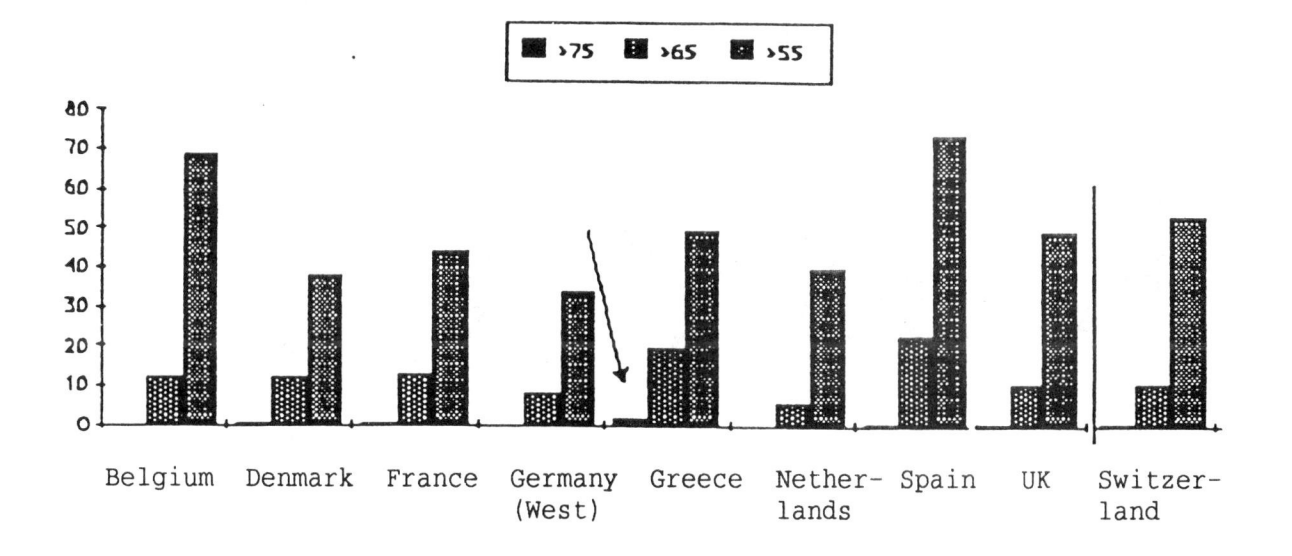

2.2 Air Pollution

Internal combustion motors and central heating systems emit:

1. Toxins which act in the immediate proximity;

2. Visible air pollutants (smokes, smells);

3. Gases which degrade the atmosphere in the longer term (e.g. carbon dioxide - CO_2).

Proximity pollution of the air - either toxic or visible - has been the object of research and reduction measures for more than 20 years; more recently, pollution transported over long distances has given rise to serious worries over acid rain, and uncertainties remain as to how much automobile exhaust fumes are responsible for damaging forests; a presumption of causation has however been made in the tightening of regulations on automobile emissions recently promulgated in all European countries. Taking account of the growth in motor traffic, these measures allow us to hope that in future the level of pollutants emitted by petrol engines in the atmosphere will be maintained at its present level, or even decreased. For diesel engines, which produce visible emissions, regulations and purification techniques are still causing difficulties. It still remains the fact that transport constitutes by far the most important source of pollution in urban areas (see the following figure). The characteristics of emissions from diesel motors and controlled ignition motors are very different, as shown in table 1.

Figure 2: Part played by motor transport in air pollution (Source: OECD)

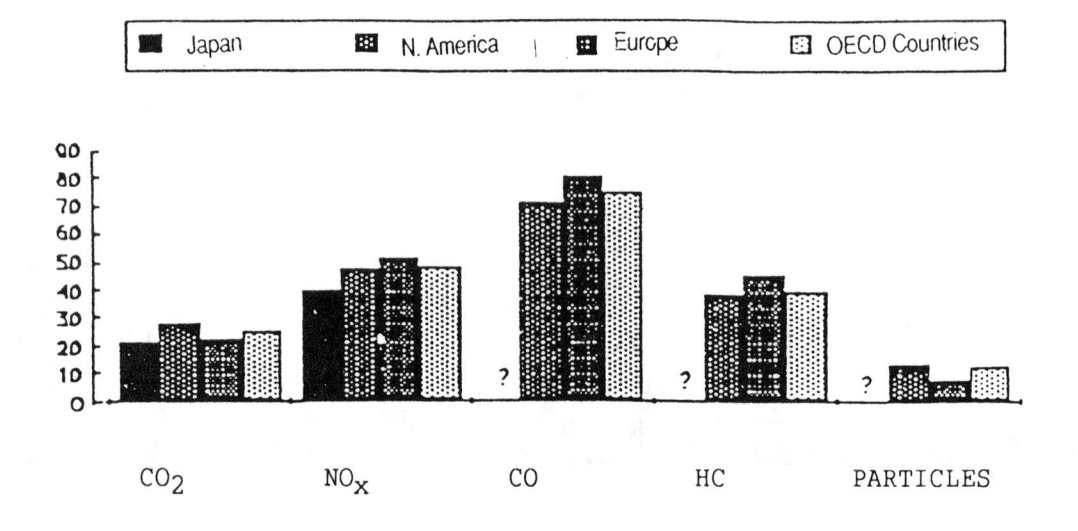

Table 1: Emissions from diesel motors and controlled ignition motors

	CO g/km	HC g/km	NO_x g/km	PAH(*) g/km	CO_2 g/km
Petrol	10 to 30	1 to 5	0.5 to 3	10 to 20	120 to 300
Diesel	0.5 to 2	0.2 to 0.4	0.5 to 1	10 to 20	120 to 300

* PAH: Polynuclear aromatic hydrocarbons

At the present time there are long-term phenomena of atmospheric degradation which are particularly likely to call into question the forms of energy used for transport. Vehicle mobility demands suitable stocks and supplies of energy. Captive to particular forms of energy, and subject to intense environmental constraints, transport will be driven to major developments in propulsion methods.

2.3 Water and Soil Pollution

Building works for infrastructural services, as well as traffic circulation and the maintenance of roads, involve pollution of water or of rivers running through towns. The following types of damage may be caused:

- Materials can be carried in suspension, following earthworks or erosion, and this may lead to clogging and effects on aquatic fauna.

- Oil and hydrocarbon (HC) spillages owing to construction machinery and vehicular traffic, and also to manufacturing plants and certain users.

- Escape of chlorine products from the salting of roads during the winter.

- Pollution following traffic accidents, with widely varying consequences depending on the location, the qualities and nature of products; ecological issues are at stake, but also economic issues when catchment waters become unusable.

- Various forms of contamination, especially through heavy metals coming from vehicles, from tyres and from fuels.

- The waterproofing of extended surfaces (roads, parking areas) leads to run-offs and sudden floods (e.g. the 1989 floods in Nîmes).

At the current time, protection techniques involve the channelling of surface water towards basins where it is decanted, where oil is removed, and the channelling of water is carried out in such a way that flow areas are spread (ditches and vegetation). Studies are also taking place on rapid alert procedures following site or traffic accidents.

2.4 Vegetation

The effects on flora are varied:

a) Cuttings through forests give rise to major worries, especially when forests are close to towns. (It is known that acid pollution affecting forests does not come particularly from nearby motor traffic.)

b) Questions are being raised about the damage which herbicides may cause to rarer kinds of plants. It should be remembered that certain species are protected by law.

c) Major motorways and their embankments have sometimes served as zones where certain types of vegetation can penetrate. One case is the ragweed which has made its way up the Rhône valley, causing allergic reactions in the urban community of Lyon.

2.5 Impact on local life - The effect is being cut off

The cutting-off effects of transport infrastructures have been considered from a sociological point of view for more than 20 years in the United States. Among European analyses, the one carried out by Professor Harder distinguishes the visual aspect, functional separation, and social disruptions (cf. figure 3). His report proposes evaluation methods for practical cases, and indicators for each effect and ways of combining them. In Sweden, recommendations from the Swedish National Road Administration involve quantitative assessments of the barrier effects and the time taken to cross roads. The disruptive role of speed grows very rapidly when vehicle speeds go over 30-40 km/h: a precise evaluation is difficult to establish, but the tendency illustrated by Figure 4 (source CEMT) may be acceptable.

A traffic road causes the following disruptive effects in inhabited areas:

- Difficulties in crossing. These affect pedestrians in particular, and thus elderly people and school-goers who are often almost entirely confined to walking; however, the difficulties may also affect two-wheeled traffic. These journeys are often necessary ones to visit traders or public amenities. The effects may cause a loss of attachment to the community centre, and even local political difficulties for public amenities.

- Disruption of the physical and social identity of certain districts. This gives rise to the general impression of a barrier, and comes out very strongly in the studies. The fragmentation of space is detrimental to the use of that space, even if the total surface area is very little affected.

- Visual barriers and nuisances. The loss of views is very strongly felt, as well as the deterioration of visual spaces, either through poor planning, or through degradation or lack of subsequent maintenance.

- Disturbance of local business. Local commerce has a double problem: the disappearance of businesses subject to compulsory purchase orders, and the lack of accessibility, leading to a lack of customers.

- Safety at crossings.

It must however be noted that areas subject to such disruption often show great capacities for adaptation.

Figure 3:   Aspects of disruption effects

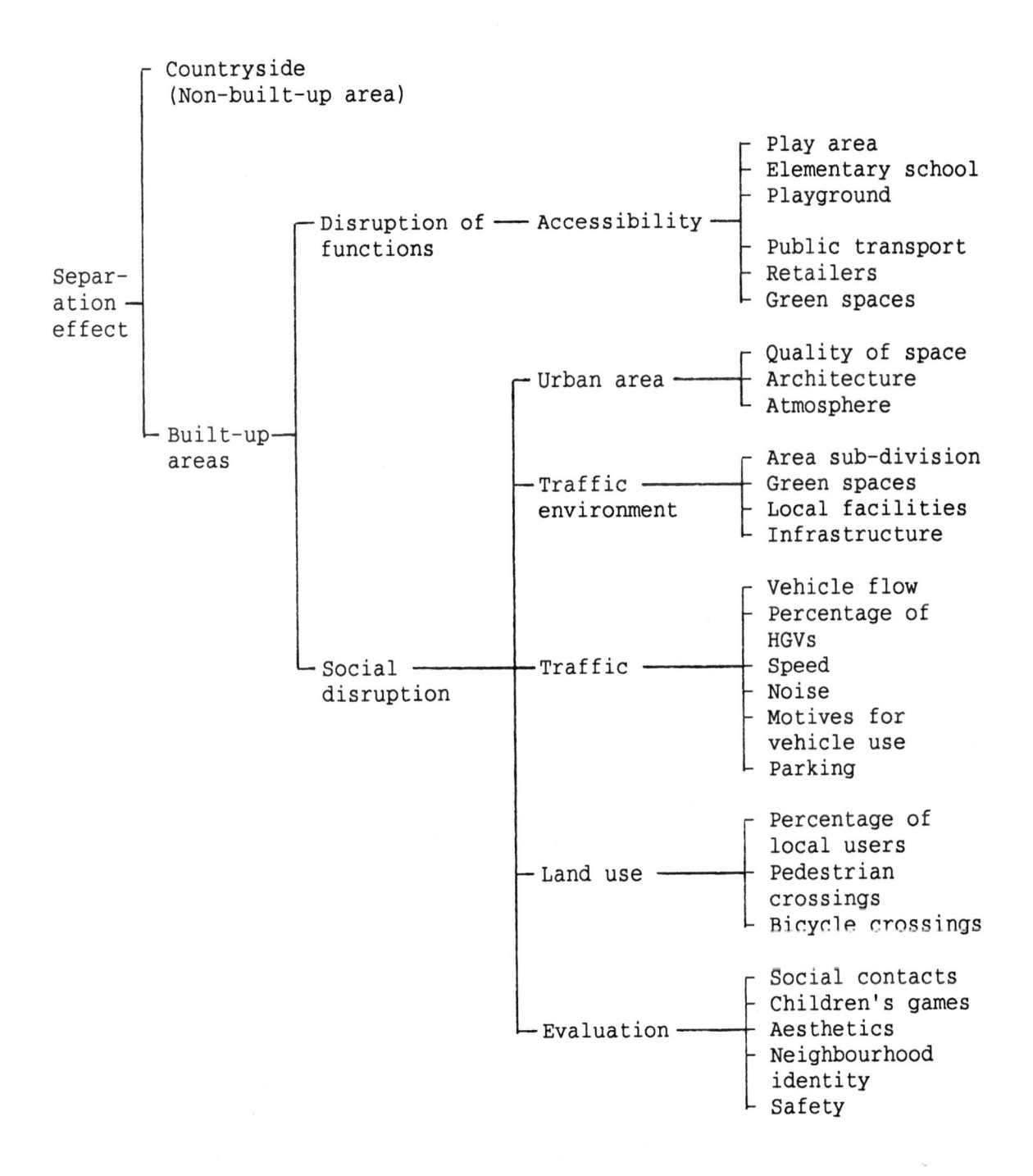

```
                  ┌─ Countryside
                  │  (Non-built-up area)
                  │
                  │                                        ┌─ Play area
                  │                                        ├─ Elementary school
                  │                  ┌─ Disruption of ── Accessibility ─┤  Playground
                  │                  │  functions         │
                  │                  │                    ├─ Public transport
                  │                  │                    ├─ Retailers
Separ-            │                  │                    └─ Green spaces
ation ──┤         │                  │
effect            │                  │                    ┌─ Quality of space
                  │                  │         ┌─ Urban area ─┤ Architecture
                  │                  │         │            └─ Atmosphere
                  │                  │         │
                  │                  │         │            ┌─ Area sub-division
                  │                  │         ├─ Traffic ──┤ Green spaces
                  │                  │         │  environment│ Local facilities
                  │                  │         │            └─ Infrastructure
                  │                  │         │
                  │                  │         │            ┌─ Vehicle flow
                  │                  │         │            ├─ Percentage of
                  │                  │         │            │   HGVs
        └─ Built-up ┤                 ├─ Traffic ──────────┤ Speed
           areas                     │         │           ├─ Noise
                                     │         │           ├─ Motives for
                                     │         │           │   vehicle use
                                     │         │           └─ Parking
                                     │         │
                                     │         │           ┌─ Percentage of
                                     │         │           │   local users
                                     └─ Social ┤           ├─ Pedestrian
                                        disruption ── Land use ─┤ crossings
                                               │           └─ Bicycle crossings
                                               │
                                               │           ┌─ Social contacts
                                               │           ├─ Children's games
                                               └─ Evaluation ─┤ Aesthetics
                                                           ├─ Neighbourhood
                                                           │   identity
                                                           └─ Safety
```

Source: Harder (60)

Figure 4:   Barrier effect of an 8-metre road (Denmark)

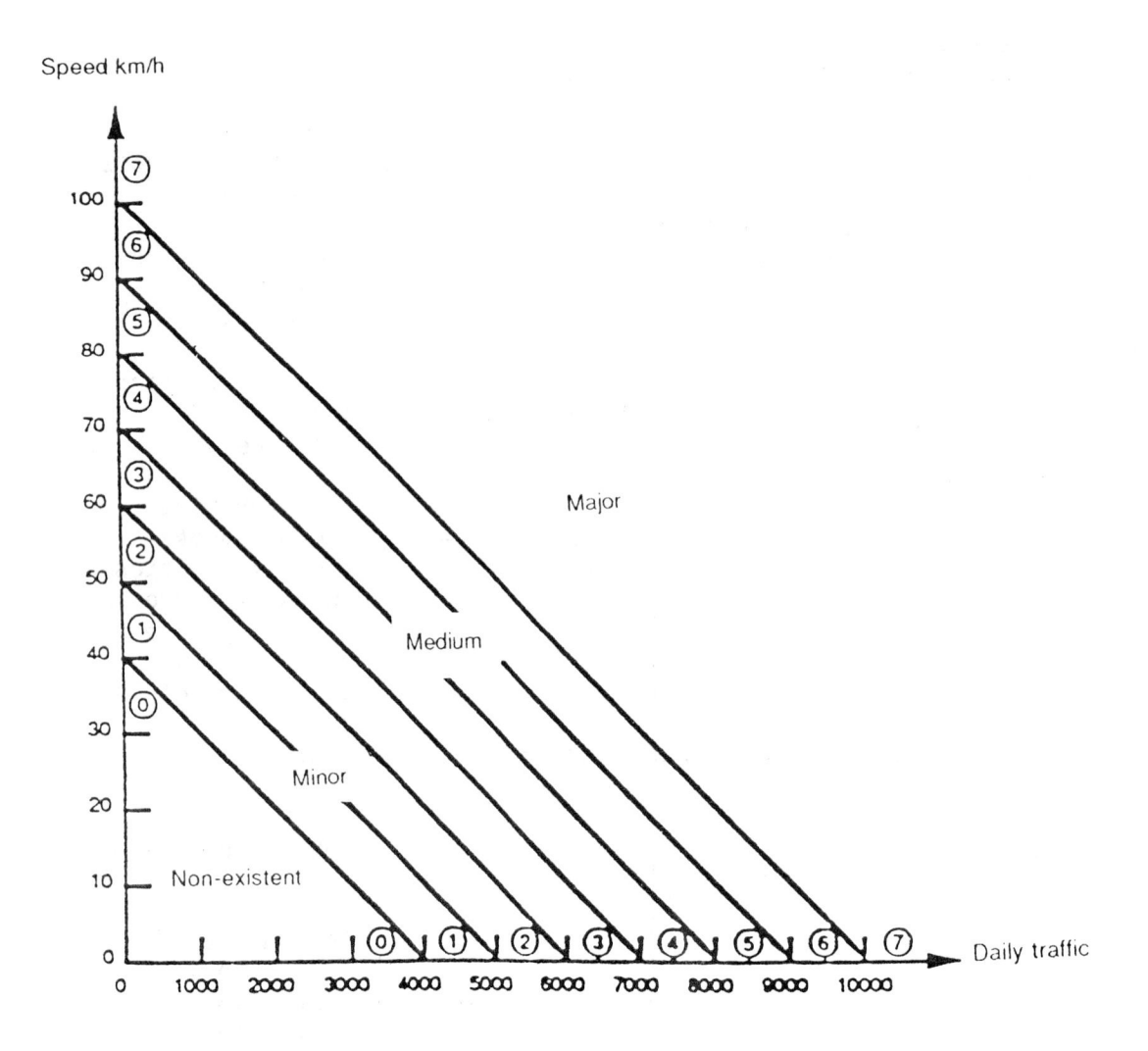

[Graph: Speed km/h (y-axis, 0 to 100) vs Daily traffic (x-axis, 0 to 10000), showing diagonal lines labeled 0–7, with regions marked Non-existent, Minor, Medium, Major]

Theoretical Observations on the Disruption Effect

Psychological research has dealt with the individual representation of spaces and landmarks. The effect of a break is to divide a space which was previously continuous. One can understand that the extended nature of a space is a source of "value", and that any break in this involves a loss or deficit in that value. This point of view can be formalised by thinking about a value-function of any convex expanse, such that the sum of the values of a reduced expanse remaining after the interruption is less than the value of the initial expanse. The difference between the two is the deficit attributable to the break.

The value-function depends on attributes contained in each expanse (surface, form, internal richness, etc.). One can also envisage an ecological aspect (disturbance to animal life, effects on genetics), an agricultural aspect (breaking up farms), a social and cultural aspect (the symbolic value of space, the recreational value, the deterioration of special sites, etc.). Another concept linked to breaks in continuity is the increased rarity of a limited resource (local spaces, number of sites preserved, etc.).

A practical aim would be to model the effect of breaks caused by roads, with a view to incorporating this factor more explicitly in decisions relating to various versions of a plan.

2.6 Transformation of the urban landscape

Surface transport infrastructure plays a considerable role in the development of urban and suburban landscapes.

In city centres, new roads are rare; in certain recent cases it has been possible to observe a de-structuring effect on the urban texture, which loses its social and architectural consistency through changes of scale.

In areas around cities, new infrastructures create new landscapes which are sometimes very extensive. They can also destroy spaces which are valuable for leisure activities and sports, such as woodland close to large built-up areas.

In residential districts, living conditions are modified by breaks, but also by changes in the direction of traffic flow, with certain streets becoming traffic corridors and losing their character as meeting-places. A growing awareness of these effects, and pressure from the Council of Europe, have been given expression by the CNRS in France, which organised a colloquium entitled "La Rue n'est pas une Route" [A Street is not a Road]. We are however still far from having methods for the assessment of modifications in the volume of traffic in streets.

3. SHORT-TERM PROSPECTS AND SOLUTIONS

The battle against the negative effects of transport may involve:

* palliative measures;
* the management of traffic, space and speed;
* a reduction in travel demands, through physical or financial measures.

3.1 Palliative Measures to Reduce Noise

The battle against noise has required the development of a number of instruments for assessment, prediction and measurement. Major progress has been made on daytime traffic noise, but it still remains to define indices and operational methods for night-time and for noises of different origin.

The evaluation of the acoustic environment, and the comparison of traffic or town planning solutions, are carried out through calculations or, more spectacularly, through small-scale models such as the ones used by CSTB in Grenoble. Unfortunately, the insertion of traffic lanes in an urban setting is subject to many other constraints other than noise, and in practice it is often a case of trying to alleviate rather than prevent problems. Acoustic barriers, partial or complete tunnelling, soundproofing of buildings are used in many noise black spots, following the suggestions provided by CETUR. As well as these black spots, many further cases of excessive noise levels could be treated, and it would be a good idea to achieve a greater spread of expert knowledge, which is all too often confined to a few administrative bodies.

Among innovative road techniques, the most promising one seems to be a porous surface coating; the porosity of the road surface brings a reduction in the noise of the contact between tyre and roadway, and the partial absorption of other noises.

3.2 Managing Traffic, Heavy Vehicles, Space and Speed

Traffic can be characterised by the speed and flow of vehicles, the proportion of private cars and HGVs; the physical characteristics of roads are of course determined by hypotheses on the traffic to be carried. We consider the role of these main parameters on noise, atmospheric pollution, the disruption effect and visual intrusion.

Distance from the Road and Average Speed

Traffic speed essentially determines noise and disruption effects, which are linked to the lack of safety in crossing the road. Noise levels are much more sensitive to traffic speed than to distance from the road. It should be recalled that average **LeqA** noise levels and peak **Lmax** levels are expressed roughly as follows:

LeqA = $20\log V - 10\log d + 10\log Q$ + **cte**
Lmax = $30\log V - 20\log d$ + **cte**

where **V** is speed, **d** is distance from the road, and **Q** is intensity of vehicle traffic.

Thus, noise levels are much more dependent on speed than on the intensity of vehicle traffic and distance. Distance is rather ineffective, as long as the road remains in a direct line of sight from the areas under consideration: one must double the distances to get a drop of 30 dB(A), which is the minimum drop perceptible by human ears. Greater distance is therefore only a solution in areas with a very low density of population. The neutralisation of noise and visual intrusion can be achieved through buffer spaces with raised mounds or the construction of buildings which are not sensitive to noise. That demands extra spaces of fairly large dimensions, 50-80 metres: raised mounds and trenches lead to considerable increases in the amount of land to be purchased.

Rather than moving the road further away, it is often necessary to consider actions of the following kind:

- Action to make building volumes less penetrable by noise;
- Action on the architecture of buildings to optimise the orientation of rooms and secure good sound insulation;

- Changes to exterior spaces, with acoustic screens where necessary.

The two extreme forms of orientation are thus:

   distance from the road;
   complete integration between the road and the buildings.

Such actions demand a single contracting authority, or at least a high degree of co-ordination. They also need extremely close co-operation between architects, acoustic and road engineers. Railway stations and road interchanges are particularly suited to this approach. Transport authorities can facilitate the promotion of major private or public planning operations; in the last analysis, the users of infrastructures can set themselves up as promoters in the vicinity of certain road sections.

In the absence of such ambitious actions, a reduction in motorway speed from 130 to 100 km/h would bring a drop in distance by about half in areas with equal exposure to noise. This would be a result worth comparing to the relative restriction of the areas under the influence of road noise in North America, as compared to those in Europe. Noise protection distances are smaller in Canada, as North American cars are noticeably quieter than European cars (see Table 2).

Table 2: Definition of Potential Areas of Acoustic Impact

Netherlands: Areas where road noise impact assessment is obligatory (Noise Nuisance Act, Netherlands 1981)

Road in a rural area	Distance from the road (metres)	Road in a non-rural area	Distance from the road (metres)
4 lanes or more	600	3 lanes or more	350
3 lanes or more	400	2 lanes with more than 5000 vehicles per day	200
2 lanes	250	2 lanes with less than 5000 vehicles per day	100

Canada (Quebec), Potential Acoustic Impact Zones (PAIZ)			
Recommended classification of roads	Maximum flow predicted (vehicles per day)	Speed permitted (km/h)	Distance on axis line PAIZ
Freeway	120,000	100	135
Expressway	100,000	70	100
Main road	40,000	60	60
Primary road	10,000	50	N A
Secondary road	5,000	50	N A
Residential street	1,000	50	N A

As regards emissions of pollutants, the effect of vehicle speed is a complex one; decongesting urban traffic reduces pollution, but on the other hand increasing speed higher than 60-80 km/h increases emissions, especially of NO_x (cf. figure 5). The introduction of new norms on vehicle emission reduces the relevance of considerations of the relationship between air pollution and local spaces.

Vehicle Flows

Levels of emissions are proportionate to traffic flows for appropriate intensities of road usage. It can be assumed that a doubling of the rate also doubles the distance of health safety zones.

3.3 Speed Limits. The Concept of Urban Enclosures and Extensions of the Concept

The maximum speed limit and the physical arrangements associated with it govern cruising speeds but also acceleration. This fact explains that speed limits of 30 km/h which have been studied in particular in West Germany ("Tempo 30") bring worthwhile reductions in noise and energy consumption. This fact was not expected by specialists, who felt that motorists would make greater use of lower gears and cause more noise. In fact, the prospect of lower top speeds leads drivers to move more quickly into the less noisy upper gears (for a brief overview, see Lamure 1988).

Figure 5:   Coefficients of emission and fuel consumption from the current stock of private cars in Switzerland, in relation to effective average speed

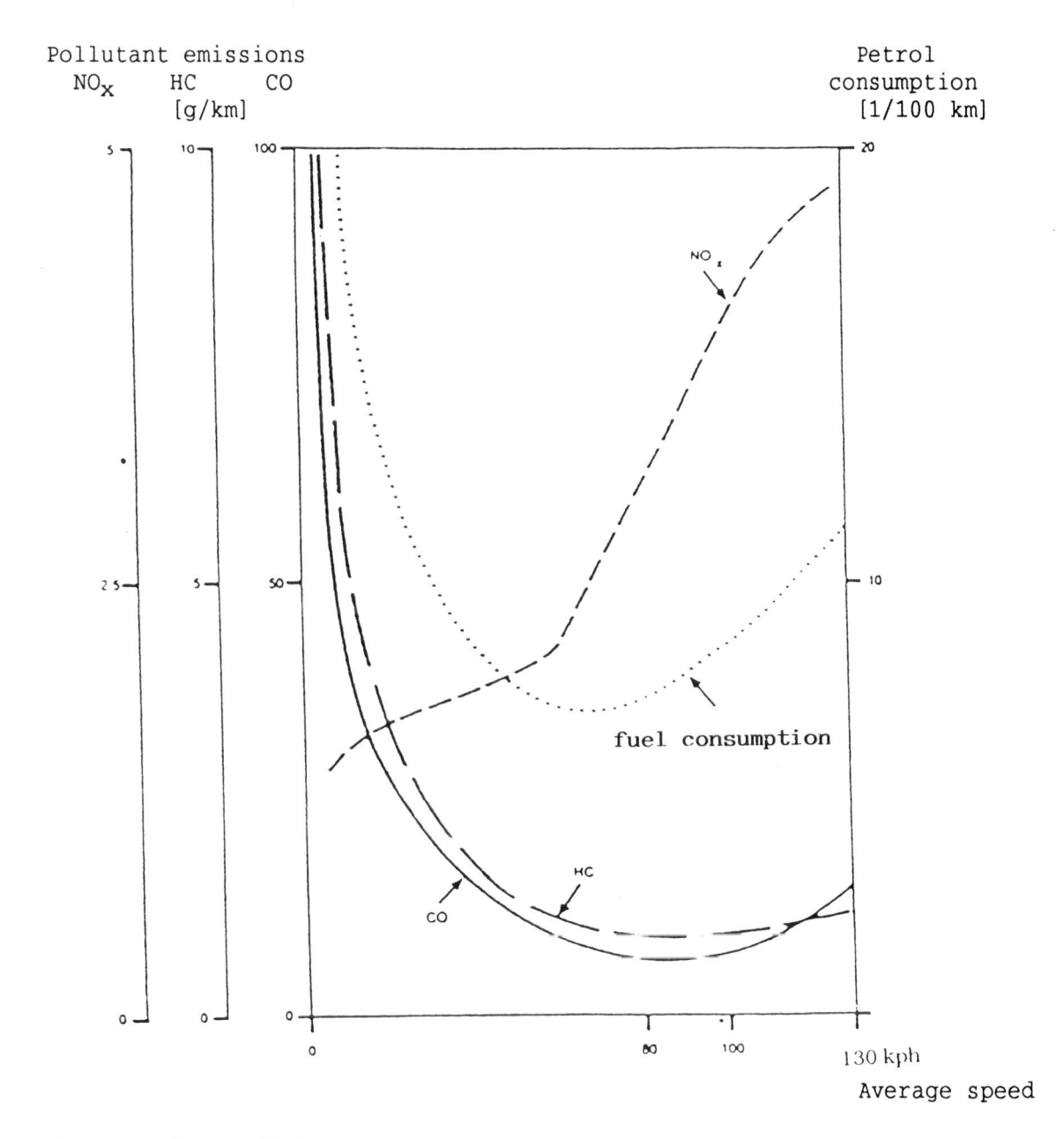

Pollutant emissions
NO$_x$ HC   CO
[g/km]

Petrol consumption
[1/100 km]

Average speed

Source: Berne (59)

Whether in terms of protective distance, or in terms of disruption by road infrastructure, speed plays a considerable role, more significant than the flow of vehicle traffic. Changes in the use of long-established roads, and especially the introduction of heavy vehicles, can greatly increase the areas subject to nuisance.

The so-called **Woonerf** movement emerged in the Netherlands in about 1970: the integration rather than the segregation of activities in streets within residential zones called for a complete remodelling of traffic space. These ideas, which were also justified by a lack of road safety, led to the adoption in West Germany, in more extended urban zones, of speed limits of 30 km/h. The elimination of through traffic, and the slowing of local traffic, are accompanied by a complete detailed planning of the road system, pedestrian and cyclist zones, and parking places with visual differentiation of surface paving and few footpaths. The improvement in the residential environment obtained in this way is considerable, and reductions of more than 20% in accident figures have been observed. There are many reports on these topics; one can consult the reference CEMT in French and English.

Top speed reductions have not been as widely extended in France as was found for example in West Germany with the Tempo 30 operations; however, safe town operations, and accident-free districts constitute good examples of remedial operations especially for roads through built-up areas.

Through Routes

After decades of neglect, the topic of compatibility between through routes and built-up areas has been the subject of various experimental research projects. Here again, the aims of road safety have generally come before the desire to improve the general environment along transit routes. The tendency is no longer to confine technical studies to the needs of traffic, but to associate architectural and environmental approaches with them. A new generation of official recommendations and publications has thus appeared (for example, in West Germany, the publications of the Forschungsgesellschaft für Strassen- und Verkehrswesen).

The slowing-down of traffic remains a constant objective as with residential streets; it is to be obtained by physical layout rather than road traffic regulations. The following devices are adopted: restricted road widths and visual appearances of width, sharp bends, varied visual marking which break up the driver's perspective (without reducing visibility), etc. Favourable effects quite similar to those in urban enclosures are obtained for safety, noise, pollution, pedestrian crossings and aesthetic appearance.

Conclusion

International exchanges on the results obtained in the Netherlands, West Germany and Denmark particularly, have tended to be confined to aspects of road safety, whereas the general environment is an essential part of the equation. It would be worthwhile, in particular, to examine the forms in which northern European initiatives could be transposed to other countries, where town planning is often very different. The main conclusion is that:

Lowering speed limits in urban areas presents simultaneous advantages of reducing disruption, and in the longer term can facilitate the introduction of transport modes or vehicles less harmful than current vehicles.

3.4 Management of Demand for Transport and Modal Transfers

Restrictions on Motor Car Use

To reduce congestion and thereby free space for public transport, there are attempts all over the world to restrict the use of cars in town. This can result in:

a) Physical obstacles: closing off town centres (for example, Göteborg), pedestrian zones, etc.

b) Financial constraints: parking charges and urban tolls. The regulation of demand by imposing travel costs is being envisaged more and more frequently: urban tolls (road pricing) adopted in Singapore and Norway, and researched notably in the Netherlands, will be extended rapidly, starting with urban tunnels (for example, Paris, Lyon, Grenoble), the progress of electronic debiting will make it easier to introduce from a technical point of view, and at a political level the imposition of these charges will be legitimated by their re-allocation to public transport; this will in fact providegreat opportunities for the development of collective transport facilities.

Going beyond constraints through pricing to reduce the number of journeys would involve coercive measures which it still seems very difficult to envisage for our societies, unless there is an extremely strong growth in awareness of the damage being inflicted on the environment by motor traffic. Hopes can be built, on the other hand, in the possible substitution of telecommunications for personal journeys.

c) Regulatory measures: prohibited access, reduction of top speeds (to 30 km/h in many European zones). The political obstacles to road pricing can - especially from the point of view of social equity[1] - make it seem preferable to use original regulatory measures: the case of Athens is well known, where motorists can only travel on days corresponding to their registration number (even or odd numbers).

---

[1] An "equitable" orientation would consist in allocating the takings from tolls to the improvement of public transport.

The rather disappointing results from the Athens experiment must not lead to an abandonment of the search for original solutions; Mexico, for example, seems set to succeed with a similar but more subtle formula (spread of prohibitions over the days of the week).

Physically blocking off town centres, with substitute parking lots on the outskirts, seems an effective formula for medium-sized cities, like many of the Italian cities. A "park and ride" policy needs the introduction of good public transport, however, as well as excellent information services, especially for tourists. This approach is being adopted in Bologna and Perugia among many other towns; they also plan innovations such as rotating parking lots, travelators for pedestrians, etc.

Public Transport

Restrictions on motor car use cannot succeed, at least from a political point of view, unless they are closely associated with the promotion of public transport.

Only big cities which are both rich and densely populated can justify the installation of underground urban railway systems. The case for metro services in Athens, Cairo, Tunis and Istanbul have been subjected to many studies recently, with different conclusions being drawn by the experts.

The Shift to Electricity

As regards air pollution, the shift to electrified rail transport is a positive development, as it eliminates local pollution. Unfortunately, this is much less certain for global or regional pollution, and regional pollution can be very worrying, particularly in the form of atmospheric smog. For the production of electricity, the countries circling the Mediterranean, for example, are characterised by a strong dependence on petroleum. Greece also consumes a great deal of coal.

The result is that for many countries, a shift towards electric-powered transport would not at the moment have a favourable effect on hazards associated with the greenhouse effect or photochemical smog.

In the short and medium term, it must be remembered that the natural gas held by many countries, especially in the South, produces combustion which is less polluting than most combustible liquids.

Buses

The most realistic and economical public transport is provided by buses. On a technical level, great progress is possible to obtain clean and quiet buses. Innumerable technical experiments have taken place in this area.

Independent electric-powered buses are still expensive, and present the drawbacks already mentioned; trolley-buses, on the other hand, are being rehabilitated. Lyon takes pride in being one of the few European towns to have preserved and developed a trolley-bus network. Athens is also planning to extend its trolley-bus network.

Internal combustion powered buses will remain in the majority for a long time. Here also one must remember the advantages of the use of natural gas, which is much less polluting, and is used without problems in Dutch and Austrian cities.

The effective use of buses such as trolley-buses calls for a careful layout of roads for circulation and stops; a restriction in the circulation of motor cars must accompany the arrangements which have now been tried and tested for bus lanes or special bus roads. Bus lanes without a physical barrier are unfortunately often taken over by other users who interfere with the functioning of the buses. In this connection, only bus lanes which run against the general direction of the traffic are satisfactory.

Separate bus roads can provide passenger flows approaching those of underground railways, with a far more advantageous cost and flexibility of use.

In many cities in developing countries, **minibus** operators provide a significant proportion of urban journeys, offering excellent pricing and frequency of service. The sometimes mediocre image of these minibuses does not seem justified by their potential in keeping up the use of public transport.

Thus a very comprehensive study of the case of Istanbul has shown that for a very modest cost minibuses in practice present qualities of consumption and pollution which are comparable if not superior to those of traditional buses.

Other forms of transport

Alongside light rail transport of a monorail or other type, one should mention cable cars for cities with a hilly terrain. For distances of two kilometres at most in a straight line, these forms of transport are economical, and only take up little terrain. They are silent, and only cause pollution through the electricity which they consume.

Terrain which is sometimes uneven, and density of habitation, can favour the introduction of systems which winter sports have helped to develop solidly. The most recent double mono-cable systems provide excellent stability for an aerial bus.

A number of towns in Algeria, such as Constantine, have thus recently ordered cable transport systems which can also give these towns an added value in terms of image and tourist interest.

4. LONG TERM PROSPECTS

4.1 Towns and health?[1]

Walking

Travelling on foot or by bicycle offers health benefits and the possibility of cutting the use of motor transport, thereby contributing to the improvement of the environment. In most European cities, more than one journey out of 3 takes place entirely on foot, and most of the others involve walking at some point during the journey. The propensity to walking is affected both by the density of the town's layout and by the quality of the pedestrian environment. Thus, the percentage of journeys made on foot can vary from 20% in zones which are not very dense, where the car provides the main means of transport, up to 50% in dense urban areas, offering easy access to pedestrians.

Most journeys on foot are however of short duration: for about half of them, the distance covered is not more than 1 km. Thus, if the percentage of journeys on foot increased from 30% to 40%, and one-third of the new walkers drove their cars beforehand, one could expect a reduction of 1% to 2% in motor traffic. These figures are low because in general, in an urban setting, the distance of foot journeys is only about one-tenth of that of car journeys.

Bicycles

Bicycle journeys offer considerable advantages from an environmental point of view; as regards health, the promotion of bicycles is as justified as the promotion of jogging, with the reservation that the cyclist must be protected as far as possible from pollution and from dangers from motor-powered vehicles.

Unfortunately, bicycles are less frequently used than could be inferred from the levels of infrastructure in certain European countries (the Netherlands being the most obvious exception in this area). In the United Kingdom, for example, one-third of all households possess a bicycle, but use it on average only for six km per week per household. It is clear that the bicycle, as a mode of transport, has suffered from the increasing rate of motor car ownership during recent decades. In most European countries, it is not usually "seriously" used (meaning outside leisure time) except by children and by men on low incomes.

---

[1] CEMT reference

The essential problem remains the bodily risk to the cyclist, especially as bicycles are largely used by children, who learn about traffic by cycling. The lack of safety explains the fairly general decrease in all countries in the use of two-wheeled transport.

The Northern European countries with a long tradition in this area have begun again to research cycle paths in towns. The general principles call for the separation of traffic by visual markings and sometimes by physical barriers. In Denmark, the Transport Minister has given grants to four municipalities for the construction of a network of cycle paths, as the classic problem is the lack of continuity in existing paths. The evaluation of the results in Odense, a town of 175,000 inhabitants, confirms that great care must be taken in planning, in designing details, in providing signalling and information to the public.

In France, after a period between 1970 and 1980 when specialist tracks were tried out, more attention is now being paid to the principle, already mentioned, of traffic calming where low speed allows a co-existence between pedestrians, cyclists and motor vehicles. This framework has seen the best results in the Netherlands and in Germany; in Berlin, the hazards connected with cycle paths running beside a rapid motor road have been pointed out. Mention should also be made of the bicycles which have been made available in La Rochelle, an experiment which has proved successful for the tourist season.

Clearly, there needs to be a great increase in bicycle traffic for it to produce a significant impact on levels of car traffic. This can only happen in countries which are already highly motorised, given the fact, in particular, that a high percentage of journeys are longer than can be conveniently made on a bicycle (for half of all bicycle journeys, the distance travelled is not more than 2 km). For countries which still have a low proportion of cars, it would be useful to research ways of supporting and encouraging the use of bicycles.

4.2 New Energies

Modifying Primary Energy Sources

The motors causing least pollution are powered by hydrogen or electricity. The only ideal solution which would not reduce mobility in our societies would be to modify our energy sources, bearing in mind that consideration must also be given to emissions arising from the production of the primary energy source. At the present time, automobile transport is almost completely tied to petroleum, and the current methods of propulsion all emit carbon dioxide.

A highly documented study which compares various types of primary energy available in the United States for road transport has pointed out the relative attractions of biofuels derived from biomass (methanol, ethanol - ref. Deluchi) (it should be recalled that methanol replacing diesel fuel eliminates the emission of particles), but Canada is more interested in extending the use of natural gas, of which it has a plentiful supply.

Rail transport, by metro or tram, has a considerable advantage over road (and air) transport, in that it can use different types of energy: petroleum, coal, nuclear, hydraulic, and at present and even more so in the future, renewable energy sources. If primary energy derives neither from coal nor from petroleum, the benefits of using rail transport become considerable in relation to all kinds of pollution. The emphasis currently placed on the greenhouse effect attributable to carbon dioxide, and on NO_x emissions causing acid rain, reinforces the attractiveness of electrified rail transport (but this may pose the problem of nuclear energy in new terms). The National Environment Protection Board in Sweden has established comparison factors for emissions of pollutants and energy consumption for different types of passenger and goods transport. The hydroelectric energy option obviously has a particular advantage for trains, but unfortunately very few countries can have plentiful reserves of hydroelectricity, and the dams involved cause major environmental dislocation.

Electric-powered, Hydrogen-powered or Solar-powered Towns?

The slow progress being made with electric batteries and fuel batteries is still giving rise to hesitations, but it appears likely that the twenty-first century will see the general use of electric cars in urban areas. In the absence of a breakthrough on superconducting materials for electric power, it may be observed that batteries already make it possible to undertake urban journeys at speeds of 30 km/h, as advocated by the proponents of "traffic calming" for residential urban areas. Only electricity provides silent propulsion at low speeds.

The authorities of the South Coast Air Basin in the Los Angeles region have forced the State of California to agree that electric-powered vehicles will be introduced at the beginning of the twenty-first century if no other solutions are found to restore the quality of the atmosphere. A call for tenders on 10,000 electric vehicles has already been launched, and the "Impact" prototype of an electric sports car (!), presented by General Motors at the beginning of 1990, is well known. The introduction of electric cars will be done gradually, by restricting access by other vehicles to zones of ever increasing size. Despite the use of methanol, which has the ecological advantage of eliminating the particles emitted by diesel engines, it may be felt that the future of combustion engines belongs to natural gas, and later perhaps to hydrogen. Among fuels, H_2 is the only one which is capable of eliminating nearly all harmful emissions, on condition - and this is sometimes forgotten - that it has not been produced on the basis of fossil energy (see figure 6). Unfortunately, nobody is perfect and even hydrogen will not avoid emissions of nitrogen oxide and OH^- ions which destroy the ozone in the upper atmosphere; noise emissions will also persist.

Figure 6a: **Percentages of growth in CO_2 emissions compared to current fuels (weighted for the United States)**

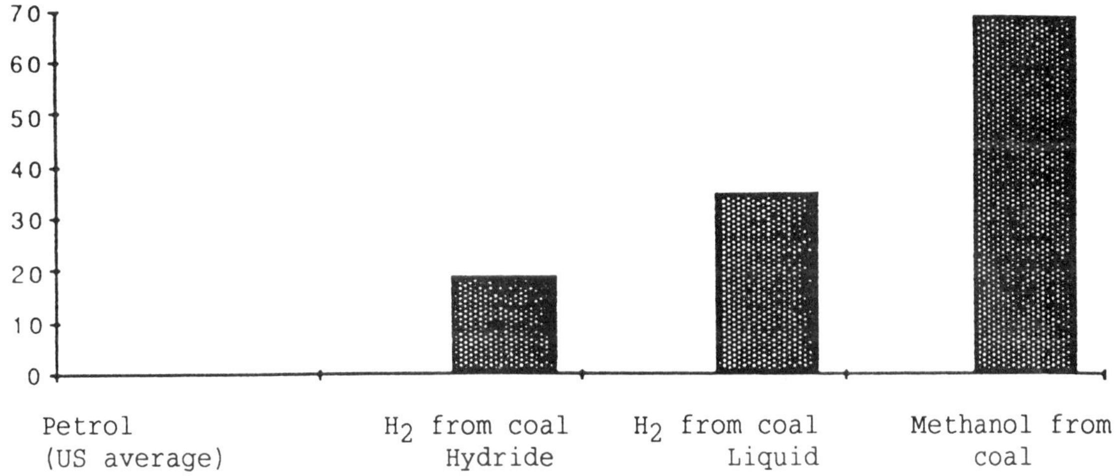
70
60
50
40
30
20
10
0
Petrol (US average)
H2 from coal Hydride
H2 from coal Liquid
Methanol from coal

Figure 6b: **Percentages of reduction of CO_2 emissions compared to current fuel consumption (weighted for the United States)**

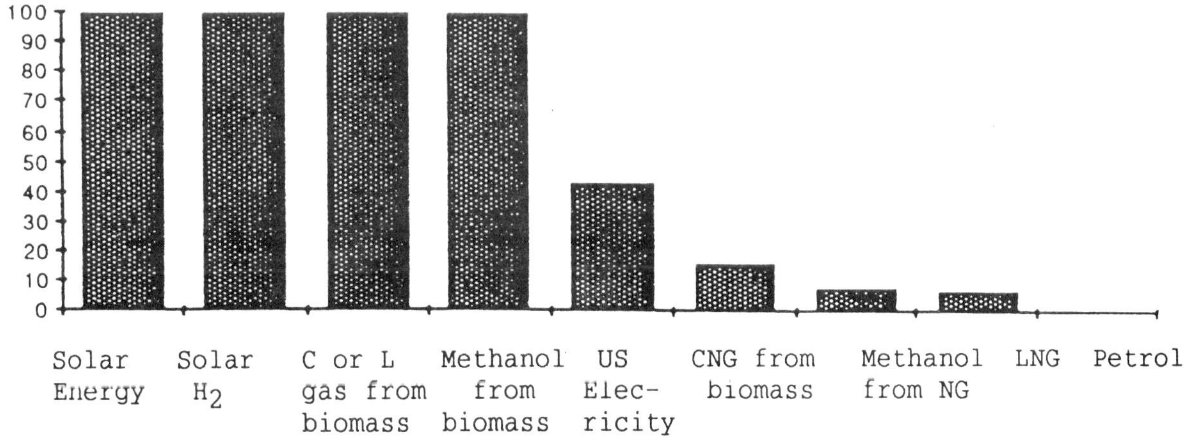
100
90
80
70
60
50
40
30
20
10
0
Solar Energy
Solar H2
C or L gas from biomass
Methanol from biomass
US Elec- ricity
CNG from biomass
Methanol from NG
LNG
Petrol

All forms of hydrogen storage - liquid, compressed or absorbed by hydrides, today offer better characteristics than those of electric batteries. The table below covers a typical tank for a large touring car or van.

Storage of Energy on Board

	PETROL	LIQUID H$_2$ LH$_2$	COMPRESSED H$_2$	HYDRIDE Ti-Fe	BATTERY Na/S	BATTERY Pb/PbO
Wt (kg)	67	130	590	1600	5400	18500
Vol (l)	83	320	1620	700	5000	6600

Storage by hydride would make it possible to have air conditioning in the passenger compartment, and recover heat loss in the exhaust. The relatively favourable weight and bulk characteristics of hydride explain the fact that almost all German motor car manufacturers are studying and even testing cars which store hydrogen through metallic hydride.

In Japan, Toyota has announced that it will soon be marketing an automobile truck powered by Ti-Fe hydride; the absence of pollution will make it possible to have vehicles moving in relatively confined spaces, in tunnels etc. (but provision must be made for the evacuation of gas in case in leakages!). The interest in the cleanliness of hydrogen in Germany has been confirmed by the signature of a contract between the EC and HydroQuebec to study the provision of liquid hydrogen to be transported on refrigerated ships to Hamburg. Plans for solar-based production are being studied for Saudi Arabia, the Sahara, etc. Hydrogen also appears as a way of transporting electrical energy over a long distance. As for distribution, it may be imagined that it will be problem free, like town gas distribution, and could be extended to filling stations along motorways. Since the last war, the Ruhr has a network of 200 km of hydrogen distribution.

Hydrogen, which can be produced from varying energy sources, centralised or localised into small photobattery units, therefore offers possibilities as a vector and storage point for energy. Unfortunately, hydrogen motors will not be as silent as electric motors, and as leakages from storage will be difficult to control, the use of hydrogen could be confined to professional fleets. To achieve silence, the hope would be that fuel batteries may yet appear - and this is still uncertain - at a weight and bulk which would be acceptable for vehicles.

Overall, in the very long term, electricity and hydrogen could share the propulsion of non-tracked vehicles; electricity stored in batteries would appear best suited to fairly slow vehicles, while hydrogen would provide the power and high degree of independence demanded by family cars, buses, aeroplanes and rapid intercity cars. This market segmentation, if it happens, could leave space for hybrid vehicles with a dual motor system, thermal and electrical, one for town and the other for the open road. Such vehicles are being intensively researched at the moment, but there are worries about their weight, their cost and the prices involved in their manufacture and maintenance.

Electricity from solar sources drives vehicles in Australian and American rallies, and the Swiss "Tour de Sol". These cars which are very expensive, and frequently uncomfortable (sometimes with drivers lying in a supine position), are very far from being marketable products. Costs and performances, which are slowly reaching 15% in practice, do not allow silicon captors to power traditional cars completely. The need to have fairly high surfaces will be a problem for land vehicles; solar captors will mainly help to decentralise the production of electricity to charge batteries or hydrolyse water with a view to producing hydrogen, lighting intercity roads, etc.

Energy Integration between Car and Home

The extraordinary rise in the equipment of cars with telematic, energetic and electromechanical resources has not yet been co-ordinated with the equipment of homes, which is leading to home automation with intelligent automatic management. Will air conditioning and remote-controlled door opening be duplicated or integrated? If one excludes the site costs, a household's investment in motor transport is not much lower than their investment in housing. Reciprocal energy packaging can bring the home and the car closer together: the heat released by hydrogen crystals being charged, could heat the house, etc. We should not forget that the average French car consumes annually the same amount as the heating for an individual, while wasting two-thirds of this energy. In any case, some of the most credible projects for solar-powered vehicles call for car batteries to be recharged by electricity produced on the basis of solar heating panels on the roofs of houses. The global management of energy, electricity and heat has already been taken on board in building in Scandinavia and the USSR; there is already an active market in co-generated small electricity stations in the United States. Will this energy integration be extended to the home-car connection?

4.3 Town Planning and Eco-Vehicles

Most current difficulties come from the fact that modes of transport are ill-adapted to cities. Only the technology of lifts is perfectly integrated with building. It is to be hoped that in future the city and its means of transport will be studied in joint perspectives, which could lead to cars being better adapted to the scarcity of urban space, and being linked with public transport, to which they should be seen as complementary. Very Small Vehicles for urban use, with good characteristics as regards space use and the environment, could perhaps one day find a market. Figure 7 and Table IV illustrate methods of organising cities and the possible specifications for three distinct types of Very Small Vehicles.

Figure 7:   Megalopoles and VSVs

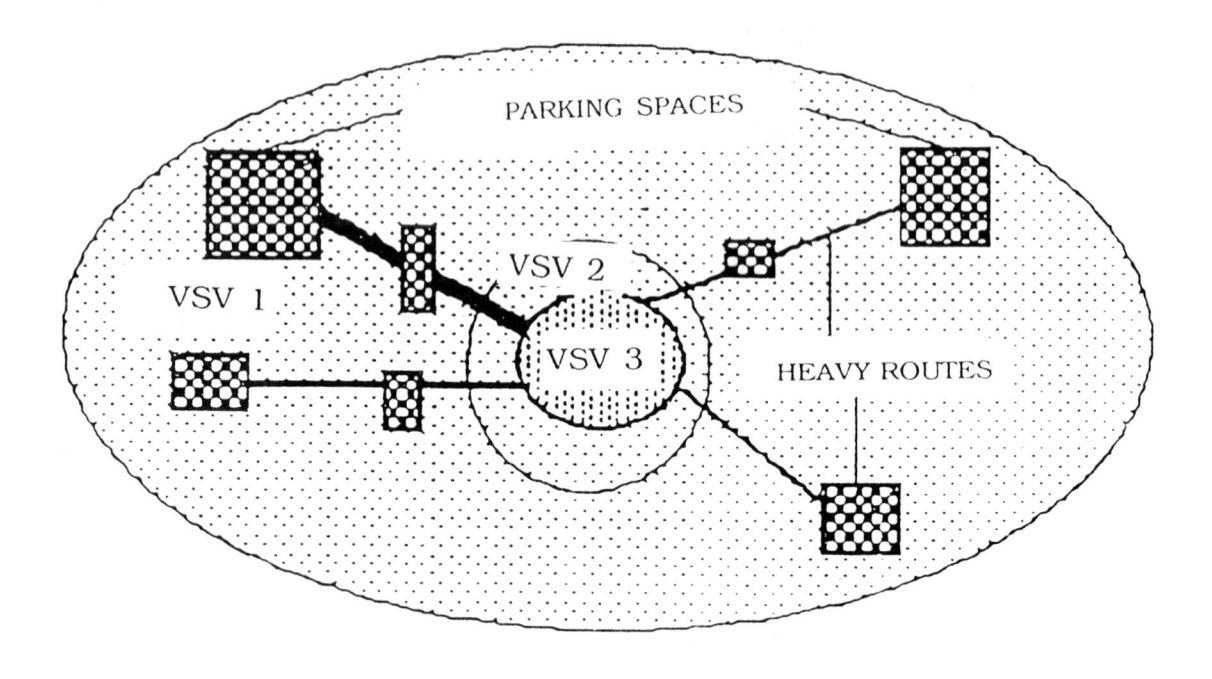

Table IV: Outline Specification for Three Types of Very Small Vehicle

	VSV 1	VSV 2	VSV 3
		Function	
	Urban - Passenger or occupational	Urban - Occupational or Delivery	Suburban - Residential
	Work and leisure zones - Hyper-centres	Urban zones, suburban zones (dense)	Residential and commercial zones
	Rental - Company cars. Taxi with or without driver	Companies	Private

Outline Specification for Three Types of Very Small Vehicle (continued)

Capacity

2 people	2 p	2 p
(80th and) 95th percentiles	same	same
Entry exit 10 secs	same	same
Luggage capacity 50 dm^3	200 dm^3	150 dm^3 (or a child)
Payload 200 kg	300 kg	240 kg
Maximum width 2.0 m	2.5	2.5
Maximum width[1] 1.2 m	1.2[1]	1.4
(Open door 1.5)	1.5	1.8
Eye level	to be specified	to be specified

Performance

Maximum speed 80 km/h	80 km/h	50 km/h
50 km/h on 4% slope	same	
Acceleration from standing start 2 m/s/s	2 m/s/s	2 m/s/s
Daily range 100 km	100 km	100 km
Consumption (urban cycle with one passenger or 75 kg) 2.5 l/100 km or 8.75 kw.h/100 km[2]	same	same
Motor idling: 0.3 l/h	0.3 l/h	?

[1] Passengers possibly positioned along drive access
[2] Measured on recharging meter

Outline Specification for Three Types of Very Small Vehicle (continued)

Pollution

HC-CO
Motor car norms

| high range | high range | low range |

NO_x - Motor car norms

Noise

- Maximum limit of cars but measured on 100 m from standing start to maximum acceleration

- Slow to stop at 7.5 m

| 55 db(A) | - 55 dB(A) | -55 dB(A) |

Safety

Impact - identical to motor car
Visibility to be specified, particularly night-time visibility
Roll-over resistance (On bends - in winds) to be specified

4.4 Transport and Telecommunications

The application of telecommunications techniques to transport is one of the topics currently favoured by transport specialists. The spread of telephones and television is reaching saturation point in most countries. Mobile radio telephones are destined for rapid expansion in a more portable car phone form; soon, with voice commands, there will be no adverse effect on the comfort and safety of drivers, and the telephone will have a calming effect on them.

The fundamental question is whether telecommunications can **replace** certain types of journeys that people make. Today, home purchase services seem to be developing despite some financial setbacks, which seem in fact to represent a consolidation of the position among American distributors. MITI in Tokyo reports a growth in demand for home deliveries, particularly of pre-prepared meals. The changing status of women, and constraints on motor traffic, may bring a slight shift in motor traffic away from purchasers and towards delivery vans. Of all the possible substitutions of telecommunications for human mobility, tele-purchasing and tele-teaching seem the most significant. For other types of substitution, what one finds instead is a simultaneous expansion of journeys and telecommunication links.

In the United States, the success of tele-conferencing is recent, and still fragile. Certain activities will be very sharply modified by telematics linked to videophones - teaching and training first of all, but also medicine, law, etc. Also in the United States, tele-conferencing is concentrated eighty per cent in training and education, but some judges are beginning to prefer passing judgement on accused persons without taking them out of prison.

An interesting question, which has been raised in the United States and Canada, is home-based tele-working, or more precisely "tele-commuting" - a term designating the position of a worker who, thanks to telecommunications, can avoid journeys between home and work (the traditional commuting trip). Alvin Toffler's forecasts could finally come true. Complete work stations for $3,000, a price which will reduce further, make it possible to communicate images, sounds and data over an ordinary digital telephone line. The reduction of trips between home and work is of interest to many individuals, but also to the authorities in southern California; for a number of years they have provided fiscal incentives, and sometimes even forced companies to set up policies to reduce automobile trips by their employees. For good reasons, tele-commuting has won their approval, and these local administrations are trying to remove all constraints on home-based working. Proponents of this idea, and especially women's groups, recently drew attention to the "ultimate home worker": the President of the United States. The probable outcome will be freedom to work at home, on condition that certain minimum standards in residential areas are met. Already, it was estimated that the United States in 1988 contained 15 million home-based workers (mostly female part-time workers), of whom 5 million were tele-commuters (a 7% increase between 1987 and 1988).

In countries where legality is less strictly respected such as in Italy and in Japan, home-based working seems already more widespread; Hong Kong has given spectacular proof of how twenty-storey buildings can be turned into hives of activity, with single-family workshops. The extension of tele-commuting seems beyond doubt in most of the countries of the world where the need for social contact can be satisfied other than through work; the role of work as a means of social integration is set to diminish.

In Europe one may consider that the need for social contact will only allow occasional tele-commuting. The public or co-operative microteleport between companies can then serve to reduce journeys for work or other reasons. Every village of 600 inhabitants used to have a post office; will every district now have its "telepostmistress"?

In conclusion, tele-commuting presents a major potential for strategies to reduce obligatory journeys in metropolitan areas. It would thereby liberate possibilities for optional journeys, thus giving practical expression to the citizen's right to free movement.

CONCLUSIONS

Electric-powered transport presents the best long-term prospects for the environment; hydrogen engines are in fact as noisy as a traditional combustion engine, and this fuel is not easy to store. Developments in electric propulsion with or without recovery of energy while decelerating should be speeded up in the case of buses, but also for various categories of urban vehicles (deliveries, etc.). There remains however the problem of the type of primary energy serving as a source for the electricity. Renewable sun or wind power have yet to show a substantial capacity, but solar batteries may see an increase in their currently very weak performance, and make an appearance in specific transport applications.

Should we conclude, for the time being, that further thought has to be given to the nuclear energy option? Ove Sviden has put forward a hypothesis of future sharing between different types of energy. The debate is not confined to transport authorities, but they must be ready to see a massive reduction in the consumption of fossil fuels.

In order to help limit the risks, it appears necessary:

- to reduce speeds and numbers of vehicles on inadequate roads;

- to encourage the use of public transport, bicycles and walking through a better management of the demand for urban mobility and the targeting of investment;

- to consider the problem of the greenhouse effect as a new energy crisis in transport;

- to promote electrification and related research for many categories of motor vehicles, and also to facilitate the use of natural gas for automobiles;

- to carry out research into the on-board storage of electricity, hydrogen and photo-electric conversion;

- and most of all to take account of environmental questions in urban planning and in investment decisions relating to transport and urban structures.

Figure 8: Hypothesis on the development of global demand for primary energy (Ove Sviden)

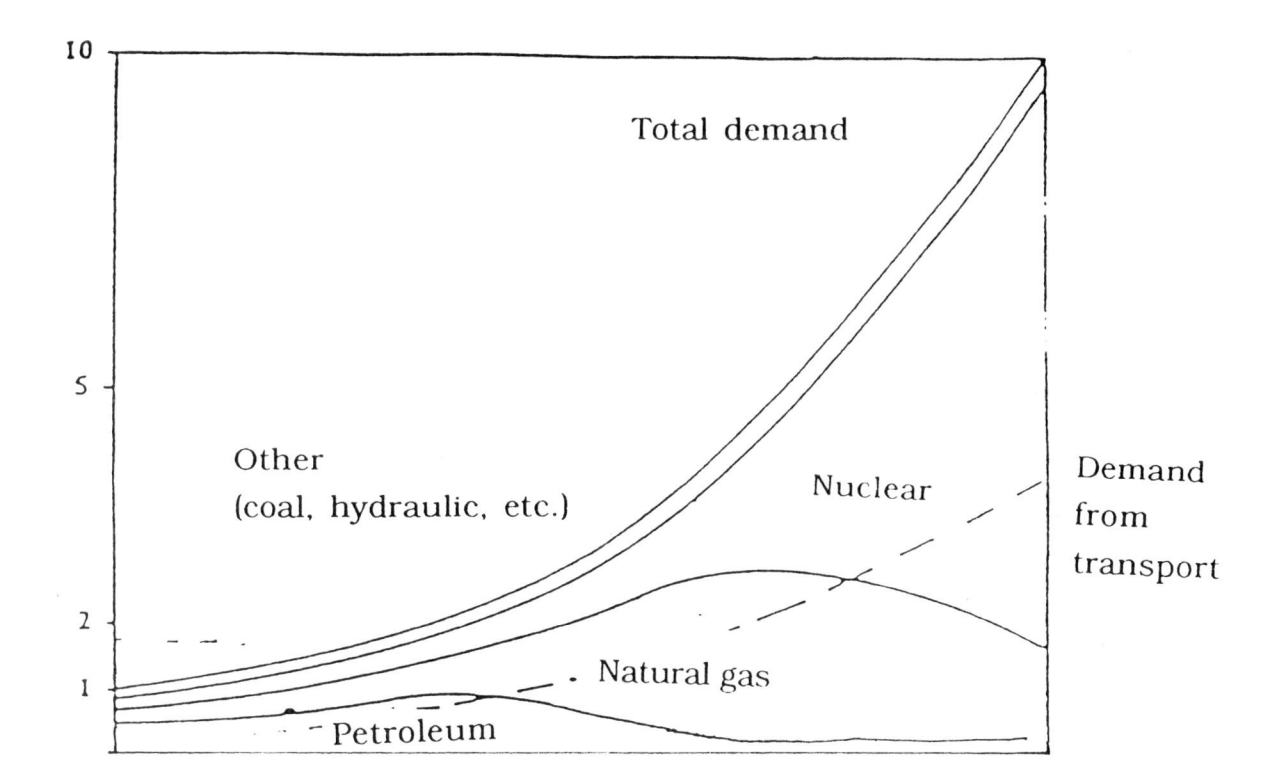

ANNEX 1

Selected effects of principal modes of transport on the environment

(Source: OECD)

PRINCIPAL MODES OF TRANSPORT	Air quality	Water resources	Land resources	Solid wastes	Noise	Accidents, risks and	Other effects
MARINE TRANSPORT AND INLAND WATERWAYS		Changes in hydrological systems when ports are built and canals are cut and dredged.	Use of land for infrastructure. Abandoning of disused port and canal installations.	Boats and buildings taken out of service.		Transport in bulk of combustibles & dangerous substances.	
RAIL TRANSPORT			Use of land for rails and stations. Abandoning of disused installations.	Abandoned track, equipment and rolling stock.	Noise and vibrations around stations and along tracks.	Derailments or collisions involving goods trains carrying dangerous substances.	Effects of disruption and deterioration of city areas, farm land and the habitats of wild flora and fauna.

ROAD TRANSPORT	Atmospheric pollution (CO, HC, NO_x). Particles and petrol additives (e.g. lead). Global pollution (CO_2, CFC).	Pollution of surface and ground water by run-off. Changes in hydrological systems when roads are built.	Use of land for infrastructure. Extraction of materials for road construction.	Abandoned deposits and materials from the demolition of road building sites. Disused road vehicles. Used oil.	Noise and vibrations caused by cars, motor bikes and heavy goods vehicles in towns and along roads.	Deaths and injuries to people or property due to road accidents. Risks linked to the transportation of hazardous substances. Risks of the emergence of structural faults in old or worn road equipment.	Effects of disruption and deterioration of city areas, farm land and the habitats of wild flora and fauna. Congestion.
AIR TRANSPORT	Atmospheric pollution.	Changes in ground water, the courses of streams, and surface flows when airports are built.	Use of land for infrastructure. Abandoning of disused installations.	Disused equipment.	Noise around airports.		

ANNEX II
EXAMPLES OF TRAFFIC CALMING SOLUTIONS

Illustrations of a speed table **above** and extended kerbs **below.**

A traffic calming scheme in West Bletchley, Buckinghamshire.

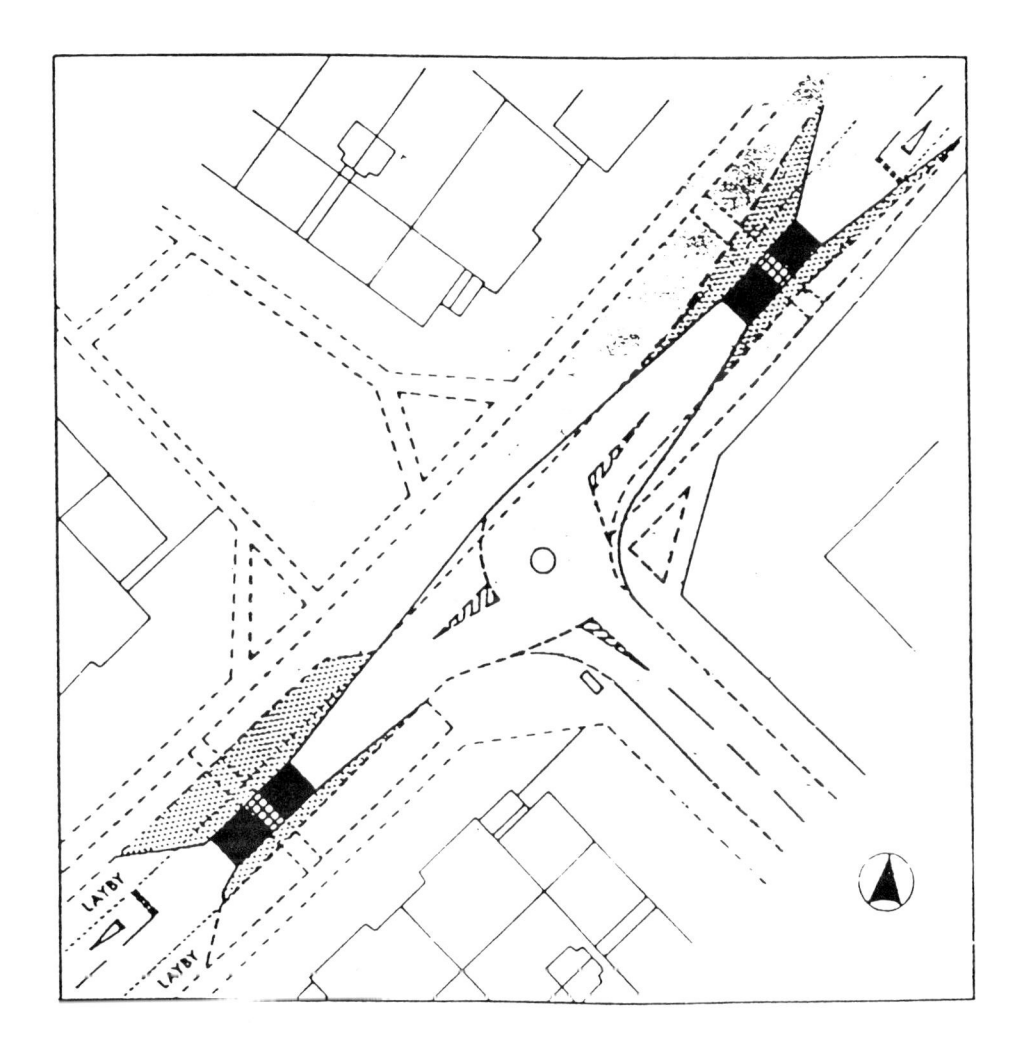

SELECT BIBLIOGRAPHY

Deluchi, M.A. - **Transportation fuels and the greenhouse effects** M.A., University of California, December 1987. TRB, Washington, January 1988

Evans, J.V.S. - **Designing Acceptable Roads.** PTRC. Summer Annual meeting. Bath, September, 1988.

Girard, Claude - **Combatrre le bruit de la circulation routière. Techniques d'aménagement et interventions municipales.** Ministère des Transports. Quebec, 1987.

Hammarström, U. - **Equivalent energy consumption and exhaust emission.** VTI topics - Volume 7, no. 3 - Swedish Road and Traffic Research Institute, Linköping, October 1988.

Harder - **Quantification of the separating effects of traffic construction measures in urban areas on social relations and urban structures.** Forschung Stadtverkehr. Bundesminister für Verkehr. April 1985

Krell, Karl - **Schutz von Strassen-verkehrsgeräuschen. 88 Jahre Strassen verkehrstechnik in Deutschland.** Kirschbaum Verlag - Bonn, 1988

Lamure, C.A. - **Speed related land transport noise.** Internoise. Avignon, 1988.

Mrass-Winkelbrandt - **Extended area consumption as example for infringements on nature and landscape by road traffic.** Roads and Traffic 2000 - Berlin, September 1988.

Sviden, Ove - **Clean fuel/engine systems for 21st century road vehicles** - ESF/NECTAR - November 1989

"Combustion et émission de polluants. Calcul des facteurs de conversion". Monographie CITEPA January 1988.

Project analysis - 15E - Calculation guide for investments in roads and streets. Jeneric Reyier. Swedish National Road Administration, September 198

Réduction des vitesses et émissions polluantes. Office fédéral de la protection de l'environnement. Berne, March 1984

Communication sur la pollution atmosphérique et acoustique. URCCE - Madrid

Conférence internationale sur l'Environnement urbain et le développement économique. BERLIN, January 1989

Athènes: la politique municipale pour la mise en valeur de l'environnement urbain. Conférence internationale sur l'environnement urbain et le développement économique, BERLIN, January 1989

Contre le bruit - Renforcer les politiques de lutte contre le bruit OECD - Paris 1986

Transport et Environnement OECD - Paris, March 1988

Les villes et leurs transports (Chapitre I - Athènes). OECD - Paris 1988

Inventaire des émissions de polluants de l'air. OECD - Paris 1990

TRANSPORT, URBAN FORM AND TOWN SIZE

Stephen Plowden
Consultant, London

1. THE NEED FOR A NEW APPROACH

The motor vehicle has existed for a little over a century. For the greater part of that time transport policy has been based on the simple principle of trying to accommodate whatever demands for its use might arise. There is now no dispute that, in towns at least, that principle will not do.

Among the reasons is the need to cut down on the consumption of energy and the resulting pollution and global warming. This consideration is so important that it might be said to have made other reasons superfluous. But it is also true that if energy were to be available for the rest of time at today's prices, and if its use brought no ecological hazards, the arguments for change would still be compelling. The cost in danger and environmental intrusion of a policy based on the indiscriminate use of motor vehicles and indiscriminate provision for them are too high, and it does not and cannot produce an efficient transport system.

Global warming has, however, produced a political impetus for changes which, however justified, were coming about much too slowly, if at all. It also increases the responsibility of developed countries towards developing ones and has heightened our awareness of that responsibility. The responsibility is of two kinds. In trying to set our own targets for reducing the use of energy and the accompanying pollution, we have to take account of the fact that developing countries are going to need more energy in order to achieve decent living standards, so that we will have to make correspondingly greater reductions. We also have a duty to provide developing countries with a better model. It is inevitable that they will take us as a model, so we have to find better solutions for their sake as well as our own.

2. BASIC CONCEPTS AND PRINCIPLES

2.1 Access not mobility

The traditional idea that mobility is desirable in itself must be discarded. Participation in activities and access to people and facilities are what matter; travel, both for the travellers themselves and for the other people on whom their journeys impinge, is a cost to be minimised.

2.2 Urban form

Good access at a low cost in travel can be achieved only if the urban form is correct. There are three requirements:

(i) **Compactness.** Towns should be of as high a density as possible consistent with the need to preserve good living standards, the provision of public open spaces within the town and a reasonable degree of private open space too in the form of gardens.

(ii) **Local provision.** People should be able to find as many of the facilities that they need for daily living within their own neighbourhoods. This requires the use of planning controls to prevent the growth of very large shops, recreational centres, hospitals and other facilities.

(iii) **Strong centres.** Facilities which generate large amounts of travel but which cannot be provided within each neighbourhood should be located only on sites well served by public transport. This means preserving strong town centres.

2.3 Selective user rules

The rules for the use of roads and parking facilities must be based on principles of selectivity. Walking, cycling and public transport should be the main modes of personal transport in towns. The use of private motor vehicles should be limited so as not to threaten or encroach upon these other modes; at the same time the rules should make it possible to use a car in reasonable conditions for those journeys for which it would still be especially convenient even when the other modes had been greatly improved.

User rules should also minimise the costs of goods distribution. In most towns, there is little opportunity for rail or water transport, but the scope for rationalising goods transport by road is very large.

2.4 Management before investment

New transport infrastructure, whether road or rail, is expensive, intrusive and inflexible. Before investing in it, it is necessary to show that better use of the existing infrastructure, brought about by reformed user rules and improved services on the existing roads, would not suffice. Because of the difficulty of predicting road users' behaviour, to explore the potential of better management will usually require actual trials and not just desk studies and modelling.

3. APPLYING THESE PRINCIPLES TO A EUROPEAN CITY

European cities predate the motor age and have inherited a suitable urban form, compact, with local facilities and a strong centre. This form must be protected against pressures for dispersal and against the tendency of facilities of various kinds to become larger and fewer. If the pressures are resisted, then, in cities which are not growing too fast, the problem becomes one of finding the best transport arrangements to suit a given land-use pattern. The following approach, which builds on the best current practice, can be applied to a large number of European towns and cities.

It is now accepted that town centres should be pedestrianised; it is important to ensure that the pedestrianisation of the centre brings as much relief as possible to the town as a whole, as well as to the centre itself. This means accepting that just as one does not drive a car within the centre one does not drive to it either. Journeys made to the centre from within the town should be made entirely on foot, by cycle or by public transport. Some journeys to the centre from outside the town can also be made entirely by such means, but when it is necessary to start the journey by car, a change to another mode of transport would be made at a park-and-ride car park at the outskirts.

The larger the pedestrian centre, the greater the relief that these arrangements would bring. At present, many pedestrian centres consist only of a few shopping streets. All towns, except the smallest, should provide districts for people who want to live without cars. The obvious way to do so is to extend the pedestrian centre to the adjacent residential areas.

These are various ways of ensuring that people do not drive right up to the boundary of the pedestrian area. Parking facilities in the band immediately round the centre could be restricted to spaces for residents and a small number of highly priced spaces for non-residents. Alternatively, or in addition, road pricing could be used, either a charge for entering the inner band or a distance-related charge for driving within it.

The bus or tram system serving the park-and-ride station would carry as well as travellers destined for the centre, a certain number travelling to premises on the radial routes into the centre. The road space freed by the removal of the cars bound for the centre or for these intermediate points could then be partly reallocated to bus lanes or to improved facilities for cyclists and pedestrians. The reduction in car traffic would also facilitate the creation of environmental areas, from which through traffic would be excluded, and the introduction of traffic calming schemes.

The rationalisation of goods distribution depends upon treating the geographical area, i.e. the town itself or some district of it, as the unit of organisation, rather than the individual firm. In this way much higher drop densities and tighter delivery rounds can be achieved, which means that the same task of getting a given amount of goods to where they are needed can be accomplished with less vehicle mileage, even though the vehicles themselves would be smaller and less intrusive than those now in use. This does not require a municipal delivery system. Some manufacturers already handle other people's goods through their own distribution systems and there are also hauliers who specialise in particular areas. The use of such services could be encouraged by bans, entry charges or mileage charges, possibly with exemptions or special rates for the use of specially designed or selected lorries, which would be small or medium in size, slow and with low emissions of noise and fumes. The road space freed by the reduction in lorry mileage could, once again, be reallocated to other uses.

Public transport should be able to flourish without subsidies under such a regime, although there could still be a case for selective subsidies (for example, to maintain a high frequency of service in the evenings) to provide an even more attractive service and so to make the regime as a whole more acceptable.

4.   THE GROWTH OF VERY LARGE CITIES.

One of the most striking phenomena of our times is the rapid growth of some very large cities, often just one city, usually the capital, in each country. It is not possible in a short paper such as this to do more than touch on this phenomenon, but a conference on cities and the global environment would be incomplete without some reference to it.

Some people appear to regard this development with equanimity, but this opinion seems to rest on a belief in trend planning and to contain exactly the same fallacies as the belief that traffic growth is desirable.

(i) The fact that the trends are the outcome of millions of individual choices does not mean that anyone has chosen, or even foreseen, the end result.

(ii) The people whose decisions give rise to the trend are thinking only of their own interests, not of the consequences of their actions for other people.

(iii) The decision makers' choices do not necessarily reflect even their own tastes or wishes, since they are constrained by the options open to them, none of which may be satisfactory. Thomas Hardy, a well placed observer, compared the migration of country people to London in the nineteenth century to water running up hill.

(iv) Governments might have intervened to check this process by improving the alternative options, but in fact they have reinforced it by concentrating investment in the cities, so increasing their relative attraction.

To my mind, there is no point in a city larger that, say, Edinburgh, Dublin or Amsterdam, which provide a full range of cultural and other facilities while still remaining human in scale and in touch with the countryside. But even if we need some cities larger than these, the very large modern cities which we now see emerging are sad, inhuman and even terrifying places. I do not believe that it is possible, especially given their very rapid rate of growth, to create good living, working or travelling conditions there.

Once cities have grown, it is almost impossible for them to shrink again; they may lose some population, as London has done, but the reduction in densities does not necessarily improve and may even exacerbate the problems. Drastic action is therefore required to prevent or, if that if impossible, at least to limit the process of growth.

The most powerful instrument available to governments is probably the location of their own facilities and of others whose location is under their control, such as universities and research institutes. More generally, investment should be diverted from very large cities to smaller towns or rural communities. Even the approach outlined in this paper, which relies on the better management of existing transport infrastructure rather than on new investment, carries some risk of encouraging undue urban growth. Investments such as the RER in Paris, or the recently approved Crossrail project in London, simply compound the problems.

SUMMARY OF DISCUSSION
RECOMMENDATIONS

The working group discussed and agreed on the following issues:

1. External costs imposed by the private motor vehicle lead to a reduction in possibilities of its general use, as it now imposes a threat to the environment and the transport efficiency.

2. Urban form and functioning of urban regions must be altered (and good urban forms preserved) in order to reduce demands on mobility.

3. Compactness and the reinforcement of activities in local/focal points should be aimed at.

4. **Physical restrictions** on access of cars to certain areas should be established. That includes complete closure of areas (pedestrianisation).

5. **Switch to other modes**/less pollutant types of vehicles should be encouraged.

    a. electric vehicles;
    b. charges for the use of cars: social equity must be respected;
    c. public transport should be given full consideration in the urban land use and transportation plans, as well as walking and alternative transportation modes.

6. When introducing regulations for restricting use of the private car, principles of manageability (political willingness) should always be borne in mind.

7. Special efforts should be made on small and medium-sized cities lacking the financial means and technical expertise to introduce measures.

8. The EC could contribute through the structural Funds to reorganise growth in cities but from a regional/national dimension. In this respect, vertical coordination between EC - national - regional - local governments should be of paramount importance.

9. Actual subsidies for car usage should be stopped by way of selective fiscal measures.

In the light of these points, the working group concludes and recommends the following:

1. As it was underlined earlier during this workshop the working group was faced with a **great issue**, but could find only small, partial, modest **answers**.

2. Transport in cities is responsible for environmental degradation, congestion and depletion of resources (space and energy): in most cities, the situation is becoming worse.

3. What should be done has been known for 15 years (in 1975, the OECD organised a conference called "Better towns with less traffic") but what happened?

    - has there been better coordination between land use and transport?
    - was there traffic restraint?
    - did public transport improve?

4. How it should be done remains debatable: some cities have improved their traffic conditions (Munich, Bologna, etc.), but most of them always "run" behind the problems. Policy instruments exist, physical measures are available. What is often missing is the political willingness, the courage to decide and do.

5. First of all, certain principles should be applied:

    - transport users should now pay the full costs of such use (the direct but also the indirect costs and especially the environmental and congestion costs),
    - any action to limit private car traffic should be accompanied, and if possible preceded, by measures to promote public transport.

6. The usual answers to traffic congestion: more roads, more technologies to assist vehicle drivers, are **inappropriate**. New roads attract new vehicles. New technologies facilitate the use of private cars.

7. However, roads and vehicles should be improved from safety and environmental points of view. In that respect the best technologies (catalytic converters, alternative fuels, etc.) should be used.

8. Present trends are unfavourable to the environment: urban growth, traffic growth, increased international trade, division of labour.

9. In the long term - 10 years? 30 years? - there will be **physical** limits to transport growth: no more space for roads and vehicles in urban areas.

10. Therefore, whatever the arguments in favour or against "freedom of movement" and "freedom of choice", a time will come when it will not be possible to use a private vehicle where and when one wishes to do so.

11. The time has come to **limit the use of private vehicles in cities** through:
    - higher cost of using such vehicles (taxes on fuel, road pricing ...);
    - public transport improvements and investments;

- physical modifications (pedestrian areas, preferential treatment of alternative modes such as bicycling and walking, reduced speeds for whole urban areas - "woonerf" concept).

12. In the long term, there is a need to limit, maybe to reduce, **travel needs**. Accessibility - at least in urban areas - is more important than mobility. In that respect, alternative settlement patterns should be considered, where the functions - work, leisure, home - are less separated. But it will take a long time to modify existing urban patterns. The situation of very big cities might be inextricable.

13. For the time being, cities should try to improve their environment for the benefit of their own citizens. But cities are also major sources of pollution for the global environment. Cities could play a major role in a more **sustainable development**. But they lack the incentives to do so. Cities should be induced - through incentives, information, subsidies - by National and International authorities to reduce the global impact of their transport systems. In that respect, traffic restraints, land use planning, road pricing, etc. all have a role to play.

14. There is no ideal, single solution. Reducing the negative impacts of traffic requires a **package of measures**, a mix of regulatory, economic and physical instruments.

15. The European Commission and other International organisations could assist National and local authorities by:
    - disseminating information and exemplary solutions;
    - developing indicators of urban environmental quality;
    - favouring exchange of experiences between cities by establishing networks or "Clubs" of cities;
    - financing certain field projects related to public transport improvements, clean vehicles and alternative models of transport.

GROUP 2

URBAN PRODUCTION AND CONSUMPTION SYSTEMS

Chairperson: Dr. Michael BANNON, University College Dublin

Rapporteur: Mr. Hugh WILLIAMS, ECOTEC Research and Consulting Ltd.

Participants:

Mr. Jupp HAMACHER, DG XVII, Commission of the EC

Dr. Richard HILTON, Department of the Environment, London

Ms. Ann McGUINNESS, Department of the Environment, Dublin

Dr. David MORRIS, Institute for Local Self-Reliance

Professor Peter NIJKAMP, Free University of Amsterdam

Mr. Juraj SILVAN, URBION, Bratislava

URBAN RESOURCE MANAGEMENT IN THE GREENHOUSE AGE

Dr. David Morris
Institute for Local Self-Reliance
Saint Paul, Minnesota, USA

SUMMARY

Global environmental concerns demand that industrialised nations dramatically reduce their consumption of raw materials. Cities can play an important role in effecting such a change. To accomplish this goal cities and higher levels of government must mix economic incentives that internalise the external costs of pollution and direct regulations where economic incentives are insufficient. The rules of international commerce must also be altered so that minimal environmental regulations do not become a competitive advantage. The principle of pre-emption should be applied rarely. Higher levels of government should be able to set minimum, but not maximum, environmental standards.

INTRODUCTION

Solving local environmental problems often means targeting materials toxic to the human body: heavy metals, DDT, PCBs. Solving global environmental problems demands that we target all materials. For it is our profligate use of raw materials, and our dependence on fossil fuels that is exceeding the carrying capacity of natural systems and is the primary cause of the present planetary crisis.

This profligacy is demonstrated by the inefficiency of our conversion systems. Even European cars, which are more efficient than North American cars, convert less than a third of the energy content of the fuel burned in the engine into car motion. Our power plants convert less than 30 per cent of the energy content of the fuel they burn into electricity in our homes. When industry processes trees into paper, as much as one half of the tree is wasted. Two calories of food energy are invested in our agricultural systems for every one calorie of food energy produced. And some 80 per cent of our products are thrown away after a single use.

These inefficiencies make the developed world the primary threat to the global environment. Ten per cent of the world's population generates more than half the world's pollution. The typical resident in these nations uses 15 times as much paper, 10 times as much steel and 12 times as much fuel as a resident of the developing world. (Durning).

The goal of drastically reducing our materials consumption can be accomplished in two ways: 1) by radically improving the efficiency with which we convert materials into useful work, and 2) by re-using products and finished materials.

Cities can play a major role in striving for this goal.

- Cities often bear the responsibility for managing or regulating materials flows, including hazardous, solid and human wastes.

- Cities may own power plants or electric or thermal distribution systems.

- Cities are the front line of public education. Waste issues are increasingly important in local elections. It is only at the local level that we can instill a new ethic of frugality and efficiency.

- Cities are active in promoting economic development and waste minimisation is one of the world's fastest growing industries. Cities tend to have the closest links to small and medium sized business enterprises, which are often on the cutting edge of "green" developments. By creating rules that make environmentally benign products and services more competitive, local governments nurture local businesses and skills that can later be exported to other communities. Moreover, improving efficiency and encouraging recycling lower operating costs and retain a greater proportion of the money in the local economy.

Testimony that cities are prepared to shoulder the responsibility for global climatic problems is the formation of the World Congress of Local Governments for a Sustainable Future, which met for the first time at the United Nations in June 1990, and the creation of the International Council for Local Environmental Initiatives in September.

THE POTENTIAL FOR WASTE MINIMISATION

To minimise wastes we must practice prevention first. In solid waste management this means emphasising re-useability. In the energy area this means improving end use efficiency.

Prevention

Re-useability is still in its infancy, yet even now refillable bottles represent the vast majority of Denmark's beverage market. In the United States, reusable cloth diapers are making a comeback. In Germany the share of the market for refillable milk bottles has reportedly risen from 0 to 5 per cent since their re-introduction a short while ago.

The concept of reusability should not be restricted to containers. Itasca County in Minnesota substituted reusable steel air filters for disposable paper filters on furnace and air conditioning units and cloth roll towels for paper towels at courthouse restrooms. Each substitution repaid the initial investment in less than one year.

The need for reusability even of durable products has led to a new type of engineering called designing for disassembly (DFD). Says David Gresham, director of design at Details, a new division of New York's Steelcase, Inc., "It promises to make recycling cost-effective for all kinds of complex products." (Business Week, September 17, 1990). DFD avoids the use of glue and screws since these make disassembly difficult. "Pop-in, pop-out" two way fasteners are used.

Electrolux Corp, already has a DFD dishwasher on sale in Italy though its subsidiary, Zanussi. BMW has a two seater car, the Z1, with an all plastic skin designed to be disassembled from its metal chassis in 20 minutes.

No studies have been done about the potential for reusability. Studies indicate that refillable containers are refilled 30-50 times before they are recycled.

The potential for reducing fuel use by improving efficiency may be even greater than the potential for reducing industrial materials consumption through reuse. Many studies have been done of the technical capacity for energy savings in buildings, appliances, cars, furnaces and manufacturing processes. Jorgen Norgard at Technical University of Denmark, for example, recently concluded that 3/4 of the electricity now used in Danish buildings could be saved at an average cost of 0.6 cents per kwh. Several other European analysts are converging on the same results (Lovins, A. 1989). A typical mass produced fridge and freezer consumes 2-3 kwh per litre annually. Models that incorporate the latest technological advances consume 0.4 to 1.3 kwh per litre. The technological state of the art is 0.2 to 0.4.

Recycling

High levels of recycling are feasible. One pilot project demonstrated 84 per cent overall recycling rates for households (Commoner 1988). Several municipal recycling efforts in the US are approaching 50 per cent materials recovery, including both household and commercial. Berlin Township is approaching a 60 per cent recovery level.

Waste Management Practices in Selected European Countries
(% of Total)

Country	Recycled	Composted	Landfilled	Incinerated
West Germany	10	2	66	22
Flanders, Belgium	--	10	40	50
Switzerland	20	2	12	66
Italy	--	10	70	20

Source: Platt, 1988.

Materials Recovery Rate in Selected U.S. Cities

Community	Population	Materials Recovery Rate (%, 1989)
Berlin, Twp. New Jersey	5,629	57
Longmeadow, Mass.	16,309	49
Haddonfield, N.J.	12,151	49
Perkasie, Penn.	7,005	43
Rodman, New York	850	41
Wellesley, Mass.	26,590	41

Excluding car hulks, white goods and construction debris.

Platt, B. 1989.

These communities are relatively small in size. However, contrary to popular belief, most of our populations live in relatively small cities, although they may be near larger population centres. Denmark's 275 cities average 18,500 inhabitants. One half are between 5-10,000. Of Italy's 8088 communes, 58 per cent have fewer than 3,100 people (Page, 1987).

Recycling and re-use saves energy and materials directly and indirectly. Re-use saves more than 90 per cent of the energy required to manufacture a new product. Recycling saves 20-90 per cent of the fuel required to manufacture a product out of virgin material. More energy is saved in reduced transportation since scrap based manufacturing units tend to be smaller and more regional than their virgin material based counterparts.

Recycling and re-use saves more than fuel. For every ton of material recycled or re-used we save several tons that were consumed or polluted to make that finished product. One ton of remelted aluminium eliminates the need to mine 4 tons of bauxite and over 600 kilograms of petroleum coke and pitch. Recycling a ton of steel prevents 200 pounds of air pollutants, 100 pounds of water pollutants, almost three tons of mining waste and about 25 tons of water use.

The analogy to recycling in energy is the recovery of waste heat from electric generation. Electric production consumes over one third of total primary energy in many industrialised countries. Two thirds of the energy now burned in power plants is lost as waste heat. Co-generation systems capture that waste heat for district heating or industrial process heating systems. District heating systems are making inroads in northern European cities.

The highest power plant efficiencies are achieved with small and medium sized power plants, for these can be matched to the base heating/cooling thermal load year round. (Cooling is done via absorption coolers). Currently the most efficient co-generation system has a power rating of 62 kilowatts, sufficient for a medium sized office building or medical facility. It has an efficiency above 90 per cent three times that of the average central power plant.

GETTING FROM HERE TO THERE

The potential for reducing our consumption of raw materials is very great. The challenge confronting us is how to translate the technical possibilities into widespread application in a relatively short time frame. The following offers specific measures that have proven necessary and successful in moving in this direction.

Data Gathering

1. A Uniform Methodology for Measuring Progress

The battle against waste lends itself to precise measurement. Scientists have developed a wide array of monitoring tools to gather information on greenhouse gas, acid rain and toxic waste emissions. A growing number of cities, states and nations require detailed manifests for waste handlers to accurately gauge how much waste is being generated and disposed.

A key problem is the lack of uniform definitions and measuring methodology. We do not yet speak a common language when it comes to waste minimisation. This lack has led several prominent observers, for example, to conclude that Japan was recycling 50 per cent of its solid wastes, when upon further investigation, the Japanese recycling rate turned out to be closer to 15 per cent. One New Jersey city in the US estimated its recycling rate at 60 per cent, but 75 per cent consisted of scrap car hulks. The practice of recovering car hulks had been going on for 15 years, and local public sector efforts had had little impact in that area. In the sectors for which the city had direct responsibility, that is, the household and small commercial sectors, the recycling rate was less than 15 per cent.

We do not yet have uniform measures of recycling rates. Moreover, we have no methodology for distinguishing between different end uses for scrap materials. Clearly in terms of global materials impact, we would prefer that paper be recycled back into itself and that bottles be reused. But we count a ton of paper that becomes compost the same as a ton of paper recycled back into paper. A ton of glass converted back into bottles is considered by planners as the same as glass mixed with asphalt for road pavements.

No methodology exists to compare the incineration of sludge to the land application of sludge to the use of sludge in integrated systems that include gas recovery and vegetable and fish production.

Without such methodologies it will be difficult to compare our performance longitudinally, or across borders and thus will slow our learning curves.

Economic Incentives

1. Change the economic relationship between producer and consumer

Until recently the consumer incurred the costs of inefficiency. We need to make these costs explicit, and impose them on the producer. For example, regulatory commissions overseeing privately owned utilities, and public sector owners of utilities traditionally encouraged power plant investments but provided no rewards for less expensive investments in efficiency. We did not include the demand and supply functions in the same accounting system.

In the 1980s utilities began to develop methodologies that allowed them to be rewarded for investments in efficiency. In some cases utilities earned higher returns for efficiency investments.

As a result of these changes at the state regulatory level in the United States, US utilities in 1990 will invest $1 billion in energy efficiency, up from virtually zero five years ago. The New England Energy System and the Wisconsin Electric Power Company in 1991 will invest more than 4 per cent of their gross revenues in energy efficiency.

In the garbage field, governments are holding manufacturers responsible for the costs of recovering their used products. In California a law called AB 2020, enacted in 1988, imposes taxes on packaging manufacturers sufficient to achieve a high product recovery level. In two years the programme tripled glass recycling rates of glass in that state.

2. Change the Comparative Economics of Efficiency and Used Materials

This can be accomplished in two ways: 1) by raising the cost of inefficiency, via waste disposal or pollution charges, or 2) by creating direct economic incentives for efficiency and recycling.

The closure of landfills and the banning of unprocessed wastes from landfills has raised the price of garbage disposal in my home state of Minnesota 1000 per cent since 1984. Avoiding the cost of these disposal fees has spurred alternatives to landfills. The scrap value of a ton of used newsprint in 1990, for example, was about the same as in 1980--$25. But "tip fees" at the landfill had risen from $10 a ton in 1980 to almost $100 a ton in 1990. The $90 increase in the "avoided cost" of disposal far outweighs the scrap value of the product and is the economic engine driving recycling efforts.

Nuremberg, Germany recently imposed a differential deposit on one way bottles and refillables. The 0.5 DM deposit on one way bottles was lowered 0.3 DM on refillables. Within months Pepsi Cola and Coca Cola, giant soda companies that previously had claimed that making plastic refillable soda bottles was not feasible, had introduced such bottles.

The same willingness to internalize the environmental costs of inefficiency and the use of fossil fuels is occurring in electric regulation. In 1978 the US, and in the mid 1980s European nations, began opening up the grid system to independent producers. In the US these producers were restricted to those avoiding fossil fuels or with high efficiency co-generation systems.

After opening up the grid, the price paid to these producers had to be set. Initially, the price was based on the avoided cost to the utility of providing alternative power. For example, if the cost to the utility of building a new coal fired power plant was 5 cents per kwh, then the independent producer, assuming similar reliability, would receive 5 cents per kwh.

Recently, countries and sub-national units have begun to quantify the externalities of power plant pollution (Ottinger, 1990) and add these to the price paid to independent producers. A detailed analysis undertaken by the European Commission prepared the way for a 4 cent per kwh premium paid to independent producers using solar or wind power (Hohmeyer, 1988).

3. Set prices to discourage high consumption

Traditionally, the more we consume, the lower the unit costs of consumption. Large users of electricity, for example, traditionally pay lower tariffs per kwh than small users. This system encourages consumption. There should be stiff disincentive to consume. Utilities are beginning to accept this principle, although most are only flattening tariffs rather than inverting them. One key problem is that the largest consumers of energy are industries and in several countries low energy prices are used as a subsidy to promote their international competitiveness.

The same declining price structure has discouraged waste minimization in the garbage field. Households, and to a lesser extent, businesses, are charged a flat fee regardless of the volume of garbage. This is changing. For example, in 1988 Perkasi, Pennsylvania required that all waste collected must be in green 20 or 40 pound plastic bags sold by the Borough. The per bag fee replaced the previous flat annual fee of $120 per residence for unlimited collection and disposal. Not surprisingly, since the imposition of volume based fees, per capita waste generation in Perkasie has declined (Platt. B., 1990).

Pleidesheim, Germany has a weight based fee structure. Household garbage cans are weighed on the truck. A bar code on the side of the can identifies the household, which is sent a computerized bill.

Efficiency investments often require an upfront capital investment which is repaid through energy savings. This creates a formidable psychological and sometimes economic barrier. Some utilities, like Southern California Edison have given away hundreds of thousands of high efficiency bulbs to low income households to overcome this barrier. Such programmes can be justified on the basis of system economies, but they can also lead to households using high cost bulbs in rarely used fixtures. The Taunton, Massachusetts municipally owned electric company is leasing high efficiency light bulbs to its customers. The customer pays 20 cents a month which is added to his or her electric bill. This is less than the monthly energy savings derived from the use of the bulbs but still provides an incentive for the household to install the bulbs where they will have high use.

Regulation

Changing the comparative prices of efficiency and recycling is a necessary, but not sufficient, step toward changing consumption patterns. Direct regulation is also needed. Businesses and households are not always guided by price. For example, more than 50 percent of all appliances (i.e. air conditioners, furnaces, refrigerators) are sold to developers, who do not pay the energy costs. Sometimes energy may be a minor part of an enterprise's production costs, and may not gain the owner's attention. Several studies conclude that households may need paybacks of less than a year before they are willing to spend more money on a more efficient appliance.

1. Procurement regulations

The public sector must lead the way. Dozens of cities have demanded that their departments purchase paper with a specific amount of recycled content. Sometimes, although not usually, they permit the department to pay a premium for the recycled paper. Unfortunately, most of these procurement regulations do not specify post consumer scrap. The result is that it encourages the use of industrial scrap, that is, scrap generated inside the factories rather than the use of recycled material from households and businesses. In the long run this is irrelevant, since once the demand for recycled paper reduces the amount of industrial scrap then it will increase the demand for post-consumer scrap. But it delays the process. This is particularly true of encouraging de-inking capacity in paper mills.

Often local, state and national procurement regulations actually retard the use of scrap materials. For example, British standards do not permit the use of recycled materials in roadways. In contrast, the state of Connecticut as of January 1991 will require that 35 percent of all materials used for public construction projects, including roadways, must be scrap.

2. Prohibition

Sometimes outright bans may be necessary. For example, in a growing number of cities and some states a moratorium on incineration has been imposed. This has occurred because of intense citizen pressure. The pressure is often a result of citizen concerns about incinerator pollutants like heavy metals and dioxins. But from a global environmental perspective, such a moratorium makes good sense.

One reason is that incineration and recycling are not compatible. About three quarters of the solid waste stream is both combustible and recyclable. Large incinerators can considerably diminish the amount of recyclable material available for recycling programmes. This in turn diminishes the potential for scrap based businesses locating in the city. Scrap based businesses, once established, will become powerful constituencies to encourage continued aggressive materials recovery programmes.

Incinerators also divert local resources, both human and capital, from recycling. For cities that do not own their own power plants, incinerators can represent the largest single capital debt incurred by or on behalf of that municipality. The siting, design, and construction of an incinerator diverts attention, time and resources away from recycling.

The second reason for a moratorium on incineration is the recognition that the front end pollution from incinerators is as important as its back end pollution. Although local battles are fought over toxic elements like dioxin the more important fact from a global environmental perspective is that for every ton of materials we burn, we must pollute, or disturb, or consume, 5-20 tons of raw materials in the processing of replacing that ton of finished product. Burning a ton of paper may generate 1500 pounds of carbon dioxide. Recycling that paper saves about 17 trees, which absorb 250 pounds of carbon dioxide from the air every year.

The issue of bans raises the question of the authority of sub-national units of government. Two hundred communities in Italy, for example, banned all types of plastic bags, but an Italian court forced them to lift these bans. The Federal Republic ruled that German cities cannot ban plastic packaging either. In the United States, for the most part, local bans on certain types of packaging, most prominently, styrofoam food containers, has been allowed.

To promote recycling one might argue for a ban on the import and export of wastes for this would encourage localities to minimize wastes and recycle them. In the U.S. the state of New Jersey enacted such a ban in the late 1970s, but this was overruled by the U.S. Supreme Court in 1982 as an interference with interstate commerce. A bill that would have allowed governors the authority to enact such restrictions was introduced but did not pass the U.S. Congress this year. The National Governors Association has recommended allowing states to establish differential fees on waste imported from other states.

Western Europe has used Eastern Europe as a garbage dumping ground for many years. In 1988, 800,000 tons of hazardous waste moved from West to East, and an unquantified but probably larger amount of non-toxic waste moved in the same direction (Christian Science Monitor, February 10, 1989). With their new found independence, Eastern European nations might ban the import of such wastes. It is unlikely that the Single Europe Treaty of 1985 would permit Western European nations from banning garbage imports from their neighbours.

In 1988 the South Coast Air Quality Management District of California enacted a sweeping clean air act that will phase out the use of petroleum as a transportation fuel within the next 20 years. The regulations cover an area of 20,000 sq. km and 12 million people. By 1991 all fleet vehicles must run on clean fuels. By 1998, 40 percent of all cars, 70 percent of all freight vehicles, and all buses must run on clean fuels. By 1998, 2 percent of all new cars must be electric, 10 percent by the year 2000. A shift to electricity, because of the improved conversion efficiency of electric cars, would modestly improve transportation efficiency. The regulations cover hundreds of household products. For example, regulations concerning volatile organic compound emissions is leading to the introduction of electrostatic spray guns, which reduce by half the amount of paint used.

3. Mandation

There is some empirical evidence that very high levels of materials recovery cannot be achieved without mandation. In gathering data for its 1989 study, **Beyond 25 percent: Materials Recovery Comes of Age**, ILSR examined 60 community programmes with recycling rates of 20 percent or more. This represented virtually all such communities in the U.S. at the time. Of the 45 that fell below 25 percent, 80 percent had only voluntary recycling ordinances.

Of those that had achieved over 25 percent materials recovery, 60 percent had mandatory ordinances. An update found that 14 of 18 communities with recycling levels surpassing 40 percent material recovery levels, or 78 percent, have mandatory recycling ordinances (Platt, 1990).

Mandatory recycling, provided the mandation includes sufficient materials, will create a large supply of used material. Attention must also be paid to the demand side of the equation. Otherwise a glut could prevail, as occurred with newsprint overwhelmed the de-inking capacity of U.S. and Canadian newsprint mills.

To create a large demand, the simplest measure to administer is a mandatory scrap content ordinance. Wisconsin is the first US state with such an ordinance, although it pertains only to packaging and is a minimal requirement (10 percent post consumer scrap content). A new programme initiated in the fall of 1990 by a private company holds promise for creating a uniform methodology for calculating scrap content while avoiding the need for cumbersome public monitoring.

The Green Cross programme undertaken by California based Scientific Certification Systems works like this. SCS identifies products that have the highest post-consumer scrap content. A manufacturer desiring certification for a similar product must be within 80 percent of the state of the art. The manufacturer pays SCS to conduct an audit of material flows in the production plant. If the product qualifies, a Green Cross label is offered. Inside the label is the actual percentage of post consumer scrap content of that product. SCS has signed up major corporations in a dozen different product areas to date.

Efficiency standards are the energy counterpart to scrap content or reusability requirements. The US is the only country to my knowledge with minimum appliance efficiency standards. These cover air conditioners, refrigerators and freezers. The standards were first introduced in 1978. The 1990 standards, which go into effect in 1993, will ban the sale of 90 percent of the fridges and freezers that were sold in 1987. As a result of these standards the annual electric consumption of a new refrigerator has dropped from 1726 kwh in 1973 to 1280 in 1980, to 930 in 1988 and 690 by 1993.

Public education

Creating an ethic of frugality demands a vast public education campaign. The message is that to be a good planetary citizen, residents of the developed nations must use only their proportionate share of the earth's resources and must use them on a sustainable basis. The Blue Angel label in Germany is a good example of a labelling programme that creates a larger awareness, for it covers not only products but such things as bus passes.

ENVIRONMENTAL REGULATION AND THE BUSINESS CLIMATE

Environmental regulations have been imposed largely for negative reasons, that is, fear of pollution. Yet one could argue that improving efficiency and recovering used materials strengthens local and regional economies. Energy related spending, for example, represents one of the worst kinds of expenditures in terms of its impact on the local economy for more than one spending cycle, compared with 40 cents for the typical dollar spent on other household goods and services (Morris, D. 1979). In other words, an additional 25 cents leave the local economy for each dollar we spend on energy as opposed to some other household goods.

Efficiency and recycling investments also tend to create more jobs than more capital intensive investments in power plants or incinerators. For every 600 tons of garbage landfilled, about 0.4 jobs are created. This rises to one job if the material is recycled, and falls to 0.05 jobs if the material is incinerated (Ruston, 1988).

The potential for using environmental investments for economic development is being seriously explored at the international level as well. For example, India's 300 million incandescent light bulbs account for about 35 percent of that country's peak electrical demand. One study suggested that investing in a compact fluorescent light bulb factory is 320 times cheaper than building a new coal burning power plant to power incandescent bulbs (Gadgil, 1990).

Environmental investments can help a local and regional economy in the long run. Yet such investments, and the creation of new technologies, will not come about without direct government involvement. "Unless government and society sets these rules ... this technical development will not come about", says Swedish Minister of Environment Birgitta Dahl.

Adds Goteborg city councillor Kerstin Svenson, "Manufacturers want to come to Goteborg and we want that, we want them there, but if they are using something harmful to the environment we say no. And then they say, "It is impossible. We must use it. We don't know anything else. It is impossible. The technique is not there yet. If you stand by and be firm, they will come with something else."

The energy efficiency and waste minimization markets are among the most rapidly expanding markets in the world. Even while some businesses struggle against environmental regulations, others eagerly embrace them as a competitive tool. Eventually, we may see a symbiotic relationship develop between businesses that embrace green concepts and government regulation. The Economist magazine recently remarked, "Most companies will be only as green as governments make them. The greenest companies will therefore try to ensure that government policies set environmental standards at levels that they can match, but their competitors cannot. The greenest governments will see such companies as potential allies".

FREE TRADE

While nurturing industries in the long run, environmental regulations can raise the cost of production in the short term. This might allow an advantage to imported goods produced in countries with a less rigorous environmental ethic. On the other hand, some environmental regulations may favour local businesses over foreign businesses. Both examples run counter to the worldwide move toward free trade.

A 1988 decision by the European Court of Justice ruled that Denmark's refillable bottle law favoured local bottlers over foreign bottles and therefore violated the Single European Treaty of 1985. The Court rules, "There has to be a balancing of interests between the free movement of goods and environmental protection, even if in achieving the balance the high standard of the protection sought has to be reduced" (Common Market Law Reports).

In December 1989, Germany introduced a compulsory deposit and return scheme for plastic mineral water, fruit juice, beer and wine containers. Only retailers are allowed to collect the returns and repay deposits. The rule discriminates against imports and favours German products. The European Retail Trade Confederation calculates that any drinks manufacturer based more than 200 km away from a retail shop could not make a profit under the system. Sales of French mineral water in Germany, for example, dropped from 250 million francs in 1989 to 30 million in 1990. Evian and other French drinks producers complained. A formal warning has been issued against Germany.

The current negotiations over the General Agreement on Tariff and Trade (GATT) also contain worrisome provisions related to the ability of nations and sub-national units to regulate on environmental matters. Even under the present GATT a nation cannot cite non-practice. Canadian

Environmental Law Association attorney Steven Shrybman notes, "The failure of a government to regulate has never been challenged a representing a subsidy, and there is no precedent for such a complaint" (Komoroski, 1988).

Recently in Europe environmentalists have suggested that GATT include a new article that allows countries to enact import and export restraints if their main purpose is to protect the environment. They would include a new category into GATT's list of unfair trade practices: ecological dumping (New Scientist, November 10. 1990). North American environmental groups echo this concern (Morris, 1990).

To accelerate the learning curve and to quickly change the habits of a century, we need as much innovation and experimentation and diversity as possible. This means that whether on an international or national level, regulations should set floors but not ceilings. Higher levels of government should be able to establish minimum environment standards but should not be able to pre-empt sub-national governments from enacting higher standards.

REFERENCES

Business Week, September 17, 1990.

Commoner, B. et al., 1988. **Final Draft. Development and Pilot Test of an Intensive Municipal Solid Waste Recycling System for the Town of East Hampton.** New York. Centre for the Biology of Natural Systems. Queens College. CUNY.

Common Market Law Reports. March 21, 1989. Re: Disposable Beer Cans: E.C. Commission (United Kingdom intervening) vs. Denmark. Case 302/86. September 20, 1988.

Durning, A. "How Much is Enough?", **World Watch,** Nov.-Dec. 1989. Washington, DC.

Gadgil, A. and Gilberto De Martino Jannuzzi, 1990. **Conservation Potential of Compact Fluorescent Lamps in Brazil and India.** Lawrence Berkeley Livermore Laboratory. Livermore, California.

Hohmeyer, O. **Social Costs of Energy Consumption,** Document No. EUR 11519, Published by Springer-Verlag. Berlin, 1998.

Komoroski, K.S. "The Failure of Governments to Regulate Industry: A Subsidy Under GATT?, **Houston Journal of International Low** 10, 2. 1988.

Lauer, P.W., June 11, 1990. **Results of Phase I, Itasca County Solid Waste Reduction Pilot Project.** Minnesota Office of Waste Management. Saint Paul, Minnesota.

Lovins, A., January 5, 1989. **Energy, People and Industrialisation.** Hoover Institution, Stanford University.

Morris, D., 1979. **Energy Self-Reliance for the District of Columbia.** Institute for Local Self-Reliance. Washington, D.C.

......., 1990. **Trading the Future: A People's GATT.** Institute for Local Self-Reliance, Washington, D.C.

New Scientist. November 10, 1990.

Ottinger, R., et al. 1990. **Environmental Costs of Electricity.** Pace University School of Law. White Plains, N.Y.

Page, E.C. and Goldsmith, M.J., 1987. **Central and Local Government Relations: A Comparative Analysis of West European Unitary States.** SAGE Publications. London.

Platt, B. and Morris, D., May 1988. **Garbage in Europe: Technologies, Economics and Trends.** Washington D.C. Institute for Local Self-Reliance.

Platt, B., 1990. **Beyond 40 per cent: Record-Setting Recycling and Composting Programmes.** Institute for Local Self-Reliance. Washington, D.C.

Ruston, J. 1988. **Developing Markets for Recycled Materials.** Environmental Defence Fund. New York.

Shrybman, S., **The Ecologist,** Vol. 20. No. 1. January/February 1990.

THE POTENTIAL OF EUROPEAN CITIES
FOR SUSTAINABLE ENVIRONMENTAL/ENERGY POLICY

Peter Nijkamp, Adriaan Perrels
Economic and Social Institute
Free University of Amsterdam

1. INTRODUCTION

In recent years the interest in urban environmental and energy policies has shown a remarkable rise. After the era of nationwide and/or sectoral energy policies it has been realised that cities and regions form important focal points for integrative and effective energy saving strategies with a view to both economising on resource expenditures and improving environmental quality. Cities and regions are usually fairly coherent administrative units, have often a joint energy production unit, have a direct interest in resource and environment issues and have usually an abundance of statistical material. As a consequence, urban and regional energy planning is gaining increasing importance as an effective strategy for ensuring ecologically sustainable economic development, as advocated in the Brundtland report (see also Juul and Nijkamp, 1988, and Nijkamp and Volwahsen, 1990). Cities offer a wide variety of energy and environmental strategies. In addition to the national level, regional and local energy measures often turn out to be indispensable additions to the national policies. Moreover, some problems are typically local in nature and therefore they may preferably be dealt with at the local level.

Demonstrations, information, consultancy and individual assistance are usually the non-price ingredients for energy policy schemes in a decentralised setting. To ensure sufficient impact these instruments should be easily accessible for the target groups. In practice this often means that the implementation of these instruments should - whenever possible - be realised at a regional or local level.

The institutional setting in which the energy system operates is of paramount importance to the feasibility and effectiveness of any local energy policy. Therefore special attention will be given in our paper to the institutional aspects, with special reference to the horizontal integration and vertical separation of energy systems in Western Europe.

In order to obtain better insight into the local potentials the EC commissioned a cross-Community review study concerning urban energy policy in all member countries in the framework of the CITIES programme of the EC. The present paper discusses the principal features encountered in this cross-Community review study. Section 2 will outline the motivation for the study. Next, some statistical information will be given concerning the economic structure and the energy consumption of the participating cities. In Section 4 the main urban energy policy issues are reviewed, while Section 5 presents various cases implemented in several participating cities. Section 6 discusses the importance of the institutional framework, while the final section 7 contains some evaluation remarks.

2. MOTIVATION FOR THE STUDY

Until very recently, the efficient use of energy did not seem to be an acute issue from the point of view of availability of energy resources. Recently the Gulf crisis has proven that this was a typically short-sighted viewpoint. The geographical and often political imbalance between spatial concentrations of oil supply and demand may be expected to be a continuous source of global oil market disturbances; hence reliable alternative sources - definitely including savings - remain a sound strategic energy policy option. To this consideration of energy availability we may add the important environmental concerns. Moreover, as long as fossil fuels dominate the energy mix, the exhaustibility of these resources should not be neglected, in particular in view of rising extraction costs. Finally, in a competitive European economy cost efficient production is of utmost importance, so that energy consumption will remain a major concern in the economic activities of firms in the next decades.

Towns are by definition centres of economic activity. Given that a concentration of activities implies a concentration of energy supply, urban areas seem to be a suitable geographical entity as a focus for energy policy (next to the international, national and regional level). Admittedly, large energy-consuming industries have usually relocated themselves from the core areas to the urban fringe, but that leaves the notion of urban areas as large concentrations of (direct and indirect) energy users (both for production and consumption) essentially unaffected.

Energy policy objectives may - at least partly - be achieved by means of national instruments, e.g., the manipulation of prices. For instance, the improvement of energy efficiency will certainly be stimulated by a rise in energy costs. Also the introduction of new major energy sources, such as nuclear energy, is usually a national policy item. However, both the residential sector and small and medium sized firms need more stimuli than just price incentives to ensure that they are actually participating in energy efficiency actions. Environmental policy has - in comparison to energy policy - also to rely strongly on non-price instruments, such as national - or preferably international - standards. Regarding the motivation of target groups, environmental policy has to take into consideration the local environmental, social and economic situation. Therefore, decentralisation of the implementation of environmental policy schemes is at least as strong a prerequisite as is the case for energy policy schemes.

Furthermore, this decentralisation argument also has an important function in a bottom-up policy strategy, as it will usually require less effort to involve and to motivate local inhabitants and interest groups for energy conservation and environmental programmes.

In summary: the following points support the establishment of and policy support for urban energy policy schemes:

- the city is a centre of economic activity and consequently a concentration of energy supply;
- local authorities have more insight and capabilities to shape the urban energy policy in a way that is custom-made to the local situation;
- establishment of local energy policies facilities the involvement of the local population, and hence motivation and public support is easier to receive;
- the municipality is often a more suitable entity as regards data collection, statistical analysis and political competence.

In line with the considerations mentioned above, the Commission of the European Communities has recognised that the decentralisation of the implementation of energy and environmental policy schemes to the urban level is potentially an important contribution to the fulfilment of national and Community energy policy targets. From 1983 to 1988 the Community has managed a programme to support regional energy studies in all member states. These studies served to provide a more efficient energy planning framework for their own region as well as an example to other regions. However, it was felt that in many circumstances the implementation of energy measures should preferably be further decentralised toward the local (e.g. urban) level in order to achieve sufficiently substantial efficiency improvements. Therefore the Directorate-General for Energy in the Commission has defined a new programme aimed at the support of energy programmes in cities. This is the so-called CITIES project, where the acronym CITIES stands for Community Integrated Task for the Improvement of Energy & Environmental Systems in Cities.

Twelve cities, one from each member state, have agreed to participate in a cross-European urban energy survey and to provide active policy support for the fulfilment of these goals.

In alphabetical order these cities are:

Amsterdam	–	The Netherlands
Besançon	–	France
Bragança	–	Portugal
Cadiz	–	Spain
Dublin	–	Ireland
Esch/Alzette	–	Luxembourg
Ghent	–	Belgium
Mannheim	–	Germany
Newcastle	–	United Kingdom
Odense	–	Denmark
Thessaloniki	–	Greece
Torino	–	Italy

Each of these cities has produced a report focusing on successful examples of urban energy policy in the city concerned. This paper will mainly highlight some important themes that emerge from the cross-Community study.

3. ENERGY CONSUMPTION IN EUROPEAN CITIES AND COUNTRIES

The population of the participating cities varies from just 30,000 (Esch/Alzette and Bragança) to more than 1 million (Torino). Some municipalities cover more or less the entire metropolitan area, such as Ghent, Odense and Besançon. Others, however, are a (dominant) part of a larger conurbation. This holds especially true for Torino, Thessaloniki, Mannheim and Amsterdam. This feature may be important as regards the interpretation of energy statistics, such as consumption per capita.

Yet, in most cases the figures presented in this section apply exclusively to the participating municipalities. However, for Thessaloniki and Dublin all figures apply to the agglomeration and for Newcastle a part of the figures apply to the region. The economic structure of the various cities differs substantially. For instance, Torino and Mannheim have large industrial sectors, whereas Amsterdam is extremely service-oriented. An overview of economic key data (as far as available at present) is provided in Table 1.

Table 1. Economic Key Data of 11 Participating Cities

city name	population (x 1000)	area (km²)	economic structure (% of labour force) industry & construction	services commercial	other
Amsterdam	720	126	19	52	29
Besançon	120	65	23	34	43
Cadiz	150	11	25	75	
Dublin	990				
Esch/Alzette	25	14	57	43	
Ghent	231	156	33	31	36
Mannheim	300	145	49	19	32
Newcastle**	286	103	31	32	37
Odense	175	102	32	35	33
Thessaloniki*	706	137	37	63	
Torino	1002	100	41	30	29

*) figures apply to agglomeration
**) labour fractions apply to region

Promotion of energy efficiency has been pursued for more than a decade in all member countries of the Community. Compared to ten years ago most countries have achieved some de-intensification of their economies. Per value unit of output energy consumption decreased with about 10% between

1900 and 1987[1]. However, the ratio of final consumption to gross consumption lowered in these years; thereby indicating the rising share of intermediate energy consumption, in particular for electricity generation. This may be regarded as a long term concern. The decrease of overall energy intensity in the European economies has been mainly brought about by conservation measures concerning combustion and heating. These conservation efforts were clearly set in motion by the high energy prices at the beginning of the eighties. Due to the low energy price levels in the last years we have seen few new efforts for energy conservation apart from new embodied (autonomous) technological progress. On the other hand we may witness a steady increase of the share of electricity in final demand. If savings on electricity continue to be relatively small and if improvements of the generation efficiency proceed slowly, the increase of electricity consumption may be expected to cause the overall energy intensity to rise again.

Although most countries managed to decrease the energy intensity of their economies, significant differences in the level of energy intensity still remain. Denmark appears to have the lowest intensity (little heavy industry), followed by France and Italy (favourable climate). The Benelux countries have rather energy intensive economies (chemical industries, steel and aluminium). From an ecological point of view energy intensity in economic terms is not always very meaningful, as the impacts on the environment depend inter alia on the specific kinds of energy used, the extent of abatement facilities and the spatial concentration of the energy consumption. In order to provide somewhat more insight into this phenomenon Figure 1 compares the energy consumption per capita in the various EC member countries and some participating cities as well[2]. Notice that the energy consumption for transport is excluded, as this appeared difficult to assess at the city level. In summary: the prevailing climate and the level of industrialisation largely determine the energy consumption levels per capita in different countries.

The different stages of urbanisation among European countries are also related to remarkable differences between urban and national consumption levels as depicted in Figure 1. Notice that in Besançon and Thessaloniki the per capita consumption levels are above the national levels, while in Amsterdam the opposite is true. Clearly this may be largely explained by the different economic structures of the cities concerned. Yet, Torino - an industrial city - illustrates (Figure 1) how carefully these generalisations should be interpreted. Finally, Figure 2 illustrates the

---

[1] Based on Eurostat, Energy Statistics 1988

[2] Total Final Energy Consumption at the City level could only be obtained for some cities. Especially, energy consumption of transport is difficult to assess at this level. More generally, energy statistics concerning the urban level are particularly reliable for network provided energy carriers.

per capita levels of electricity consumption for the twelve cities and their related countries. Compared to Figure 1 Mannheim and Torino are more intensive than the country average. The extreme electricity orientation of Besançon is remarkable. Probably this may be explained by a high penetration of electric heating. Perhaps to a lesser extent, electric heating explains the shifts of Mannheim and Torino compared to Figure 1.

Figure 1: **Final energy consumption per capita excluding transport in EC countries and participating cities**

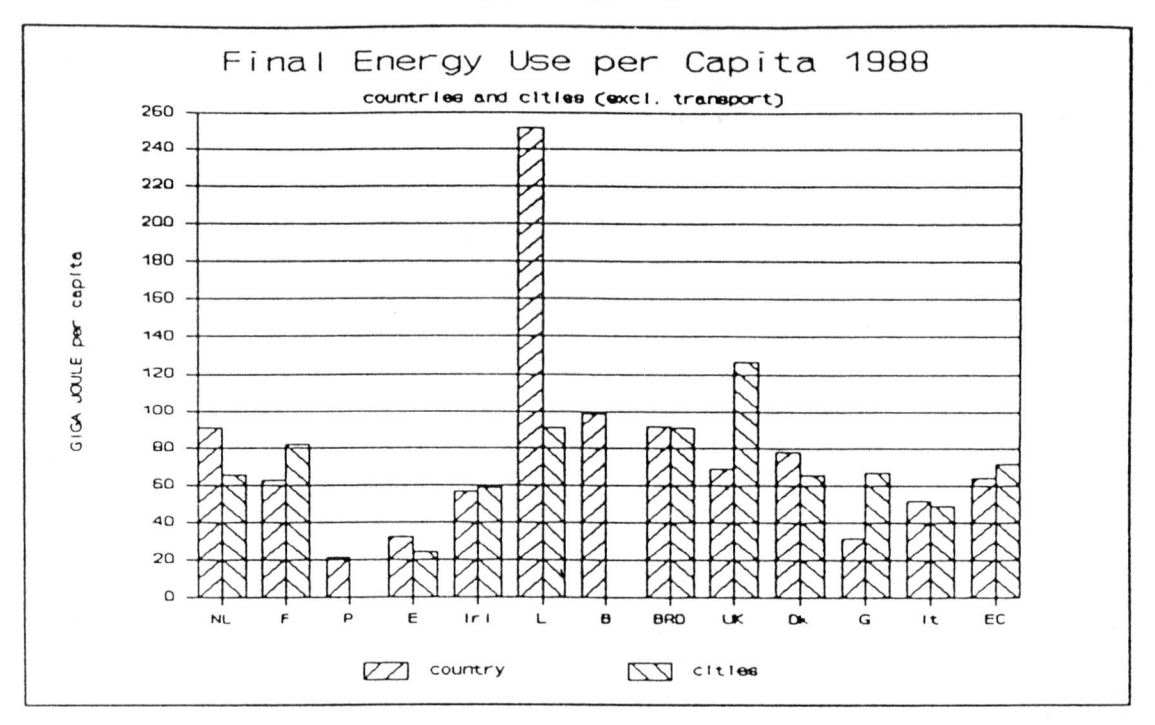

Figure 2: **Final electricity consumption per capita in EC countries and participating cities**

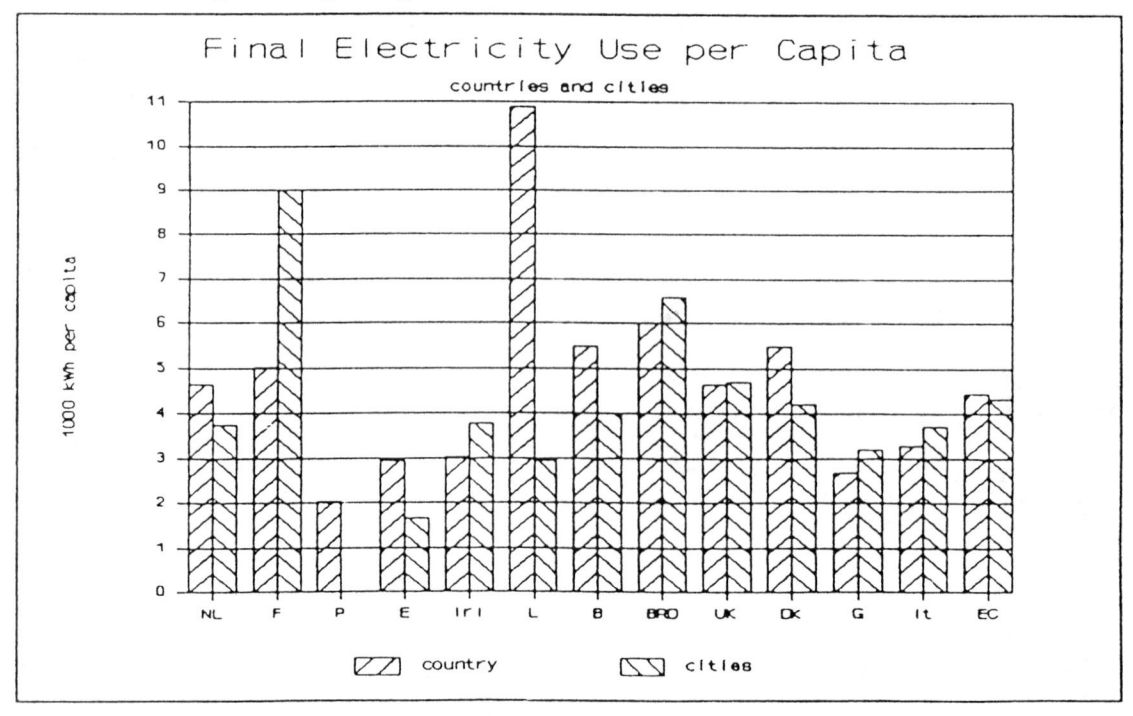

4. AN OVERVIEW OF ISSUES IN URBAN ENERGY POLICY

During preparatory talks with the various city teams and supported by various publications on energy (inter alia, Europlan, 1988; Lundqvist, 1989) the following policy areas were identified as largely making up the urban energy policy "space":

- urban energy supply systems (UESS), e.g. district heat systems based on combined heat and power units;
- urban waste management (UWM) e.g. urban waste recycling schemes;
- urban transport systems (UTS) e.g. promotion of public transport, traffic flow management;
- information, communication and marketing (ICM) e.g. customised consultancy on insulation for/by small consumers;
- management of municipal building and vehicle stock (MBVS) e.g. measuring, data collection, targets, monitoring of energy use in public buildings;
- development of integrative urban energy concepts (IUEC) e.g. the balancing of economic, social and energy concepts (IUEC) environmental costs and benefits of offering connections to two or more alternative energy networks.

Twelve cities participate in the CITIES programme. Table 2 shows the choice of energy policy areas made by twelve of the participating cities. This choice by no means implies that the city concerned is not active in other entries of the table. One policy area may cover more than one project in a city, while some projects are related to several policy areas.

Energy management of the municipal capital stock is common practice in all participating cities, but is discussed at length in only a few reports. It may be regarded as the lower limit of a local energy policy. Obviously, a municipality should at least be capable of improving the efficiency of its own buildings and equipment. Usually this serves two objectives. First it reduces the operating costs of the municipal capital stock and second it serves as a good example to local firms and citizens.

The upper limit for local energy policy is an effective local management of the energy supply systems. In the case of local management of the energy supply system, the municipality (or its energy subsidiaries) has the opportunity to shape the system in a way that is optimal in terms of local environment, efficiency and reliability. Clearly, it should be acknowledged that sometimes the surplus revenues of local energy companies are used to cover financial deficits in municipal budgets, although this is not reported in the documents of participating cities.

Table 2. An overview of programmes and projects discussed in twelve city reports per policy area

	UESS*	UWM	UTS	ICM	MMCS	IUEC
Amsterdam	*			*		
Besançon			*		*	
Braganca	*					
Cadiz	*					
Dublin	*					
Esch/Alzette	*				*	
Ghent	*	*			*	
Mannheim	*					*
Newcastle		*		*	*	
Odense	*			*		
Thessaloniki		*	*			*
Torino	*					

*) UESS - urban energy supply systems; UWM - urban waste management; UTS - urban transport systems; ICM - information, communication and marketing; MMCS - management of municipal capital stock; IUEC - integrative urban energy concepts.

In countries with strongly centralised (i.e. national) energy supply companies, cities often do not have much influence on the local supply system. Consequently, the municipalities concerned appear to focus their energy policies on other fields where they are capable of exerting significant influence. On the one hand, a municipality may decide to create local energy consultancy agencies aimed at the support of small commercial and residential energy consumers. By doing so it circumvents to a large extent the monopoly power of national energy companies.

On the other hand, in cases where a municipality chooses not to challenge the other major actors, it usually prefers to deal with issues that have a derived impact on energy consumption and the environment. Urban transport systems appear to be a popular alternative, although spectacular results are only rarely found. Nevertheless, the urban transport system is undoubtedly a meaningful option, as the transport sector happens to be an important energy consumer in urban areas (approximately 25%). Moreover, the environmental consequences are substantial in terms of both pollution and space. Generally the energy and environmental aspects of urban transport policies result in the stimulation of public transport, the exclusion of private cars in some inner city areas, the creation of park and ride facilities near main gateways to the city, the encouragement to use clean engines (preferably electric), and demonstration projects concerning the introduction of environmentally less unfavourable (public or para-public transport) vehicles.

5. SOME CASE STUDIES

5.1 Urban Waste Management

Due to its inherent lack of appeal and the concomitant low social value given to work related to refuse processing, both individuals and institutions have tended to neglect the processing of waste. For a long time it was common practice throughout Europe just to deposit the waste at the urban fringe in large pits. Due to the growth of cities, the increase of individual wealth and the expansion of industrial output, the "production" of urban waste has grown to enormous quantities. Sooner or later, national and local authorities realised that this practice could not be continued forever. Initially numerous local authorities resorted to rather evasive solutions. For instance, the refuse was transported to remote areas or it was burnt in large combustion units lacking any filtering. Clearly these "solutions" merely transferred the problems to other regions or to another part of the biosphere.

In order to establish real solutions the value of waste as well as the disvalue (costs) of environmental pollution have to be recognised. It turned out that as soon as this was the case, a range of technical solutions became feasible. All these solutions have the following characteristics in common:

- identification of the components that make up the refuse;
- separation of components in order to recycle components (e.g. paper, glass, various metals, biological refuse)
- isolation of environmentally hazardous components (e.g. batteries)
- volume reduction of remaining unrecyclable components causing as little damage as possible.

In fact, prior to the above mentioned steps a comprehensive waste policy should also pay attention to the "production" of waste. That is, industries should be encouraged to use recyclable non-noxious materials and both producers and consumers should be encouraged to produce as little waste as possible. Yet, these waste prevention measures require a lot of co-ordination (between industries, etc.). Therefore such measures may preferably be dealt with at the regional or national level. In many cases even international co-ordination may be necessary (viz. the Montreal agreement on CFC's).

As there are so many producers of waste the organisation of urban waste management is not a very easy task, especially as regards the motivation of citizens, firms and institutions to participate in a disciplined and environment-friendly way. In this respect separation and isolation seem to be key issues for successful urban waste management.

Newcastle-upon-Tyne has developed an advanced method to process a kind of pelletised fuel out of urban refuse. According to the Newcastle report these refuse fuel pellets turn out to be cheaper than any other combustion fuel. However, initially the production process for the pelletised fuel encountered many problems especially with regard to a reliable separation of the usable elements from the collected waste.

Separation at the source, that is at home, office, etc., seems to be a valid strategy to prevent difficulties with the separation in subsequent stages of waste processing.

In this respect, the Belgian city of Ghent has made much progress as regards its treatment of refuse. It has established a sophisticated separate collection of the various waste components. Since 1988 four public refuse container parks are operated, that allow the separated collection of glass, paper, tyres, construction and demolition waste, biological waste, oil and oil products, and metal wastes. In addition to these waste collection parks, there exists a door-to-door collection service for paper and glass. Furthermore, there are several collection networks for crown caps, batteries and mercury thermometers. In order to attain high retention rates for recyclable components, several information bulletins are regularly distributed among households and companies.

Since 1964 the municipality operates compost units to treat household refuse. More recently (1985) the municipality installed a pilot fermentation plant, which produces bio-gas from household refuse. Another kind of bio-gas generator has been installed in a large hospital. For the near future a reorganisation of the incineration of urban waste in Flanders should be effected. The new refuse combustion plants, of which one is to be located in Ghent, are designed to produce electricity.

5.2 Information, Motivation and Price Incentives

Households and small enterprises often do not have sufficient knowledge about effective ways of improving the energy efficiency in homes, shops and offices. Therefore price incentives have to be accompanied by information and consultancy instruments. Information may be given both via mass-media such as (local) television and newspapers and by means of personal advice to individual consumers. Most countries in the Common Market have national energy information and energy consultancy agencies. Fortunately, more and more cities or other local (energy) authorities are establishing local energy information and consultancy agencies as well. Sometimes these agencies are part of the municipal information department, but in most cities the consultancy and information task is delegated to the local energy company. However, the delegation of this task to the local energy company requires that the promotion of energy efficiency should be defined as an official company task. The motivation of the local energy company to promote energy savings will be significantly enhanced if the local energy company deals only with distribution and not with energy production and/or if the local energy company operates according to an overall energy plan including efficient production, transport and use of energy. A recent phenomenon in several cities is the very active marketing toward households in conjunction with an enlargement of the scope of energy consultancy services, including, for instance, mediation in case of debts to the energy company.

In conjunction with informing the public most municipalities have made enormous efforts to improve the efficiency of their own capital stock. One should not forget that the municipality itself is an important energy consumer. In order to be effective these internal energy efficiency programmes require a thorough organisation of information flows. Initially general guidelines were issued, while subsequently many municipalities started to monitor energy budgets. In order to explain differences in energy consumption ratios between departments, buildings etc., detailed metering schemes were installed. The next logical step was to move from automatic metering to automatic control. Consequently, nowadays a lot of municipal buildings are fitted with energy management devices, contributing to an impressive increase in the energy efficiency. For instance, the energy consumption for heating in all municipal buildings (including schools) in Besançon in 1989 is 67% of the amount of energy needed in 1979. The investments in energy efficiency appear to be very cost effective. The accumulated investments in Besançon since 1979 amount to 20 million FF, while the accumulated energy savings since 1979 represent a value of 33 million FF.

Time of day rates are the most well known instrument to bring about changes in the load shape of an electricity network. Numerous studies have been published on this subject (see inter alia Sexton et al, 1987; Train et al, 1987). On the other hand, the assessment of an appropriate rate structure as well as an appealing introduction to the consumer are quite complicated activities. The Amsterdam Municipal Energy Company has found an interesting opportunity to accomplish both some levelling off of the early evening peak and saving electricity in households. Because of earlier residential consumption surveys it was relatively easy to identify residential lighting as one of the important contributors to the evening peak. This is illustrated in Figure 3 below. This figure represents a diurnal load shape of the national grid; in Amsterdam the early evening peak is more marked.

Figure 3: **The load shape of the Dutch Electricity Network on Thursday, January 21, 1988**

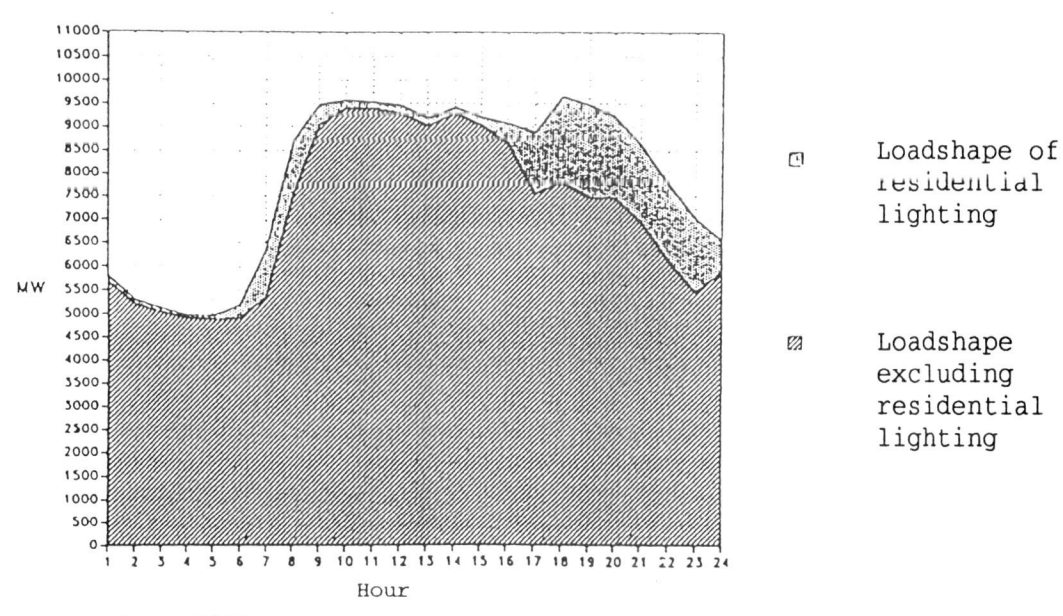

Source: Sep, 1989

Before the action started, energy saving lamps (SL and PL) had hardly penetrated the household market. This poor penetration rate is largely attributed to the relatively high initial costs of SL and PL lamps compared to conventional light bulbs (Hfl. 20.- to Hfl. 30.- and Hfl. 1.- respectively). The resulting long pay back times discourage most people to buy such lamps. Therefore, the Amsterdam Municipal Energy Company arranged with several electric bulb producers and relevant local retail organisations to issue a special offer to households. Households were able to buy a limited number of SL or PL bulbs for a reduced price during a period of six weeks. The customers could choose for either direct payment or payment by cheque issued by the Energy Company. In the latter case the cheque had to be repaid by adding the costs to the next ten monthly bills. Assuming direct payment of the lamp the approximate break-even point compared to the ordinary light bulb is 22 months. About 150,000 lamps were sold, most of them by direct payment. The Energy Company expects a reduction of aggregate annual demand of approximately 11 GWh. Further stimulating actions for the promotion of this kind of lamps are foreseen.

6. THE SIGNIFICANCE OF THE INSTITUTIONAL FRAMEWORK

As indicated above, the institutional setting in a country determines to a large extent the maximum, "policy space" available for an urban energy and environmental policy. Based on the information from the twelve city reports two aspects are identified as being of particular importance. These are the degree of (de-)centralisation of the management of energy systems as well as the ownership status of the energy systems. A large variety exists among member countries of the European Community. An overview for both aspects for various member countries is given in Table 3.

Generally, countries have specific institutional and organisational forms for their energy systems. However, mixed situations may exist as well, for instance, when one energy system is primarily nationally managed, while another system is mainly locally managed. Furthermore, some energy supply systems, e.g. the high-voltage electric power transportation grid, have necessarily a national status.

In Denmark integration of production and distribution is often established at the local (urban) level. The same concept exists in several German cities. However, regional power companies also exist. Usually these are private companies, though a significant part of the shares may be owned by local or regional administrations. Sometimes the integration at the urban level includes district heat and natural gas distribution. Recently production and main transport of electricity and natural gas in Holland has been completely separated from distribution.

Table 3   Degree of centralisation and ownership status in various EC member countries (the prevailing situation in each country is diplayed)

	Electricity production	distribution	Natural Gas main transport	distribution
Belgium	private-central	ppp-regional	ppp-central	public-local
Denmark	public-local	public-local	public-central	public-local
Germany	*private-regional	*private/public-regional/local	*private-regional	*private/public-regional/local
Greece	public-central	public-central	public-central	public-central
France	public-central	public-central	public-central	public-central
Italy	*private/public-central/local	public-local	*private-central	public-local
Holland	*private-regional	*private/public-regional/local	ppp-central	*private/public-regional/local
U.K.	public/private-central	private-regional	private-central	private-central

ppp - public private partnership
an asterisk (*) before "private" denotes ownership of shares by public authorities

In various countries, (through merger and buy-out) horizontally integrated regional or urban distribution companies have been created taking care of electricity, natural gas and district heat (if present). Where energy companies are private, (e.g. all power production companies and various regional distribution companies), shares are owned by the regional and local authorities concerned. France and Greece have completely centralised vertically-integrated public energy companies covering virtually the whole country. In Belgium the production of electricity is mainly a private business, but the distribution of both gas and electricity shows various alternatives including joint ventures between public and private institutions (public private partnership). If the electricity supply industry is privatised like the other components of the British energy system, the UK undoubtedly will have the most privately owned energy networks. Notice that the natural gas grid is operated within one nationwide organisation,, while the power distribution sector is organised on a regional basis. Italy shows quite a hybrid picture: on the one hand there is a very large state owned energy holding company including production, main transport and distribution of electricity and natural gas; on the other hand there exist various regional or local (urban) distribution companies for electric power, district heat and natural gas. Some of these local companies also possess electric generation power.

In all countries strategic planning and research for the various energy systems is carried out by national organisations or by a co-operation of regional and local companies. In some countries, like the UK and Holland, the production (extraction) of natural gas is operated by private - not state owned - international firms, such as BP, Exxon and Royal Dutch/Shell. In other countries, such as Italy, this is done by state owned companies. In wholly centralised systems such as in France and Greece, electricity distribution companies are usually not allowed to operate small scale generation units (including district heat). In the decentralised or separated systems distribution companies usually have this right and make use of it. The arguments to install small scale local power units are manifold, such as local optimisation of supply, peak shaving, countervailing power vis-à-vis the large power supply companies, demonstration and experimental purposes and environmental considerations. Clearly, these arguments may be mutually complementary.

From the case studies in the preceding section as well as from the information above we infer that scale economies in the electricity sector require much larger generation companies than distribution companies. Consequently, the electricity supply industry is usually organised on a national or regional level, while - due to recent decentralisation tendencies - distribution companies operate often at a local or regional scale. Moreover the separation of production and distribution enhances competition in a manageable way and opens up better opportunities for energy saving measures.

Undoubtedly, privatisation is developing most strongly in the UK. The regional electricity companies in, for instance, Germany, Belgium and The Netherlands also have - in varying degrees - a private sector character.

In these cases regional and local authorities ensure their influence between the management of the wholly privatised energy companies in the UK and the Limited companies in Germany, Netherlands and Belgium. The latter companies will usually be able to attract external capital by paying normal long term market interest rates and sometimes even lower. In the UK however, the energy companies have to compete fiercely with other investment alternatives, which implies currently real rates of return of about 15%. Consequently, British energy companies are very reluctant to invest and on the other hand they have to be very keen on a high utilisation level of their capital stock. Under certain conditions such incentives may frustrate energy conservation strategies. For instance, so called "valley filling" for electricity companies may be an attractive option. In those cases where this "valley filling" is achieved by attracting new demand instead of shifting demand - and especially in case of substituting natural gas or district heating - this practice is incompatible with long term energy efficiency programmes.

The state of the local economy is of course another important restriction on the actual possibilities to carry out local energy programmes. Even if the "policy space" is available and benefits are evident, other local problems may be perceived more important to the municipality. For instance, several large cities suffering from urban and concomitant social decay prefer to focus their efforts on the improvement of the social and economic situation of the population in those parts of the city concerned (see inter alia Nijkamp and Perrels, 1990). These efforts may include energy measures such as insulation in order to cut heating costs. Remarkably enough, the same kind of priority options may arise in economically extremely successful cities. Usually the growth of the metropolitan area induced by the economic thrift absorbs most attention of the municipality. Moreover many municipalities do not dare to risk any decline in urban growth by introducing measures aimed at the improvement of the energy efficiency and/or the environment.

Yet, apart from the long term benefits, the short and medium term benefits of comprehensive energy programmes should not be underestimated, both in financial and environmental terms, especially if this includes the lifting of institutional impediments. For instance, the reorganisation of the utility sector in the Netherlands has clearly contributed to a situation that allowed (and allows) for efficiency improvements in the electricity supply sector as well as stimulated the establishment of energy efficiency programmes by the local and regional energy distribution companies.

7. CONCLUDING REMARKS

The cross-Community review of urban energy projects has revealed that virtually every city recognises the importance of local energy policy. Yet, the policy space is very much influenced by the institutional organisation of the energy systems and responsibilities concerning security of supply, price level, environmental standards, etc. The responsibilities just mentioned are usually a national matter and may be influenced depending on the degree of market functioning and the ownership and taxation of exhaustible resources, such as fossil fuels.

Given any national energy policy framework, additional local and regional energy plans always seem necessary to offer a detailed implementation framework in addition to often rather generally formulated national policy goals (e.g. an overall efficiency improvement of 20%).

As regards the institutional organisation scale economies may be a sensible indicator, as far as they are separately assessed for constituent parts of the system, i.e. generation, distribution, etc. The separation of generation (or main transport) from distribution may be accompanied by integration of the distribution of several network provided energy carriers at the local level. In other words vertical integration is to some extent substituted by horizontal integration. As regards the ownership status, there is some tendency to forms of private companies, although public influence remains decisive in most cases except for the UK.

The various cases presented here underscore the importance of a comprehensive approach of every project. Though a concrete project may aim at specific goals related to a particular aspect of the energy market, it always involves other items included in the list of most crucial issues presented in section 4. For instance, information and communication including updating and feedback are relevant aspects for any project.

The overall conclusion from this document is that urban energy policy may be an effective strategy in the framework of both economising on energy costs and improving urban environmental quality.

REFERENCES

Eurostat, **Energy Statistics 1987,** Luxembourg, 1989.

Eurostat, **Energy Statistics 1988,** Luxembourg, 1990.

Juul, K. and Nijkamp, P., **Urban Energy Planning,** DG XVII, European Commission, Brussels, 1988.

Lundqvist, L., Introduction in Lundqvist, L., Mattson, L.G. and Eriksson, A. (eds.) **Spatial Energy Analysis,** Gower, 1989, pp. 1-10.

Nijkamp, P. and Perrels, A.H., **Urban Space: From Refuse Deposit to Promising Area,** paper presented at the conference "Environment and Urban Development", Bremen, January 24-26, 1990.

Nijkamp, P. and Volwahsen, A., New Directions in Integrated Regional Energy Planning, **Energy Policy,** vol. 8, no. 8, 1990, pp. 764-773.

Sep, **Verlichting in Huishoudens** (Residential lighting), report TVB/PdG/SMW 0536G, Arnhem, 1989.

Sexton, R.J., Brown Johnson, N. and Konakayama, A., Consumer Response to Continuous Display Electricity Use Monitors in a Time-of-use Pricing Experiment, **Journal of Consumer Research,** vol. 14, 1987, pp. 55-61.

Train, K.E., McFadden, D.L. and Goett, A.A., Consumer Attitudes and Voluntary Rate Schedules for Public Utilities, **The Review of Economics and Statistics,** vol. 69, no. 3, August 1987, pp. 383-391.

SUMMARY OF DISCUSSION, RECOMMENDATIONS

The working group discussed first the context of environmental aspects of urban production and consumption (A), then came to recommendations.

A. THE CONTEXT

1. There is a globalisation of ownership and control of production systems.

2. There are consumer and efficiency and legislative pressures (national/international) for cleaner production methods (but not necessarily minimisation of energy/materials).

3. There is a tendency for structural change from manufacturing to services etc.

4. The internationalisation of environmental standards and legislation continues.

5. National/local power structures are changing.

In cities a vast majority of the European population is represented. There is a need for dialogue and co-operation, for acting together.

The city is a provider of quality of life. The issues of the **city in relation to the global environment** are only part of this role.

B. RECOMMENDATIONS TO CITY MANAGERS IN RELATION TO CITIES AND THE GLOBAL ENVIRONMENT

The city as manager/owner of production systems

1. Cities should be managed/designed to minimise energy use, materials use, pollution; and to maximise re-use/recycling, promoting integrated systems (waste/energy).

2. There are already many examples of good practice; cities should seek to learn from existing experience and take up dialogue between cities.

The city as framework for manufacturing/service production systems

1. Cities should ensure implementation of environmental standards.

2. They should initiate programmes to help industry convert to cleaner processes.

3. Cities should act together to identify product standards/areas affecting cities and initiate ideas. Initiate open dialogue with producers, standards institutions etc. (in the area of cars, packaging, hgv's, energy suppliers) and be pro-active not re-active.

4. Cities should ensure the provision of adequate infrastructure and community services (sewerage, centralised/common waste treatment) to allow industry to meet environmental standards most efficiently.

5. Cities should seek closer co-operation and relations with industry, chambers of commerce, trade associations etc.

The city as a spatial organiser

1. Cities should include in their assessment of alternative development strategies a consideration of the more global environmental implications - energy use, material use, infrastructure requirements etc.

2. Cities and systems of cities should be considered against objectives such as maximising access while minimising movement.

3. Cities should integrate environmental/pollution control standards and requirements with planning and building permission process.

4. Cities should co-operate to promote environmental quality and to reduce the dangers of intercity bidding.

The city and its citizens as consumers

1. Cities should play an active role in educating and encouraging their citizens to become environmentally friendly consumers - collectively and individually.

The locus of responsibility

1. Cities are the appropriate level at which to implement the above policies towards sustainability.

2. The role at national, EC and international level is to set overall targets, standards, goals, and arrange for research, S & T and investment strategies.

3. National and EC levels should use instruments for applying policies which allow flexible and appropriate implementation procedures at the local level.

GROUP 3

URBAN RESOURCES AND WASTE MANAGEMENT

Chairperson: Mr. D.W. PURCHON, Director of Health and Consumer Services, Sheffield

Rapporteur: Mr. Serge KEMPENEERS, Institut Bruxellois pour la Gestion de l'Environnement

Participants:

Mr. Daniel BEGUIN, ANRED

Mr. Bjørn ERIKSON, Norwegian Confederation of Trade Unions

Mr. Jake GOMILNY, ELEICH

Mr. Michael R. JACOBSEN, Århus Municipality

Mr. Kawmars KHOSH-CHASHM, World Health Organisation

Mr. Neil MORTON, Rotherham Metropolitan Borough Council

Mr. José QUINTERO GARCIA, Izquierda Unida, Ayuntamiento de Huelva

THE ADVANTAGES OF GLOBAL MANAGEMENT OF URBAN WASTES
(Summary)

Daniel Beguin
ANRED/Les Transformeurs

There is no "miracle solution" which can make the waste that we produce disappear - in particular, the household wastes thrown out every day by consumers. All that we have are a few techniques which make it possible to get rid of these wastes, with or without treatment. Depending on the individual situation, these techniques fit in more or less effectively with the constraints faced by the local authorities who are in charge of managing the wastes.

These techniques are the traditional methods of treating household waste - incineration, sorting/composting, controlled dumping - supplemented by newer techniques (methanisation), but also systems for recycling, such as multi-material selective home collections, "refuse banks" which are at the same time a means of collection and a means of sorting, etc. All these tools are available to local authorities to give them, in principle, a way of managing their waste problems satisfactorily.

According to the findings of the recent national inventory (1988 figures), more than 90% of the population are served by an "authorised" treatment facility. One could therefore almost believe that a solution has been found to the problem posed to local communities by waste. This idea is belied, however, by the growing numbers of requests for help on this topic, and the growing number of local situations which are blocked, conflict-laden, or even explosive. In what ways are waste treatment facilities failing to resolve local problems completely?

They are failing, on the one hand, because taking waste products to a treatment facility never eliminates the totality of household garbage, and the dump still remains at the end of the line as the almost inevitable destination of the last residue of treatment, whether one is dealing with clinkers from incineration or materials which could not be composted. All too often, the "disposal" side of the system is not handled with the same care as the installation of the treatment facility - which is, of course, much more attractive to both technical specialists and elected representatives.

The other reasons why they are failing is because household garbage is not by any means the only challenge posed to local authorities by wastes. There are also bulky wastes, wastes from pruning, sludges from water purification facilities, wastes from markets, toxic wastes held by households or small-scale producers, etc. The failure to manage all these products is not without consequences for the environment: the unauthorised dumps which one still finds far too frequently provide the most striking proof of this, but one can also imagine the pollution attributable to toxic elements dispersed into the environment either directly or through treatment networks or facilities.

In the search for solutions to these problems, two basic concerns of local authorities also come into play:

1. **The growing desire to improve the quality of service provided** for the population; in the area of waste, this leads to the establishment, alongside the traditional household garbage collection service, of a complete service which can respond to the problems which wastes cause for the various categories of people under administration;

2. **The equally growing desire to rationalise the management of local finances**, stimulated by current economic difficulties; this provides an incentive to reduce by all possible means the major expenditure heading represented by waste elimination - and as well as the optimisation of the system, this concern enhances the attractions of considering possible ways of recovering raw materials or energy from this mass of matter.

Faced with this set of questions, one may be tempted, after having prioritised them - according to criteria which are peculiar to each community, such as the quantity of wastes involved, the nature of the pollution which they cause, the prevailing regulations or the economic context in the locality - to seek appropriate responses to each question, and implement them on a piecemeal basis. That is how household garbage, as a priority problem, was first to capture the attention, and the budgets, of local administrators.

But such a systematic approach may, under certain circumstances, involve some risks - that is how, in some cases, separate consideration of collection and treatment led to the setting up of a collection in plastic bags of household garbage which was intended for composting - and in any case fails to use the many advantages which are made available by a more global consideration of these questions.

That is why those in charge of these problems within local authorities are tending more and more often to supplement their technical considerations by a management approach aimed at defining a local policy for waste handling.

THE MANAGEMENT OF HOUSEHOLD WASTES

Daniel Béguin
ANRED/Les Transformeurs

INTRODUCTION

In France today, 94% of the population are served by authorised household waste treatment facilities. The figure has never been higher. At the same time, there is an explosion of problems on the ground, linked to waste management by local communities.

This explosion is expressed, in particular, by:

* a major growth in the demand for technical assistance on the part of communities, mostly when they are confronted with the problems of their dump being full to capacity or their treatment facilities being obsolescent;

* many blocked projects and controversial local situations, with an pervasive emergence of voluntary group movements (whether of an ecological nature or on the initiative of residents), opposed to plans for new installations of whatever kind (the well-known NIMBY syndrome).

This apparent contradiction requires a detailed analysis of the causes or themes underlying the problems which occur on the ground; these problems are partly explained by the proliferation of these themes, by comparison with the not-so-distant past when the preservation of public health was almost the only concern of a service which was confined to collecting household waste and nothing else, for elimination based usually on a single criterion - the lowest possible cost.

1. CHANGES IN THE APPROACH TO WASTE MANAGEMENT

Among all the elements, external or internal to the will of local communities, which influence these problems today, the following may be noted in particular:

* **the increased quantity of waste produced** (about 3% per year per inhabitant), and especially the volume of waste, connected particularly with the proliferation of packaging.

* for household wastes, **a frequent awareness of the inadequacy of the service provided** by a treatment facility on its own, of whatever kind: thus, in particular, difficulties arise after the event with the elimination of incineration clinkers or compost waste, because all too often the "disposal" part of the system has not been handled with the same care as the establishment of the factory, which is of course a more interesting topic both for the technical expert and the elected politician.

* **the increasing severity of regulations** and their application to all forms of treatment; this increasing severity often causes a rise in the cost of treatment - sometimes a very large rise.

* **the recent awareness of the absolute necessity to be economical with disposal sites**, both for technical reasons such as the suitability of the hydro-geological characteristics of the sites for this use, and for reasons of a more psychological type, described below.

* **the increasing emergence of problems caused** to local communities, apart from the management of household wastes, by **all the other types of urban residues.** These include, in particular, **bulky wastes** resulting from an "extreme" consumer society (short lifetime of household electrical equipment, changing fashions, etc.), garden refuse, whether originating from private households or from public open space areas; whose volume and characteristics (seasonal production and low calorific power) pose serious problems when it comes to elimination; **sludges from water purification facilities** which still remain difficult to use for agricultural purposes; **hospital wastes** for which it is now agreed that elimination cannot properly be carried out - with some exceptions - by means of solutions within the establishments concerned; **ordinary industrial wastes** which of course are not legally the responsibility of the local municipality, but still weigh heavily on treatment capacities and therefore cannot be excluded from the reckoning. Indeed, it may also be borne in mind that even from a moral standpoint, the local community cannot refuse to take any interest in the management of **toxic wastes** produced in its area.

* **ecological awareness** both national and individual, faced with **squandering of resources and pollution**: today there is no longer a tolerance of disposal systems which do not involve at least some degree of recovery of raw materials and energy contained in wastes; likewise dumps which are badly run, or uncontrolled, polluted beaches and dirty roads are no longer tolerated.

* following from the preceding point, **the promotion, even the obligation, of recycling** (draft EC directive imposing a minimum rate of recycling of liquid food packaging in member States, for example), and the resulting debate on the responsibilities and respective roles of the economic actors involved: basically producers, distributors and local communities.

* **the psychological aspects** linked to wastes, and which arise on at least two levels in the NIMBY phenomenon - on the one hand, provoking a natural reflex of disgust linked to waste products, which are perceived as nothing more than society's excrement - and on the other hand because they have contributed to the downgrading of this activity among all public services, often reducing its management to the bare minimum, which leaves a number of unsatisfactory situations on the ground today, reinforcing the worries of opponents.

* **general raising of the standard of living and comfort among local communities,** which involves a growing demand for quantity and quality of service provision: in the area of wastes, this influences the frequency of collection of household wastes, and the need to establish services for all other forms of waste produced by the population.

* for some years now, and particularly since the first oil crisis, **the need for the economic optimisation of community services,** which provides an incentive to reduce by all possible means the major expenditure connected with waste elimination; as well as optimising the systems currently in place, this concern increases the importance of considering the possible recovery of this deposit of raw materials and energy.

2. THE TOOLS AVAILABLE TO LOCAL AUTHORITIES

Faced with this context which is characterised by growing complexity, not only on a technical level, it is clear that there is no simple solution, still less any "miracle" solution which would make it possible to make this waste which we all produce disappear cleanly. All we have is a range of techniques which could be used at different stages in the process: collection/transport/sorting/treatment, leading to elimination which in the last analysis is always based on recycling, incineration or burial.

It should be borne in mind first of all that recycling, which consists in reintegrating material within a production cycle, is often by far the best way of eliminating waste. In the dustbin, this recycling could cover 20 to 25% of raw materials (paper, cardboard, glass, metal) as well as about 25% of organic matter, which can be put back in the soil in the form of compost. The rest of the dustbin is made up of non-recoverable materials, often of a complex nature, part of which can in principle be recovered in the form of energy through incineration, while another part is made up of non-recoverable inert material, and has no other possible destination at the present time apart from being dumped.

It is worth noting that the techniques available today can combine several stages in the process, and on this basis can no longer be classified among "treatment techniques" or "collection techniques": thus, selective multi-material home collections ("Ecopoubelle"[*]), as well as garbage deposits, are at the same time methods of collection and sorting.

The following review of the main tools currently available is intended to point out their limitations, advantages and drawbacks.

---

* "Ecopoubelle" is a trademark registered by ANRED

Controlled Disposal Site

Controlled disposal sites offer a method of elimination based on the burial of waste products.

Household waste is spread in layer upon layer over a site where the hydro-geological features make it possible to avoid all risks of pollution or nuisance. A recent circular from the Environment Ministry (11 March 1987) establishes the following rules, in particular:

There are two types of dumps:

*   the traditional dump which needs waste to be covered over on a daily basis;

*   the compacted dump: in this case, special machinery reduces the volume of household waste by compacting it, and avoids the need for the site to be covered in daily.

Any authorisation to run a controlled disposal site must be subjected to an impact assessment including, in particular, a hydro-geological study of the chosen site. In addition, a controlled disposal site must have specific features such as:

*   management of access;
*   installation of fencing, gate, supervisor's hut;
*   planting and visual screening.

The specific facilities for the site reduce the zone of activity by eliminating pits or holes by means of ditches. Peripheral channels and a drainage network carry off surface water.

Assuming that it is properly run, the main advantages of a controlled disposal site are its reliability in relation to other procedures, its great flexibility of adaptation to the quantities to be treated (an area with high seasonal variation), and it can be an excellent way of reclaiming otherwise unusable land over a period of time, or restoring damaged sites (quarries, for example).

In France this is the least expensive technique (60 to 120 francs per tonne). On the other hand, it does not allow the recovery of materials nor - apart from some exceptions - the energy contained within waste products, and it has become in a way the symbol of squandered resources. Moreover, the availability of sites is limited, and a sound management of wastes must try to reserve controlled dumping as the last resort for waste products which have no other possibilities of elimination.

Sorting and Composting

Sorting and composting aims to recover a portion of household wastes (about 50%) as a compost which can be used for the organic improvement of soil. The waste must be shredded (opening sacks and sorting) and must then undergo aerobic fermentation. This fermentation can happen in heaps outdoors over two or three months (slow composting) or in enclosures over a period of two to fifteen days (accelerated composting) before a final sorting designed to refine the product and the maturation which is necessary to stabilise it.

The non-compostable products emerging from the sorting process, (about 50%) are sent to a dump or incinerated (high calorific power, taking account of the high level of plastics).

Before setting up any sorting/composting facility, it is necessary to involve the potential users so as to arrive at a precise definition of needs as regards the quantity of compost, but especially the quality of the product to be sold, and decide consequently on the sort of installation to be established. The cost comes to between 150 and 300 francs per tonne.

Incineration

Incineration is the treatment process which allows the greatest reduction in the volume of residues to be eliminated. It consists in burning household wastes in special furnaces suited to their characteristics: variable calorific power, fairly high humidity.

Combustion must be carried out correctly to avoid any transfer of pollution or nuisance. Moreover, the gases produced must undergo special treatment (de-chlorination) so as to meet the norms on atmospheric emissions defined in the Decree of 9 June 1986, norms which will be reinforced by the application of the latest European directives.

In the case of energy recovery based on burning household wastes, the outlet must be large enough to absorb the maximum production of the incineration facility, a production which fluctuates in practice, given the variable flow of household wastes. The outlet must also be sufficiently close to the factory, and guaranteed for the lifetime of the incineration unit.

The questions arising today about incineration are essentially concerned with the risks of pollution transfer which they cause: questions are being asked on the quality of fumes and the elimination of the residues of treatment (ashes, etc.). The cost keeps increasing: 200 to 400 francs per tonne.

Methanisation in a Digestor

Fermenting household wastes in a digestor produces a gas made up of methane (50% to 70%) which, after purification and compression, can be fed into the French national gas grid, and an enriching agent which can be used in agriculture (40% of the input tonnage).

The waste products are crushed and go through a simplified sorting process. The crushed wastes, after readjustment of the humidity level, are put into a digestor where they stay for 10 to 15 days (mesophile regime t. 36°C). Coming out of the digestor, the fermented substratum (known as the digestate) is dehydrated through compression, then cleared of the inert materials (plastic, glass) which are still present. The liquid lost during this pressing is used to increase the humidity rate of wastes before their insertion in the digestor. The incineration of wastes can also allow energy to be recovered.

Methanisation in a digestor is a relatively recent technique; the first industrial use of it in AMIENS ran into technical and economic difficulties, which led in fact to a bankruptcy petition by the original company (VALORGA). A new company (VALORGA PROCESS) took on the installation, and is planning substantial modifications in the procedure. It is thus too early to offer a reliable judgement on its development potential and economic significance.

Transfer Centres

Transfer centres or "transit stations", which do not constitute a treatment technique, take in waste products from collection bins. Household wastes are stored in a ditch, on storage lots or in containers. They are eventually compacted, then evacuated by a high-capacity transport mode (heavy lorry, railway, barge) to a treatment facility.

Local communities often use transfer centres when the following conditions prevail:

* It is impossible to find a site which can take a treatment facility or controlled dump;

* There are advantages in sending waste products towards an existing facility some distance away, rather than having to set up a new unit which might cause harmful risks;

* It is desirable to use a far distant disposal site in order to preserve the environment.

"Ecopoubelle"

This is the name which the ANRED agency gives to door-to-door multi-material selective collection. In the present context, this must be taken as one of the elements in the treatment scenario. Pioneers in this field, a proportion of the inhabitants of the urban community of Dunkirk have, in addition to the "traditional" bins, a "blue bin" collected once a week, in which they place their recyclable wastes: paper, cardboard, glass, metal, plastic bottles.

The sorting centre (TRISELEC) which receives these products recycles about 25% of the wastes produced by this population into economic reuse.

The limitations of this technique may consist in the local situation regarding outlets, and the greater or lesser difficulties in working a specific collection into the existing system.

In Dunkirk, where it has proved possible to set up this collection in substitution for previous services, thereby generating no other additional costs apart from the purchase of a second waste bin, the overall cost of the operation is estimated at 200 francs per tonne today.

Garbage Depots

The essential aim of this method is to offer users a place for waste products which are not covered by traditional collection systems. Essentially, one is dealing with bulky waste items, gardening and DIY waste, etc.

This method can also allow a separate reception of toxic wastes from households: batteries, medicines, solvents, used oils, etc. In addition, it can accept recyclable waste (glass, paper) without thereby setting itself up as a selective collection resource.

In other words, this is an instrument designed above all to combat unofficial dumps, and which allows users to do their own sorting and direct waste products towards the destination best suited to their nature.

The success of this type of resource lies in its attractiveness to the public (reception, aesthetics, layout, dimensions), and in a precise study of the outlets or opportunities for the products involved.

The cost of running such a facility comes to 10 to 15 francs per inhabitant per year, for an investment of between 400,000 and 1,000,000 francs.

Specific Instruments

Specific treatments for certain waste products can either be put in place, or used, or at least known and promoted to resolve particular problems: for example, toxic waste treatment facilities, which the community can use for the output of toxic household waste collection systems, or specific installations to deal with contaminated hospital waste.

One may also mention the treatment of waste from green spaces through composting; the Agency is currently testing an optimised version (the VEGETERRE procedure), in co-operation with local authorities.

3. FACTORS IN AN OVERALL MANAGEMENT OF URBAN WASTE

Dealing with this problem, and having this range of instruments at their disposal, the people in charge of these problems within local communities are tending more and more frequently to supplement their technical considerations by a management approach, aiming to define a local policy for waste control.

Without claiming to present a methodology for drawing up such a policy here, the following are some key points in the considerations involved:

* The bases of this approach inevitably involve a prior examination, from a qualitative and quantitative point of view, of the extent of wastes produced in the area. This examination may require a campaign of analytic measurement, as undertaken by an increasing number of communities (the Urban Community of Lille, of Dunkirk, the Urban District of Nancy, etc.). As well as wastes produced by individuals, small businesses and traders, etc., at this stage the waste products from industry must also be considered. In fact, although communities are not legally responsible for their management, what elected representative could today completely ignore the production, in the area under his or her administration, of waste products which are sometimes toxic, representing a potential risk for health or the environment? As for common industrial waste, a better knowledge of them can only improve conditions for their elimination in a treatment facility or the municipal disposal site.

* The approaches to be adopted should in principle lay emphasis on recovering or eliminating waste products according to their nature, giving priority to recycling whenever possible. There is no single solution for this problem, but a set of solutions towards which the various waste products concerned have to be steered. In other words, one can say today that the question is no longer one of choosing between incineration, composting or controlled dumping, but of combining two or even three of these techniques, each of which should process the proportion of waste products which are suitable for it, after a sorting process at the input stage which is developed to the maximum possible level (the "Ecopoubelle" system in Dunkirk seems the most promising technique today), in order to diminish the volume to be treated. Obviously it is not a question here of preaching a systematic implementation of mixed solutions, which are always expensive in the case of household wastes, but one could for example quite plausibly imagine that within a community where pruning or gardening wastes are normally treated by incineration there is a composting unit specifically reserved for this type of waste. As for controlled dumps, which seem to be getting increasingly difficult to open, both on account of technical problems of unavailability of adequate sites, and

political problems arising from hostility among neighbouring populations, this solution must obviously be used to the minimum extent possible, and only for waste products for which it is impossible to find a better destination.

* A certain number of solutions can make it possible to resolve several problems at the same time. Thus, composting brings household waste and sludges from water purification stations together, and this can be an elegant solution for recovery in certain cases. In the same spirit, a "garbage depot" makes it possible to diminish or even resolve completely the problem of uncontrolled dumps, giving the public a supplementary service which meets a need - the need to be able at any moment to get rid of a waste product which cannot be dealt with by the collection service, but also to complete a system for the collection of recoverable materials, thus making it possible to steer waste products towards the best treatment process. One could even imagine "industrial garbage depots" which, in an industrial zone, would sort materials on the basis of their nature and their destination. We already have an example of this on the disposal site belonging to the town of Angers, where there is a sorting centre for these types of waste, with a separation between recoverable products (metals, cardboard), incinerable products, and products for dumping. At any event, the sorting process, which is necessary for optimising recovery and elimination, should be given a prominent position towards the beginning of the process, whether one is dealing with households or industries. "Garbage depots" appear clearly to provide a particularly efficient instrument in this context.

* The internalisation of costs is something to be considered for the whole system. It is by considering all the costs, for example, that selective collection can be seen no longer as an isolated action which must find its own self-contained financial viability, or even provide economic benefits; instead, it can be seen as one element taking its place in the overall framework of waste elimination, and syphoning off its own proportion of the flow of materials. Thus, it would be economically attractive so long as the cost of this selective collection does not exceed the cost which would be involved in joint elimination with the rest of waste products, and reserving the right to pay for the service provided by the provider of this collection. The same approach can be tried for recovery operations which could be directly conducted by communities, such as the sorting of clinkers in order to recover them; the attractions of this approach can be measured particularly by the savings made over the lifetime of a disposal site which these products would otherwise clog up.

* Such a policy presupposes a growing sense of responsibility on the part of each producer of wastes, and works most effectively when accompanied by a suitable campaign to raise awareness among the different categories of people being administered; they not

only need to have an explanation and a reminder of the different outlets which are available and the conditions of reception, but also to receive a clear explanation of the issues at stake and the consequences of their own actions.

THE NEW WASTE SYSTEM OF ÅRHUS, DENMARK

Michael R. Jacobsen
Århus Municipality

"Environmental Van"

Collection of environmentally dangerous waste (oil, chemicals, etc.) from private households has a very high priority.

At present, the Municipality of Århus has two specially equipped vans to collect environmentally dangerous waste. A box for storage of the waste has been distributed to every household. The box is provided with sorting instructions as well as a collection timetable. The environmental vans visit every household 10 times a year. They drive around after working hours and when a signal is given with the horn, the residents can hear that the van has arrived at its usual stopping place.

On average, each household delivers 1.4 kg/year. The waste is delivered to the Municipality's receiving station for oil and chemicals, from where it is sent for disposal to Kommunekemi A/S, Nyborg, Denmark.

The environmental van system was established in April, 1990, and all 120,000 households should be included by the summer of 1991. At the moment the two vans cover 55,000 households.

Separation at source of green household waste

In October 1990, the Municipality established a system for collection of green household waste from 10,000 households (4,000 flats and 6,000 single-family houses). They were supplied with free sorting racks and black and green waste disposal bags as well as information material.

The households sort the waste in a "green" section consisting of leftovers, wet kitchen paper, etc., and in a "black" section consisting of other waste, for instance empty boxes, etc. The bags are deposited in two out-door containers of various size. The green waste is collected once a week, while the rest of the waste is collected every fortnight. The rest of the waste is delivered for incineration. The Municipality has established a new high-technological composting plant for the green waste.

The plant, the first of its kind in Europe, is a development project implemented by the Municipality of Århus and the engineering company Krüger.

The composting process itself has been calculated to last 1 month. In order to prevent possible working environment problems the composting takes place in an entirely closed system. It is the intention that the compost be used on an ecological farm as replacement for liquid and solid manure.

Building and construction waste

In order to limit the quantity of building and construction waste to dumping grounds by re-use of the materials, a new pre-sorting plant for building and construction waste was put into service by the Municipality in October 1990. The plant is expected to handle approx. 80,000 tonnes/year. After sorting, the materials are expected to be re-used by, for instance, new construction projects.

Hospital waste

The Municipality has a special collection of hospital waste, for example contaminated waste, biological waste, used blades and needles. The waste comes from hospitals, the primary health sector, laboratories, etc. The producers have to separate the waste from other waste and pack it in special wrapping or containers.

Collection of the waste is done by the local sanitation department (Århus Renholdningsselskab) which delivers it for incineration in a special furnace at the municipal refuse disposal plant.

In collaboration with Vølund Miljøteknik A/S, Århus Renholdningsselskab, and Århus County, the Municipality of Århus has initiated sale of the entire collection and treating system.

CFC (Freon)

The Municipality of Århus has established a Recycling Factory which has developed a system for reclaiming freon from cold storage plants, etc., for instance, refrigerators and freezers. The Recycling Factory is the only one of its kind in Denmark.

Recycling stations

The Municipality has 3 community recycling stations, where private households can deliver all sorts of waste, except household waste, free of charge.

The community recycling stations have been organised with a number of containers for paper, cardboard, plastic, glass, furniture, wood, household equipment, garden waste, etc. Households sort the waste at home and place it in the right containers, so that as much as possible can be re-used.

The community recycling stations are open on weekdays as well as Saturdays/Sundays. In 1991 two new community recycling stations will be opened so that all households have at maximum 7 kilometres to travel to the nearest station.

ARHUS TO BE TEST CITY FOR INTENSIVE RECYCLING

The Council for Recycling and Minimally Polluting Technology (The Danish State) has resolved to conduct trials involving some 17,000 households (private houses, apartment blocks and farms) in part of the Municipality of Århus.

Each household is to sort its rubbish into four portions: food residues; glass; paper and residential refuse. In this way we hope to recycle some 60 to 70% of household refuse. The system is based on individual householders sorting their rubbish into various categories of material suitable for processing and recycling. For this purpose, all households will be supplied with 2 rubbish-containers, each divided internally into two, giving four compartments, as follows:

1. Food residues
2. Residual refuse
3. Glass
4. Paper

The containers are emptied into a compartmentalised rubbish cart with a built-in compressor system.

The containers are expected to be emptied once a fortnight.

The food residues, kitchen waste and other organic materials will be composted or used for the production of bio-gas. Jars and bottles will be sorted for cleaning and re-use; broken glass to be melted down. Paper and cardboard to be sorted by type and used in paper manufacture. The residual rubbish, about a third of the original amount, will be burnt, the heat produced being utilised for e.g. central heating (communal district heat distribution).

This trial is an example of the kind of Sorting at Source which the Minister of the Environment, Lone Dybkjær, has frequently called upon local authorities to carry out. During the trials, new types of refuse container and rubbish carts are to be tested, and new sorting facilities will be constructed. During this user trial period, a crucial point will be the establishment of a satisfactory working environment. One result will be that the "dustman", or refuse collector, will have a new part to play, being entrusted with inspection and advisory functions, for which he will be given special training.

Detailed planning, including selection of the experimental area of Århus, is now under way, the collection is planned to start in a year or eighteen months, when the necessary facilities have been constructed.

The Recycling Council will support the project financially, up to a maximum of DKK 20 million, i.e. about 50% of the total cost.

SORT YOUR REFUSE

A leaflet on what you, the individual citizen, can do to further the cause of recycling in Århus.

Århus City Council, 2nd Department,
City Engineer's Office
Refuse Disposal Department
Denmark

Contents

	Page
Foreword By Councillor Olaf P. Christensen Convenor of the Council's Dept. II.	145
Central composting Two bags for one Sorting your kitchen refuse	146
Home composting Recycling in your own garden Kitchen and garden refuse	146
Larger items Furniture, mattresses, cycles etc. Collection arrangements	147
Refrigerators and freezers Freon (CFC) destroys the ozone layer Collection arrangements	147
Environmentally dangerous refuse The Battery Box and the Environmental Van	148
Paper and glass Recycling	148
Local recycling stations Recycling, incineration, the rubbish dump and destruction	149

FOREWORD

On behalf of your City Council, I have pleasure in informing you what you, the citizens of Århus, can do to ensure a cleaner, purer environment. As you will see, we can do a lot! For Nature, and thus for ourselves. The aim of this leaflet is to aid and advise you, so do keep it to refer to any time you need help with any particular refuse disposal problem.

It is the responsibility of your Council to dispose of all refuse in an environmentally correct manner. Århus City Council have thus adopted a Refuse Plan. By the year 2000, the aim is to recycle about 50% of all refuse, use another 30% or so for producing energy - and only deposit some 20% in controlled refuse dumps.

The Council therefore intends to utilise refuse far more efficiently than in the past, when dumping or incineration were the usual methods of disposal. Instead of being recycled, enormous quantities of raw materials ended up on the tip or went up in smoke in the incinerators. This was a waste of natural resources.

Better utilisation of refuse needs each individual citizen's co-operation. Recycling requires unmixed materials, and we can only get these if we all sort refuse into its different categories.

The watchword is "Sorting at Source".

In future, householders must ensure that paper, glass, garden refuse, larger items of refuse and so on are deposited in the right place (in the correct containers).

It is also important that refuse which can damage the environment should be separated out. For this purpose you can either use the Environmental Van or one of the 200 or so places where you can hand this sort of refuse in. If you have large quantities of rubbish, it is a good idea to use the municipal local recycling stations. It is never more than 7 km to one, wherever you live.

In the autumn of 1990, as a complete innovation, your Council introduced Sorting at Source of kitchen waste, into a green portion for composting and the rest for incineration. This system comprises 10,000 households to start with, but will eventually be extended to the entire municipality.

Experience gained so far convinces me that the citizens of Århus are in favour of the new Refuse Plan and are taking an active part in Sorting at Source. Always remember: "Many a little makes a nickle".

It is worth being environmentally conscious - Århus has made a start.

Olaf P. Christensen
Alderman of the 2nd Department of the City Council

Central composting

Århus City Council has resolved that green kitchen refuse is to be kept separate from other household waste and recycled as compost.

Two bags for one

In future, every home will have two rubbish-bags in the kitchen - one for green refuse and one for the rest.

Green refuse, about a third of the total, comprises tea-leaves, potato peelings, dead flowers, used kitchen-roll, etc. The rest is such things as tins, cartons, dirty tinfoil and plastic wrappings.

The Council has built a high-tech composting unit at Lisbjerg Incineration Plant. An initial 10,000 households in selected suburbs will be sorting their kitchen refuse in 1990-91. If this experiment works satisfactorily, it will be extended to all households.

Composting turns green refuse into soil-improving material which can be used in gardens, parks and agriculture.

Residual refuse which can neither be composted nor recycled will be collected for incineration as before. The energy released by incineration is utilised for district heating.

Sort your refuse - for the sake of the environment.

Home composting

If we did not take our garden refuse to the tip, we could do without one in twenty of the rubbish dumps in Denmark.

Garden refuse comprises nearly a tenth of all private household waste. Instead of returning their refuse to the natural ecological cycle as free fertiliser, many people send it to the rubbish dump - and then spend money buying peat moss and artificial fertilisers instead.

Århus City Council calls on all gardeners to make compost heaps for their garden refuse. Suggestions for making containers are available in various leaflets.

Most of your garden refuse can be composted in specially made compost containers which prevent vermin gaining access to it.

Green kitchen refuse which may be composted includes flowers, stale bread and cake, fruit, vegetables, tea-leaves and coffee grounds, eggshells and peel.

Food residues containing meat, fish, delicatessen, gravy, grease and lard etc. attractive to vermin must NEVER be put on a compost heap.

Large clippings from trees and bushes may be taken to your local recycling station. It will then be taken to the compost unit at Hasselager, where it will be ground up and composted with refuse from the parks.

Non-compostible refuse such as earth, stone, flagstones etc. can also be taken to the local recycling station.

Recycling in your own garden - pure joy!

Larger items

This compost covers anything that will not fit into an ordinary dustbin, e.g. furniture, mattresses, TV sets, bicycles, etc.

You can dispose of your larger items of rubbish at your local recycling station. In addition, Århus City Council has two collection systems.

The Recycling Works
   (phone 86 176 677) will collect such items as old furniture, stoves, washing machines and scrap metal for recycling, by previous arrangement.

Århus Renholdningsselskab
   (phone 86 151 600) will collect large items for incineration or dumping, by previous arrangement.

No charge to private householders.

Garden refuse and builders' rubble will not be collected. These may be taken to your local recycling station.

A series of voluntary organisations have containers in which you can place old clothes and second-hand shoes. We recommend you use these facilities.

Protect the environment by recycling.

Refrigerators and freezers

It is illegal to dump refrigerators and freezers on tips. They contain freon (CFC). The CFC leaks out of scrapped refrigerators and freezers and adds to the destruction of the ozone layer.

You can make sure your old fridge ends up in expert hands. Ring the Recycling Works on 86 176 677 and it will be collected free of charge.

Or you can have it taken away with other large items by phoning Århus Renholdningsselskab on 86 151 600.

The Recycling Works has established a new company, Dansk CFC Genvinding, which reclaims and purifies the CFC from refrigeration systems so that it can be used again.

If your refrigerator or freezer are in need of repair, please ensure that the electrician collects the CFC and sends it in for recycling - e.g. by Dansk CFC Gevinding.

Protect the Ozone Layer - it protects you.

Dangerous refuse

Under 1% of all rubbish from private households can be regarded as directly detrimental to the environment, but even such small quantities as this can do a great deal of damage, so it is important to separate it out.

Delivery facilities

In association with the shops, the City Council has established a series of ways of getting environmentally dangerous refuse under control.

Batteries

The Battery Box is a special container for used batteries. There are 175 Battery Boxes in the municipality, e.g. in supermarkets, at schools, at photographers and at other places selling batteries.

Car batteries can be handed in at petrol stations and garages.

Paint residues, chemicals and pesticides can be handed in at paint dealers.

Unused medicines, broken thermometers and used hypodermic syringes can be handed in at chemists.

The Environmental Van

is a special refuse collection vehicle which collects environmentally damaging refuse from near your home. Every household will be sent an Environment Box for keeping environmentally dangerous refuse in. The box contains instructions for sorting and the Van's timetable.

Local Recycling Stations

With the exception of unused medicine, you may hand in any type of environmentally dangerous refuse at your local recycling station or the Oil and Chemical Residues Reception Station.

Use your Environment Box - for a cleaner environment.

Paper and glass

Practically one fifth of all private refuse consists of paper, newspapers and periodicals, advertisements etc. plus bottles and jars. This is a good argument for collecting them for recycling.

In 1989, a total of 2,500 tons of glass and 6,500 tons of paper was collected for recycling in Århus.

This is about half the paper and glass which we reckon gets thrown out, i.e. recycling could be a lot better. So Århus City Council is going to set up even more containers for paper and glass.

The paper is sent to Genfiber in Assens, which removes the printers' ink. The cleaned paper then goes to other papermills for making such things as kitchen-roll, lavatory paper, egg cartons and wallpaper.

Half the bottles collected are cleaned and re-used. Jars and the remaining bottles are melted down for re-use at Holmegaard Glassworks.

Panes of glass must not be put in the containers but taken to the local recycling stations.

Recycle your glass and paper - use the containers.

Recycling and container stations

Recycling stations with containers for various types of refuse have been set up on Lystrupvej, Birkegaardsvej and Nymarken. Any kind of rubbish may be taken in free of charge. EXCEPT KITCHEN REFUSE.

Environmentally dangerous refuse must be handed to the staff on duty.

The Eskelund and Ølstedvej stations will be established in due course. Until then, there are container stations with times of opening as shown on the map.

Do sort your refuse before leaving home. Time spent there is time saved waiting at the containers - for yourself and other people.

The stations are arranged so that it is easy to put your refuse into the correct container. Just follow the coloured signs:

Recycling:

- Plastic - empty bottles and clean film only.
- Iron and other metals.
- Cardboard - corrugated cardboard boxes to be handed in squashed.
- Papers and periodicals including advertisements.
- Mixed paper, e.g. old books, writing or typing paper, telephone books, bundled printed matter etc.
- Bottles and jars: drinks bottles, jars (NO LIDS, please) etc.
- Compostible garden refuse only: clean refuse with no stones or wrapping materials.

Incineration

- Mixed combustible rubbish, e.g. furniture, mattresses, fittings, carpets, expanded plastic boxes, wood, soiled plastic and paper, etc.

Rubbish dump

- Mixed non-combustible rubbish, e.g. impregnated timber, insulating materials, asbestos tiles, windowpanes, plasterboard.
- Rubble (soil and stones).

Destruction

- Electrical equipment such as radios and TV sets, wiring etc.
- Consumer durables: washing machines and stoves.
  All such articles to be recycled to the greatest possible extent by the Recycling Works and the scrap merchants.
- Environmentally dangerous refuse, e.g. batteries, car batteries, paint residues, household chemicals, pesticides, fluorescent tubes etc.

In addition to being taken to your local recycling station or the containers, environmentally detrimental refuse may be handed in at the Oil and Chemical Residues Reception Station on Aabrinkvej 51, 8000 Århus C, phone 86 153 624. Open daily from 8 to 3; closed on Saturdays, Sundays and Public Holidays. All environmentally dangerous waste is collected here for inspection prior to despatch to the National Destruction Unit, Kommune Kemi.

SUMMARY OF DISCUSSIONS, RECOMMENDATIONS

1. THE NEED FOR SYSTEMATIC MANAGEMENT

Four key issues should be considered:

- Increasing the efficiency of the use of raw materials and energy used in cities;
- Economy of materials and energy;
- Promoting recycling and reutilisation;
- Integration of regional and urban planning in managing flows of materials and energy.

2. CONSIDERATION OF ALL STAGES OF A FLOW

There have been discoveries and progressive solutions to the problems of managing flows:

- collection;
- treatment;
- recycling;
- prevention.

The stage of reflection is not the same in all cities of the world. In the Third World there is an attempt to resolve the problems of collection and reclamation, while in Europe the discussions centre on integrated management.

A sorting procedure must be developed as far as possible upstream in the flows, so as to obtain homogeneous flows guaranteeing the high quality of materials recovered (organic matter, metals, paper, etc.).

It is necessary to develop treatment facilities at the most effective points within flows, while maintaining other treatment options at other levels of the flow.

Another necessary step: to develop ecological and economic evaluations of all the strands involved in collection, treatment and elimination.

As regards the composition of wastes, certain materials and products are being replaced on account of new consumer habits and sales networks (for example: a drop in organic matter and an increase in packaging, as a consequence of the sale of ready-to-eat meals). This situation applies also to water and energy.

3. DEVELOPMENT OF A COMMON VOCABULARY

No comparisons are possible without a shared terminology in terms of vocabulary, the definition of statistics, etc. (e.g. wastes, recovery rates, etc.).

4. REGIONAL ADAPTATION OF MANAGEMENT

According to the geographic, urban, social and other features of the area, it is possible to establish levels of vulnerability, resistance, participation, etc. Management procedures must be adapted to regional characteristics.

5. DEVELOPMENT OF INFORMATION, EDUCATION AND RESPONSIBILISATION

Information to families and companies; evaluation of its impact. For this reason:

- development of the education of young children;
- development of the example-setting role of the public services;
- development of databases on practical local actions for local managers.

6. DEVELOPMENT OF AN ECONOMIC STRATEGY WITH INTERNALISATION OF COSTS

This includes:

- development of research on this topic;
- development of fiscal and parafiscal instruments suited to the needs of towns;
- economic incentives to recycle and economise, on the basis of a certain treatment cost for wastes;
- definition of the real costs of waste treatment.

7. DEVELOPMENT OF STRONG POLITICAL OBJECTIVES IN ALL COUNTRIES

This includes:

- general agreement on the priority in reducing quantities of wastes and the introduction of technologies which do not cause high pollution levels;
- an obligation to use recovered materials;
- constraints in the use of disposal sites;
- introduction of management plans.

8. ECOLABELLING

There is a need to define and harmonise the criteria (recyclability, re-utilisation, durability, repairability, harmlessness).

9. EVOLUTIVE MANAGEMENT

This includes consideration, in the policy-making process, of the real timescale for the amortisation of facilities.

Prevention policies are too recent to offer reliable tools and provide convincing results in the short term.

10. IMPACT OF ECOLOGICAL DECISIONS ON TRADE AND INDUSTRY

Policies should carefully indicate:

- the impact of recovery policies on the protection of trade and industries in a country (transport, deposits, etc.);

- the impact on trading in products which have been recovered.

GROUP 4

ATTITUDES, BEHAVIOUR AND ENVIRONMENTAL CHANGE

Chairperson: Dr. Jacqueline MILLER, Free University of Brussels

Rapporteur: Ms. Edith BRICKWELL, Ministry for Urban Development and Environmental Protection, Berlin

Participants:

Mr. Jean ALEGRE, DG V, Commission of the EC

Mr. Michael COOKE, Leicester City Council

Mr. Ricardo GARCIA HERRERA, Gobierno Vasco

Ms. Heather MacDONALD, World Health Organisation

Ms. Carmen SERRANO GOMEZ, Ministerio de Obras Públicas y Urbanismo, Madrid

Mr. Henny KETELAAR, International Institute for the Urban Environment

Mr. Sybren SINGELSMA, International Union of Local Authorities

Ms. Nédialka SOUGAREVA, Ministère de l'environnement, Paris

Ms. Karola TACHNER, BEE, Expert for the European and Social Committee

THE HEALTHY CITIES PROJECT

Heather MacDonald
Consultant, Healthy Cities Project
WHO Regional Office for Europe

Healthy Cities is a vision as well as a concept and a starting point is the recognition that:

1. health is a state of complete physical, mental and social wellbeing, and not merely the absence of disease or disability;

2. the major determinants of our health are the social and physical environment in which we live and work and our lifestyles;

3. a city is more than an economic entity. It is a living, breathing changing organism that has a key role in promoting and maintaining the health of its citizens and a unique capacity to implement an ecological public health programme.

This means that health is everybody's business and there is a role for everyone in health promotion; the policy maker, the town planner, the social worker, the traffic and housing administrator, the community activist, the environmental officer, the business employer, the public health professional and many others.

So it was that unique capacity of cities to promote health that triggered WHO's interest to go local, and it did so but not empty-handed. WHO's strategy Health For All by the year 2000 and the Ottawa Charter for Health Promotion provided the backbone strategy for such a venture. Thus it was possible to define the desirable qualities of a Healthy City and furthermore the process through which such a vision could become reality.

A city must:

- provide a clean, safe, satisfying and supportive physical environment and a sustainable ecosystem;

- have a diverse, vital and innovative economy;

- meet people's basic needs (housing, income, food...);

- provide access to a wide variety of experiences and resources;

- provide a sense of connection with the history, culture and biological life of the city; and

- offer good and accessible public health and health care services.

The project strives to achieve its goals through a process of:

- **political commitment** by moving health high on the social and political agenda of the city and by providing the necessary legitimisation, direction and resources for the project;

- **organisational and institutional changes** that encourage co-operation between departments and key sectors and promote the active involvement of the community;

- **recognition and appreciation** of the health impact of city policies, the environmental conditions and the needs of those who are more vulnerable and socially deprived;

- **innovative action for health** that aims to promote equity, sustainability, supportive environments, community action and healthy municipal policies.

In a nutshell, the project must change the way cities understand and deal with health if it is to have a long term impact, and this requires new structures, styles and processes.

The project involves a network of European cities who have endorsed the principles and policy directives of the Health For All strategy and who are politically committed to a five-year plan (1988-1992) and to jointly developing and implementing action strategies for health.

The project is based on a spirit of true partnership and has well established mechanisms that promote information exchange, sharing of experience, mutual support, adjustment of existing plans, development of new strategies and dissemination of ideas and products.

The first 11 cities were designated at the end of 1987. Then another 14 cities were designated in February 1988 and another five (total of 30) at the end of 1989. Our analysis covers the first half of the 1988-92 phase and it was geared towards investigating and analysing how and to what extent the cities had fulfilled the criteria for joining the project, the structures and processes that were introduced and the types of activities for health and the environment that were initiated or linked to the project. The analysis was based on in-depth structured interviews with representatives from Project Cities and the Healthy Cities Project annual progress reports. The information from this evaluation process was also used to prepare individualised consultation reports for the political and managerial leaders of our Project Cities.

The project has been very successful in accumulating practical knowledge about the strategies and structures that can help promote the Healthy Cities idea. It is now possible to prepare a composite picture of the organisational and managerial processes that predict success in developing new approaches to public health at the local level.

The mayors and senior political representatives of the WHO Project Cities have issued a strong declaration of political support (Milan Declaration) and several Project Cities have already devoted significant resources to the project.

The success of a local Healthy Cities Project depends on the social, economic, environmental and organisational features of a city, the extent of political commitment to develop and implement the project and the availability of practical knowledge from international experience. The legitimacy that is achieved by being part of a growing world wide movement is a key factor for the success of local projects.

About half of the Project Cities have successfully developed a new organisational model of strategy for addressing health.

Several cities have been successful in mobilising a high degree of political support, but more experience is needed to establish the approaches and structures that generate broad community control over the project.

There is considerable experience in establishing multi-sectoral committees. Cities that locate the project office outside the health department make more rapid progress in generating community action and co-operation between different city departments.

Knowledge is growing about the ways to define the role and functions of local project offices in relation to their goals. Some cities are generating initiatives that will have long term significance and impact and several have defined their role as contributing to the establishment of new ways of generating knowledge (such as community profiles, maps of health equity etc.). Many cities have actively and courageously undertaken to legitimise projects and ideas that were previously viewed as marginal.

Collectively, the cities have a comprehensive set of structures, mechanisms and practices related to community participation, but very few of them have an overall strategy for community participation based on the internal structures of the project itself.

Managerial accountability for health and long term planning for the project is so far limited to very few Project Cities.

Several cities have experienced conflict and some have begun to develop methods to diffuse this conflict.

The analysis clearly suggests that projects need to have a specific set of qualities or characteristics to perform their role effectively. These qualities are present to varying degrees in the projects that have achieved significant success so far: strong political support, effective leadership, broad community control, high visibility, strategic orientation, adequate resources, sound project administration, co-operation between sectors and political and managerial accountability.

Drawing on the experience of Project Cities we have been able to formulate solutions on how to achieve these qualities. Assessing and documenting progress and producing handbooks of practical strategies and know-how applications and training modules have now become imperative. This is one of the Project Office's major tasks to be fulfilled by the time of the 1992 WHO Healthy Cities Symposium in Copenhagen.

The WHO Healthy Cities Project Office has now published the Review of Project Progress 1987-90 (and an analysis of project progress conducted by the Research Unit in Health and Behavioural Change).

At present we are discussing with our project partners the process, schedule and products of the second round evaluation of the project (1990-92) and developing a computerised database of models of practice and resource persons in the Project Cities.

Evaluating a fast growing and changing role such as the Healthy Cities Project requires new methodological approaches, new criteria and a deep appreciation of political and organisational behaviours. What does the project, or being involved with it, mean to local politicians, planners, businessmen, community workers, citizens? Is it not a criterion of success that in April 1990, 900 local citizens, professionals and academics in one of our Project Cities signed a petition asking the municipal authorities to implement project plans faster and to organise a community conference to discuss and agree how the project can best meet perceived community needs and wishes.

Cities should first and foremost be about people. Economic and technical issues must no longer be our overriding concern - human development, health and wellbeing must be our focus.

Citizens need to have control over those factors that affect their health and have a right to an environment that supports them to make healthy choices, realise aspirations and satisfy their needs.

THE "HEALTHY CITIES" PROGRAMME IN THE BASQUE AUTONOMOUS COMMUNITY

Ricardo Garcia Herrera
Director
Jenaro Astray Mochales
Health Promotion Division
Department of Public Health
Basque Government

SUMMARY

This communication describes briefly the Healthy Cities programme now in operation in the BASQUE AUTONOMOUS COMMUNITY, one of Spain's 17 autonomous communities. The programme includes some aspects which make it different from similar programmes:

1. It has been promoted by a regional government.

2. It integrates the health policy already in operation in the region.

3. It puts special emphasis on the perception of the urban environment and other subjective factors.

We will explain the process which led 20 Basque cities to take part in the programme.

Special attention will be paid to the population perception diagnosis.

A survey on 2188 residents in the eight largest cities has been carried out. Some results are presented on:

- The ideal healthy city.
- City perception by their residents.
- Priorities in a healthy city.

Finally a general perception index is built. It explains the global opinion of the people about their own city.

1. INTRODUCTION

This paper describes the healthy cities programme now in operation in the BASQUE AUTONOMOUS COMMUNITY, one of Spain's 17 autonomous communities. The programme includes some aspects which make it different from similar programmes:

1. It has been promoted by a regional government.

2. It integrates the health policy already in operation in the region.

3. It puts special emphasis on the perception of the urban environment and other subjective factors.

Below, we will explain the process which led 20 Basque cities to take part in the programme.

2. ANALYSIS OF THE SITUATION

Spain is a country which is divided into 17 Autonomous Communities, with legal competence in: education, health, agriculture, etc... The Basque Autonomous Community in the north of Spain has a common border with France (Figure 1), and is divided administratively into three historic territories: Alava (12% of the population), Guipuzcoa (33%) and Vizcaya (55%). Total population is 2.1 million, in an area of 7,261 km² with a population density of 294.18 inhabitants/km². It is an industrialised region with 15 cities over 25,000 inhabitants, where 61.2% of the population lives. Apart from a small minority these cities expanded at a time of industrial growth, generating a harsh urban environment

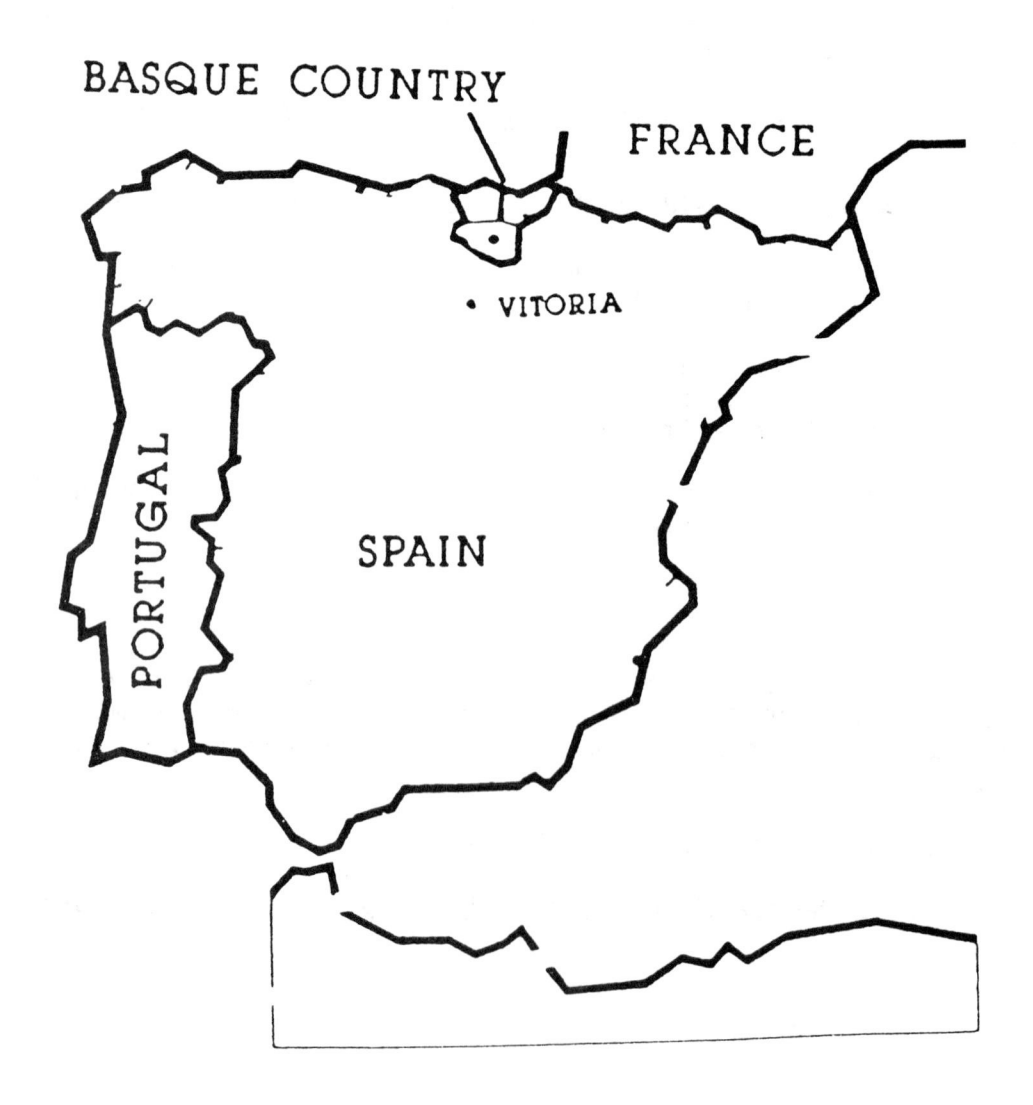

Figure 1: Geographic location and administrative division of the Basque country

(environmental deterioration, unemployment, drug addiction problems, etc...). Characteristic of the cities is the way in which industry is incorporated in the town's structure, provoking a deterioration in the environment and a negative population perception. Therefore residents demand strong intervention measures to oppose environmental deterioration. There are also a large number of psycho-social risk factors as a result of the economic crisis of the seventies, still present in the region.

Of all these cities, only the capitals of the Historical Territories, have the necessary technical equipment to analyse the environmental and health situation. Others need technical assistance to develop a programme such as the "Healthy Cities". For this reason the Basque Government, through the Basque Health Service (OSAKIDETZA), decided to start the programme, encouraging participation of local councils, giving them all kinds of informative support. At the same time it provided important human, economic and technical resources to help the cities in the accomplishment of the programme. The Department of Health also helps local councils asking for assistance and agrees to work with them in a co-ordinated way to promote health in the city. In 1988 the Public Health Division of the Basque Department of Health and Consumer Affairs started a Public Health Programme covering the following areas (Public Drinking Water, Pesticides and Chemical Safety, Radiology Protection, Beaches and Swimming Pools, Sewage, Food Hygiene, Zoonosis, Slaughters, Occupational Health, Accidents, Epidemic Control and Nutrition). The existence of these programmes, helped the methodological development of the Healthy Cities programme (DIAGNOSIS AND HEALTH PLAN) and allowed the channelling of the different health problems existing in each city.

3. STRATEGY

Three lines of work were established for the strategic development of the plan.

3.1 Promoting the Programme

20 local councils in the Basque Country have already decided to take part in the programme. The Department of Health and Consumer Affairs promoted the programme the following way.

A. A programme was drawn up adapted to the realities of the Basque Country's Local Councils. It clearly explained the line of work to be assumed by the participants.

B. Once it had been approved, the programme was presented to the town's council, and studied by the local councillors. It was important to achieve a political consensus to facilitate the development and implementation of the programme. After the local council had approved the plan, the mayor signed a collaboration agreement with the Basque Government's Department.

C. As a next step the Department of Health undertook and financed the town's health risks analysis.

The city could then have access to subsidies and grants from the Government to finance the public health problems prioritised in the town's study.

D. Larger towns, which had sufficient resources and services, controlled more directly the Study and the Programme, but the challenge for the Department of Health and Consumer Affairs were those towns between 25,000 and 125,000 inhabitants which did not have adequate structures to put the programme into operation. We put most of our efforts into them.

3.2 Methodology

3.2.1   Diagnostic Phase

The diagnostic phase is based on the town's health risks analysis and includes environmental and social aspects.

- Environmental sectors

    * Water
    * Soil
    * Air
    * Plant life
    * Energy
    * Housing and city planning
    * Socio-economic indicators

- Analysis of negative health indicators

    * Mortality rate
    * Morbidity rate

- Analysis of subjective or soft indicators of residents' Perception of the City. This is an attempt to determine the degree of acceptance residents have of their city.

    * General Perception of the city
    * Integration in the city
    * Perception of the town council's management of city
    * Public spaces in the city
    * Social pessimism

- Immediate surroundings. This defines the individual's interaction with his immediate surroundings.

    * Home
    * Family
    * Personal relationships
    * Work
    * Personality

- Compensatory Behaviour. This refers to life styles, considered as damaging for health.

    * Drugs
    * Alcohol
    * Other drugs
    * Tobacco
    * Food
    * Health perception

- Leisure and free time. This refers to the amount of free time available and how it is used.

    * Active leisure time
    * Passive leisure time
    * Intellectual leisure time
    * Social leisure time

- Needs. This tries to define the priorities for intervention expressed by the people interviewed.

    * Environmental
    * Urbanistic
    * Public spaces
    * Cultural and social

With these health indicators we combine objective and subjective factors obtaining a joint vision of the state of the community and the basis for a correct planning of its health policies.

3.2.2 Health Plan

Once the problems have been identified, they are grouped into intervention strategies:

A. Participative: Includes the different aspects of local life, as well as the different institutions acting in a particular area.

B. Dynamic: incorporates new information.

C. Monitoring: evaluation through objectives and indicators.

As the Local Council is responsible for the implementation of the Programme, the Department of Health and Consumer Affairs will only participate if the Council accepts the guidelines of the Programme.

3.3 Training of the City Health Councillors

We wanted local council representatives to be present in the design of the plan. Before, we found it necessary that they receive basic training in health planning and promotion.

With this in mind, in 1989 a continuous training workshop was set up for local politicians, consisting of more than 100 hours of classes and 15 monographic sessions. This course enabled the local councillors responsible for health and the technicians of the Basque Health Service, to know each other and to work together, in the Healthy Cities programme.

After two years the programme has rapidly expanded, and now more than 65% of the Basque population is included. In addition to that risk analyses are available at municipal level allowing the detected problems to be given an order of priority.

4. RESULTS

Two different concepts of an ideal clean and healthy city came out of our surveys. One based on the opinions of residents of the eight largest Basque towns but excluding Vitoria and the other, more practical, based on the surveys undertaken in Vitoria-Gasteiz. In the other cities, the same process was done, with very interesting results. We detected significant differences in mortality and morbidity rates in the highly industrialised areas of Vizcaya. This is at the present time our main work priority.

4.1 What do Residents Consider a Healthy City

When we started the project, one of the key questions was, what do residents consider a healthy city.

To find an answer, we carried out a survey of residents of the eight largest Basque cities (2188 questionnaires), with an margin of error of 2.5% and a confidence level of 95.5%. The survey showed what people considered an ideal healthy city (Figure 2).

1. An area completely free of pollution, with special emphasis on water, air and noise (88% of the survey).

2. The existence of public areas for leisure-time activities as well as adequate medical services (50% of the survey).

3. The improvement of public transport network, working conditions, and citizens' information (30% of the survey).

4. The desire that the residents' opinions be taken into consideration (30% of the survey).

This variety of replies is a consequence of the city's objective realities, as we commented above, and no significant differences between the cities were found. On the other hand, differences do appear when we take age into consideration:

- The youngest people surveyed (12-25 year olds) gave more importance to the existence of leisure and sports facilities (55%).

- Those over 65 gave special importance to an adequate health care system (55%). The rest of the priorities appear in second place.

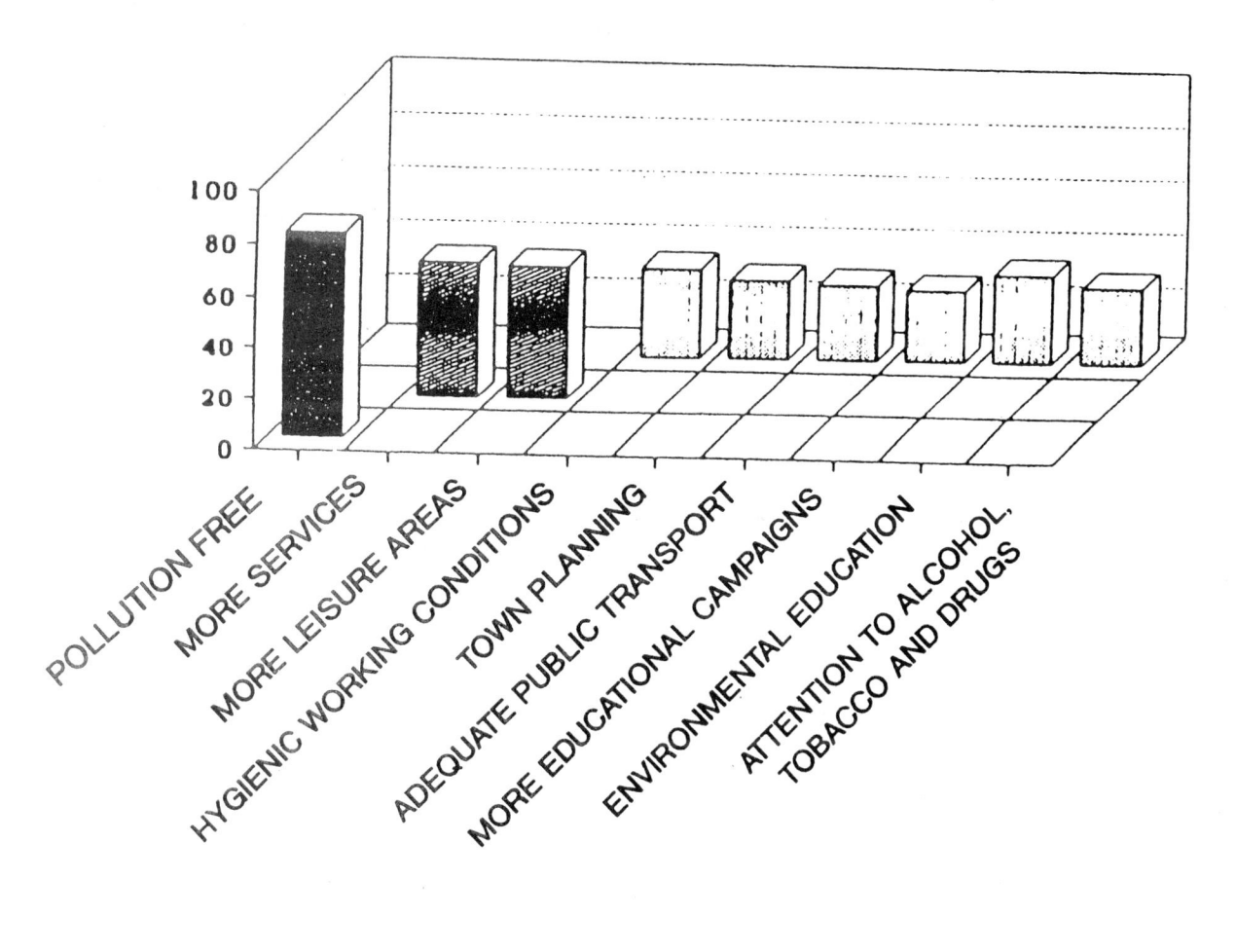

Figure 2: Priorities in a healthy city as seen by residents of 8 Basque cities

FIRST PRIORITY   SECOND PRIORITY
THIRD PRIORITY

These differences in the two extreme age groups surveyed are logical and represent the different expectations. On the other hand the perception of an ideal city is practically the same in all of the cities surveyed, keeping in touch with the reality of the Basque cities.

4.2 The Example of Vitoria

The Vitoria health survey analysed the physical and social situation of the city, capital of the Autonomous Community with a population of 200,000. It set up intervention priorities for the next 2 years in different fields.

For the implementation of these priorities an agreement was signed between the Local Council and the Department of Health and Consumer Affairs on "Healthy Cities". The document was divided into 3 parts:

A. The first established the programmatic lines of the agreement, centred basically in the five action areas of the Ottawa Conference.

B. The second set up a "follow-up" commission, to keep an eye on the programme's development, and provide the necessary information to evaluate its progress. The commission is formed by:

- A President, the mayor of Vitoria-Gasteiz.

- 3 Councillors, responsible for the areas involved.

- 2 representatives from the Department of Health and Consumer Affairs.

- 2 representatives of neighbourhood committees and associations appointed by the Vitoria-Gasteiz town council.

The Vitoria-Gasteiz local council agreed to set up a new Public Health Service in 1989, dedicated to:

* Develop environmental protection plans encouraging the formation of local groups.

* Promote healthy habits amongst the population.

* Promote collaboration between the different departments in the city council in order to achieve a "healthier city".

On the other hand, the Department of Health and Consumer Affairs was to co-ordinate the healthy cities programme by:

1. Giving technical and informative advice on the activities to be carried out by the local Health Department.

2. Carrying out Vitoria's health risks analysis.

3. Supporting demands of the city to obtain funds from other Departments of the Basque Government involved in the "Healthy Cities" programme.

C. Finally, in the third part of the agreement, an intervention plan was proposed for 1989 based on the problems detected in the environmental health survey.

It proposed a series of specific actions in all the analysed sectors. The local council agreed to hire in 1989 a public health expert and a technician to work on the programme. They were located at the local Institute of Health and Consumer Affairs.

As an example, we will resume some of the agreements reached in the environmental areas:

1. Drinking water

Problems were detected in the reservoirs, where water is collected to supply Vitoria. They were not protected and an increased eutrophisation and chemical pollution was found. Part of the water was not filtered, and high levels of Lambliasis were recorded in the infant population. Once the problem was known it was given priority and action was taken by the organisation responsible in this area. A multisectoral commission was also created to analyse the problem.

2. Liquid wastes

Sixteen companies working in the area were found to dispose of chemical wastes with high heavy metal content. Once the situation was known the responsibilities of the organisation participating in the agreement were discussed. The town council decided to control the dumping of the wastes. The Department of Public Health supported the allocation by other Departments of the Basque Government of zero or low interest loans to the industries responsible for the toxic waste.

3. Solid waste

The following problems were detected in the city's legal dump site:

* Run-off water circulates in the open and discharges directly in a small river running nearby.

* The dump-site is not isolated and no check of the incoming waste is made.

On the other side of the city many illegal waste sites were detected with no control at all on the source and content of the wastes.

An intervention programme was designed. After two years of work the problems have been solved.

4. Noise

* The Local Council of Vitoria-Gasteiz approved an Order to control the acoustic level in the city.

* A study of the noise problem in the city was carried out and a city acoustic map was drawn.

* The town council started a campaign to make the public aware of this problem.

5. Fauna and food hygiene

The inspection and control of food in Vitoria-Gasteiz was considered adequate, nevertheless, the local council collaborates in any way necessary with the territory's Health Department, specifically in Salmonellosis and other food related programmes (retail trade, transport, microbiological meat control and animal health).

6. Atmospheric Pollution

* In 1989 the Vitoria-Gasteiz local council increased the number of pollutants monitored; NO_x, CO and hydrocarbons were included.

* An atmospheric clean-up plan for the local area was also studied. Its viability will be decided next year.

* The relocation of the company FUNDIX S.A. (the only company situated within the town area), was decided as a consequence of an agreement between the local council and the company. It left its location on December 31st 1989.

7. Other Areas

* Any special action necessary will be carried out in programmes already under way such as drug addiction (alcoholism, smoking, etc).

* Information programmes were designed to improve the population's behaviour towards cleaner surroundings, pollution, healthy habits, life styles, etc.

8. Social Area

The Department of Health of the Basque Government and the Public Health Service of Vitoria-Gasteiz are to carry out a study in the local area of how to encourage the necessary participation of the population in the "Healthy City" programme.

4.3 Population Perception

Vitoria-Gasteiz (according to its residents) does not only have a need to improve its environment (green areas, etc.), but people also feel a great need for improving its social aspect. Vitoria is a new city, which had a high population growth in the seventies (the second re-industrialisation). It surroundings have been unaltered but obviously this contributes to other problems, such as the absence of real integration networks in the city, which could help in difficult family situations or personal problems.

This problem can only be studied from the point of view of social science and it is so important that we cannot seriously approach the planning nor the development of local health policies, without taking into consideration local psychosocial realities. For this reason, it is necessary to have access to indicators which can condense all the information available. We also need some reference levels and points of comparison between cities.

We briefly explain the situation in Vitoria-Gasteiz, using only two indicators, **"the general indicator for city perception"** and the **"citizens' demands"** indicator, (at the present time we are working with 24 subjective indicators), which we think sum up the reality commented on previously.

These indicators stem from the analysis of opinion polls specifically designed to work with a multivariate analysis and to draw up complex indices afterwards. Therefore we have indicators peculiar and unique to each local council, and others which are general indicators.

The city's general perception indicator refers to the real perception people have of their city, i.e. it is a measure of the city's objective environmental situation (Clean City, polluted, noisy, overpopulated, built-up, installations...). This indicator makes each individual take a clearly negative or positive attitude towards his city, giving a global value from which it is difficult to extract all the components.

The general perception index is a value between -100 (all respondents have a negative image of the city) and +100 (all respondents have a positive image of the city). The average of the 8 cities studied was 31.7. This shows a generally negative perception, and makes us think about the environmental situation of the cities (Figure 3). The variance analysis indicates that there are significant differences between the perceptions of the different cities analysed. Hence in VITORIA-GASTEIZ, we find a reading of 59.8, showing a city with the best perception of its surroundings, followed by SAN SEBASTIAN, with an index of 27.0, whilst the rest of the cities have negative values, BILBAO (-68.6) and SESTAO (-79.9).

The factors which weigh most in this negative impression are noise (-46.2) and atmospheric pollution (-37.2). If we analyse the scores given to the general index and the pollution level, we see a high correlation level between them, hence the "Pearson r" is 0.9874, which indicates that 97.7% (r2) of the general index can be explained by the perception or non-perception of pollution and vice-versa.

In any case, if we analyse the index by its different components in Vitoria they are all positive (healthy, clean, little pollution, somewhat noisy, not over-populated, correct town planning and adequate facilities) (Figure 4), obtaining the lowest values in noise (+9.1). The industrial cities give negative results in all these factors.

Figure 3: The General Perception Index in 8 Basque cities

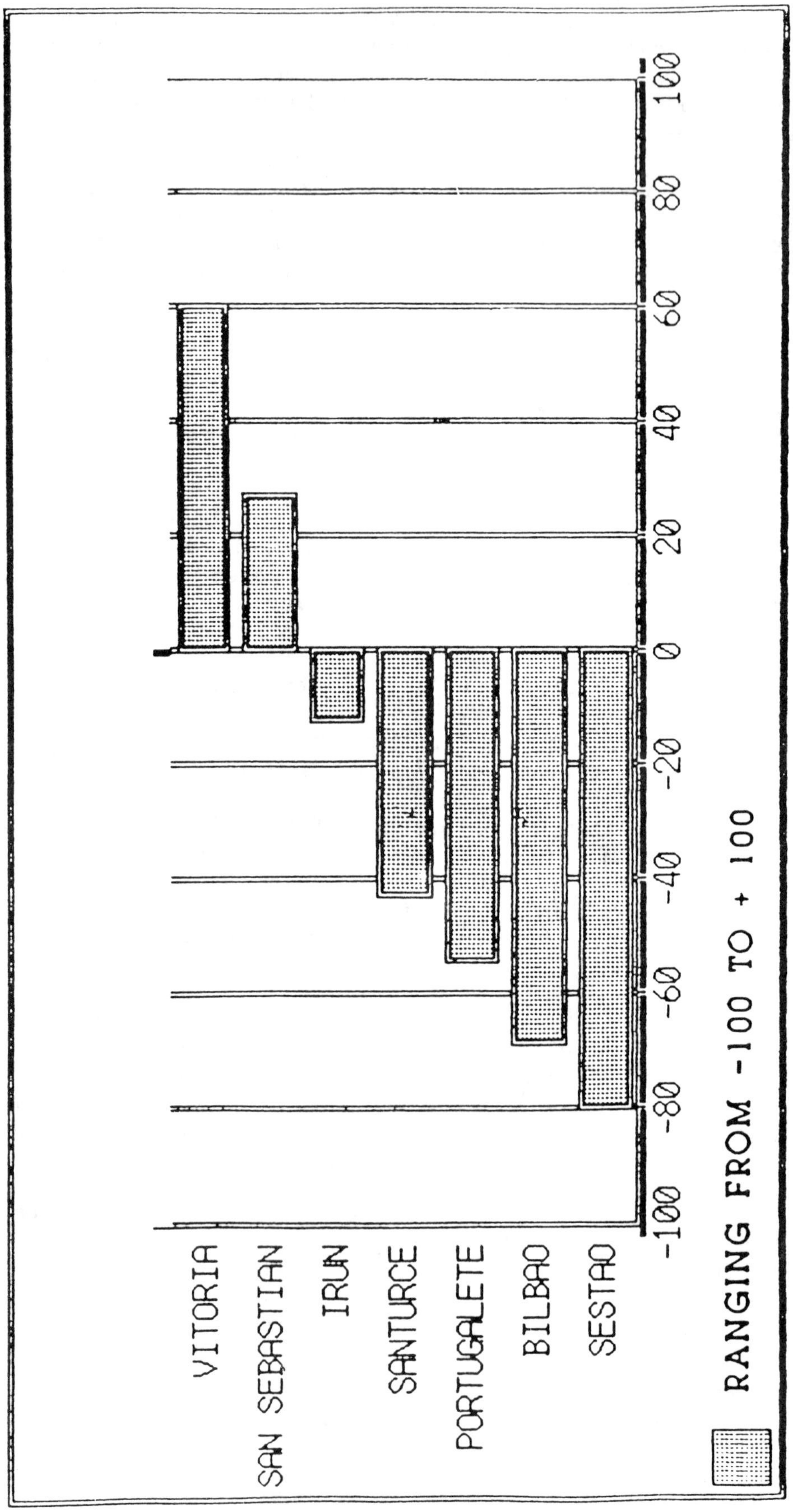

RANGING FROM -100 TO +100

The "citizens' demands" indicator attempts to explain the needs felt by the population. Five factors are considered: pollution - including air, water and noise pollution, road and traffic improvements, improvements in education, improvement in free time facilities and drug control.

Vitoria-Gasteiz (Figure 5) shows that 30.2% of respondents were for a reinforcement of measures to reduce general pollution. If we consider the different types of pollution, we find 15% wanted atmospheric pollution to be reduced (in industrial areas this was over 30%), 7.7% noise pollution and 7.4% water pollution.

Figure 5: Indicator of population demands in Vitoria

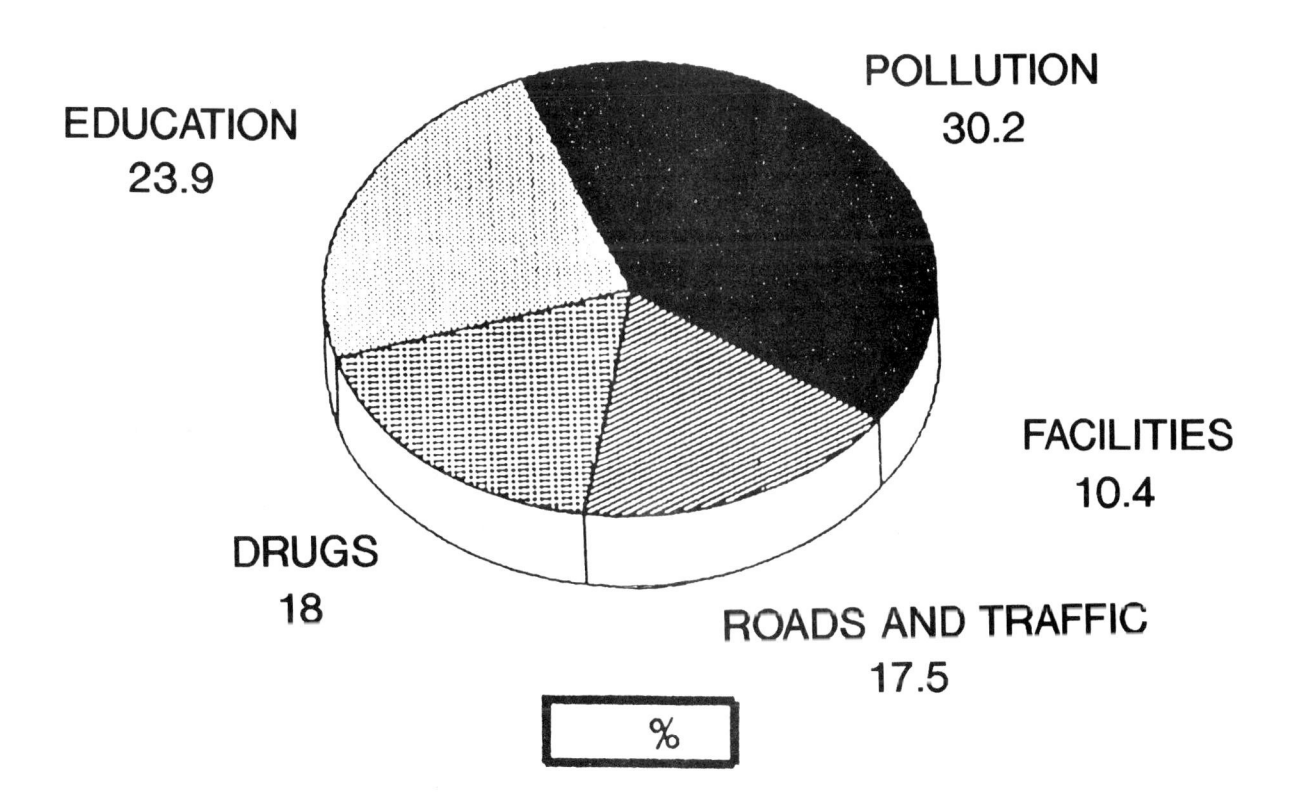

Education, with 23.9% was the second factor amongst the population demands of Vitoria. Alcohol, tobacco and drugs control came in third place. In fourth place were improvements in the traffic situation, with 17.5%. Of them 9.4% indicated the need to improve the public transport system.

The improvement of facilities was in last place (10.4%), at a long distance from other cities in the Basque Country where it was first.

Looking at the surveys, it is worth noting that complaints about pollution in Vitoria are ten points below the average, and in the case of free time facilities, almost seven points below. The opposite happens in the need for an improvement in education and drug control.

Thus we are faced with two different types of cities: those which have not solved the problems considered by the population as important or primary (showing a negative perception index) and those with a positive perception, where the priority demands of the population may be considered as secondary: access to information, the need for childrens' education, problems with drug, tobacco or alcohol consumption, or the development of areas for leisure-time activities, etc.

The development of these indicators has changed the situation in Vitoria. All the problems discussed in the agreement have been or are going to be solved soon and in a very efficient way. There has also been an important change in the priorities of the city's health department. Before, they had been basically centred around hygiene problems. Now priority is given to an improvement in lifestyle (alcohol, tobacco, etc.), and other problems which may influence the quality of life of its citizens.

Two years after the project has begun, we are now convinced that it has had a positive effect, not only in VITORIA-GASTEIZ, which is a well planned city and an example of good local administration in our country in the seventies, but also for the rest of the local councils taking part in the programme.

URBAN ENVIRONMENTAL IMPROVEMENT AND ECONOMIC DEVELOPMENT

Emilio Gerelli
University of Pavia
Italy

1. THE ROLE AND QUALITY OF THE CITY

1.1 Cities have always been the main place of cultural, social and technological development, especially because of agglomeration economies. Their inhabitants are about one half of the total world population and they are expected to grow at an increasingly fast rate: from 1 billion in 1960 to more than 2 billion at present, to reach 3 billion in the year 2000 and 5 billion in 2025. However spatial concentration also brings about costs, including environmental ones. An acceptable balance of benefits and costs must therefore be sought to achieve sustainable growth, i.e. a growth which is consistent with environmental quality. To this end this conference has been concerned with the innovative approach of exploring the links between the economy and the environment of cities, therefore considering environmental protection not only as a burden to polluters and a welfare increase for citizens, but also as an economic opportunity.

1.2 Many factors determine whether or not a city is economically buoyant but in cities where polluted air, foul water and derelict land are concentrated, it is generally the case that the economy is weak. A poor environment creates two kinds of economic burden. First, it affects the profitability of the industries that have caused it because they are faced not only with the costs of cleaning up their own production processes but also with contributing to the cost of making good damage done in the past. Second, it discourages new investment in the area because firms looking for locations in which to establish themselves (particularly the modern types of "footloose" industry which are most influenced by environmental considerations) are put off by the presence of a poor environment.

Yet even flourishing cities are constrained by environmental problems. In their case further economic growth promises e.g. to increase road traffic and raise energy consumption - both of which add to air pollution. Left unchecked, this growth in toxic emissions threatens the economic expansion that underlies it.

The future of all cities is thus dependent on improvements to the environment - a relationship now acknowledged by government and business alike.

1.3 It is however nowadays fashionable to state in an often uncritical way that environmental quality can be smoothly accommodated together with urban economic development.

Many cases discussed in this Conference prove that this is indeed possible, provided however that the difficult task of overcoming two failures is successfully performed. The first is of course market failure in accounting environmental costs through the price system. It follows that public intervention may fail as we see in our everyday experience and as it is fairly successfully stylised in the theory of Public Choice (where, apart from uncertainty in decision-making, to interpret reality it is assumed that politicians' and bureaucrats' goals do not necessarily coincide with social optimum). Our case studies show how in different situations and using various approaches we can make a success by skilfully combining two mechanisms (the market and public sector decision-making) characterised by partial failures.

1.4 In fact, compared to the grim situation of the early industrial conurbations the current situation of the modern metropolis in advanced western countries is better. Where deliberate policies have been implemented, encouraging results have been obtained. Using enough ingenuity, the two above-mentioned failures can be overcome. To this end the teachings from this Conference, based on real life experience, are particularly relevant.

2. MATCHING URBAN ENVIRONMENTAL IMPROVEMENT AND ECONOMIC DEVELOPMENT: THE EXPERIENCE

2.1 From the analysis of both the practical experience and the forward-looking approaches of more than 20 OECD countries actively facing the challenge of improving urban environmental quality, this Conference has shown that there are promising opportunities for market economies with efficient government intervention (which are the common framework for OECD member countries) to successfully tackle urban environmental problems.

2.2 Our discussions have also shown that a unique instrument to improve the urban environment and at the same time achieve economic development does not exist; rather, a well thought out strategy based on specific situations must be planned and implemented. However, at least a general approach may be used as a Leitmotiv.

The second part of the title of our Conference, i.e. economic development, is led by the market which has the advantage of making scarcity known through prices. No one would dream of using energy, labour, or any other production factor without paying a price. Since, as we have reminded, the invisible (but somewhat crippled) hand of the market does not work to also ration environmental resources, it must be supplemented by another hand which can be operated by implementing the Polluter Pays Principle (PPP). In its general meaning, this principle states, in fact, that we must pay for the use of the environment a price which is sufficiently high to guarantee that it is not overused, taking into account also the interests of our neighbours and future generations. The PPP can be applied through the traditional direct regulation (standards plus monitoring and penalties), but to face complex situations such an approach can be usefully complemented by more imaginative methods such as the "bubble approach" (i.e. the selling of pollution rights, which however, has not been examined in our Conference) or the area licensing scheme to which we refer now.

2.3 Road transport is at present one of the most important sources of pollution and congestion in urban areas. An as yet unpublished study (updating a previous OECD assessment) estimates at 2.5-3% of GNP the external cost of road transport due to pollution, noise and security (the total social cost of road transport amounting to about 18% of GNP, of which half is the private user cost and about 7% is the cost of time. Remember, for comparison, that pollution control expenditures in advanced countries amount to 1-2% of GNP). Here is an area where the magnitude of damage costs makes room for efficient market simulation. In this connection the Stockholm case discussed yesterday is of particular interest. The impact of changes in transit fares (either a decrease or an increase of 50%) and of an area licensing scheme (cordon toll fee of 25 SK per passenger car per round trip) has been evaluated for Stockholm county. The most favourable policy with respect to the reduction of car pollution is area licensing combined with traffic fare reduction. This policy reduces car NO_x and CO discharges by 25%, and also the cost of time (which as we have seen is an important part of social cost). A similar scheme has been successfully applied in Singapore since 1975.

An important characteristic of the above schemes (and of all direct externality charges) is that they must be area-wide, otherwise congestion and pollution are reduced in the area where the road price is enforced, but this can spread traffic to other areas. It is encouraging to note in this connection (although in a different context) that, e.g. in Milan, a few months after an extended car-free zone has been created in the central district, the use of private cars has been reduced also in the outside districts.

Our session on **urban transport** has also shown that to deal with this problem policy-makers must recognise the functional and financial interdependence of the various modes of transport in a city and they must act on them so as to reduce pollution and congestion at the same time. This is a very difficult task since there are still very few cases of urban transport schemes resulting in both less congestion and less pollution.

It has also been shown that urban transport can be improved through appropriate management schemes, e.g. allowing certain categories of vehicles at certain times and in certain areas, restraining parking or through traffic, etc.

2.4 A second relevant result of our work here is that (as mentioned above) **efforts to upgrade the physical environment and amenities will positively influence the attractiveness of urban settings for business** and, conversely, a prosperous business community will yield more revenues which can be used to finance environmental improvement.

This is the case of such different places as, e.g. Rotterdam, where in planning the city centre around the river the emphasis is placed on the attractiveness of the city, both in the functional and spatial sense; in Manchester where the derelict Salford Quays are being renewed so as to produce dramatic improvements in environmental and economic regeneration in an inner city context; in Vancouver, where in the once heavily polluted and declining area of the False Creek Basin, water quality has been improved drastically and Granville Island has been turned from a highly polluted industrial area into an internationally successful urban park. In most cases an appropriate mix of locations for production and dwellings has been sought.

2.5 A further important and general result to be drawn from our case studies is that one of the recurring elements in success stories is the co-operation among public and private organisations. Although we fully recognise the importance of this instrument, we must not forget that, in general, business efficiency and creativity can be turned in favour of environmental improvement particularly when the public sector sets clear goals and can manage the appropriate intervention even if they are implemented by private bodies. Once this ability is present, a very fruitful and close co-operation can take place.

This is the case, e.g. of Salford Quays, Greater Manchester, where also in order to attract private sector investment the City Council commissioned a development plan; deals were made with private developers and central government released funding to reclaim the docks and provide infrastructure.

In general, the creation of urban development agencies working under private business conditions has proven to be successful at combining both efficient project management and safeguarding public interest. Given a strong political commitment from the local community and appropriate support from national authorities to restructure derelict areas, private investors will find economic opportunities with possibilities for job creation.

2.6 Another field where not only public-private co-operation, but also a comprehensive approach is necessary is energy conservation. **Urban energy management** requires in fact action by utilities, building owners, companies and households (see e.g. the cases of Aalborg and Helsinki).

The first step is for government, the energy utilities and their engineering consultants to produce an urban energy management plan. Finance for implementing the plan will come from both the government and the private sector. Banks are likely to be involved in financing large-scale, capital-intensive projects; energy consumers will upgrade the services in their homes to conserve fuel. At times when energy prices are falling, the investment of public funds in such measures can be justified on the grounds of the benefits to the environment.

3. THE NEED FOR INCREASED CO-OPERATION

3.1 Public/private co-operation, as stated above, becomes strategic, but the different actors involved must perform within their respective fields of competence. It is important too to keep the public well-informed.

The case studies are useful in clarifying the roles of the various participants in joint actions to improve the environment of cities.

3.2 By transferring individual values for environmental quality into social choices, the **public sector** sets the objectives and the framework of laws. It also defines the rules for co-operation with business. By means of this process resources are allocated for environmental improvement. Inequalities may therefore arise (e.g. polluting industries bear abatement costs and producers of pollution abatement equipment increase their sales). Such temporary distributional problems must also be faced by the public sector.

3.3 **Businesses** have an important role in efficiently implementing public guidelines for the sustainable development of urban areas in a market context. They are becoming increasingly aware that the environment of cities affects their profitability and that commercial opportunities exist in reducing pollution and reclaiming derelict land.

3.4 **Individuals**, whether cast in the role of householders or consumers, can reduce their loading on the environment by altering their patterns of consumption and travel in order to create less waste and reduce vehicle emissions. They can conserve energy. They can also form pressure groups and there may be scope for them to co-operate locally with government and business to pursue environmental goals.

3.5 **International organisations** can play an important role in increasing public awareness, in initiating co-operation among countries and cities, in transferring experience in the field of urban environmental improvements and in assisting national governments efforts to stir investments in those cities which are in greatest need of improvement. With the support of International Organisations, "best practice" in environmentally conscious urban management should be made available with least possible delay to as many urban decision-makers as possible.

3.6 Germans use the fascinating word **"umweltfreundlich"** to define the positive behaviour of business and citizens described above. Such a behaviour may be voluntary and education and moral persuasion are very important tools to foster it. However in a competitive world of pervasive environmental diseconomies, the carrot of subsidies (borne by the tax-payer) and the stick of regulation and charges must still be used. All our case studies have confirmed the first and fundamental law of both ecology and economics: "there is no such thing as a free lunch"; on the other hand they have also shown that most successful are the à la carte lunches where appropriate arrangements involve all the actors on the stage, using the specific ability of each of them.

4. CONCLUDING REMARKS

4.1 Cities with foul air, unclean rivers and swathes of derelict land are at an economic disadvantage. Their poor environment is not only a burden for citizens, but also a drag on established firms and a deterrent to investment by new ones. For such cities environmental improvements are a key to economic revival.

4.2 Yet even prosperous cities need to be conscientious guardians of their environments. Their very success is likely to bring increased traffic, rising energy consumption and worsening air pollution. If environmental conditions deteriorate in these cities, they too might hinder their long term prosperity as has been the case in many old cities.

4.3 Preliminary assessments of current damage costs in advanced countries are of about 4-5% of GNP (which is probably an underestimation because of the difficulties of measuring long term (e.g. greenhouse) effects). Control costs range between 1 and 2% of GNP. As shown in the OECD Conference on Economics and the Environment, control costs of a clean environment will have to rise, and this will particularly affect cities, where most of the population lives. This unavoidable burden will not be too heavy if it will be met using the intelligent conclusions to be drawn from this Conference, based on real life. In my opinion, and in a telegraphic way, they are the following:

- City governments have the main responsibility of initiating the process of integrating environmental improvement and economic development.

- Public policies as well as private business strategies need to include environmental considerations not as marginal additional items but as thoroughly integrated concerns at all steps of decision-making (setting of objectives, definition of strategies, implementation and monitoring). In this way, environmental goals will become basic, intrinsic values in economic decision-making.

- Given the pervasive nature of environmental problems regulations are becoming very wide-ranging, and indeed even cumbersome. Environmental policies may therefore have to rely on more flexible economic instruments such as pollution charges, cordon tolls, marketable permits, etc.

- Improvement of the urban environment also creates business opportunities, which must be fully exploited to increase the efficiency of environmental policies.

- The environmental dimension brings about new models for urban management, since the development of cities must be substantially restructured. It is no easy task, but experience shows that success can be reached.

URBAN PLANNING AND THE ENVIRONMENT:
A GLOBAL APPROACH IN SEARCH OF A NEW URBAN
BALANCE FOR FRENCH TOWNS

N. Sougareva
Official Representative
Agency for the Environment and the Prevention
of Major Technical and Natural Hazards
Quality of Life Office, Neuilly

The search for a new balance in urban life in France emerged in the 1970s and 1980s, when planning problems came to be considered in a more general framework, taking in all aspects of economic, social and cultural life.

This approach made it possible:

1.1 to balance the social composition of districts;

1.2 to link urban development to the features of local economic development;

1.3 to take account of environmental concerns in seeking a more qualitative management of town life;

1.4 to improve the quality of projects undertaken, especially in the area of assisted housing;

1.5 to secure better integration into city life for vulnerable social groups (young people, the elderly, etc.);

1.6 to improve the services provided for citizens (transport, education, leisure, culture).

DECENTRALISATION

Since 1983 the decentralisation of urban planning in France has given local authorities complete responsibility for the planning of their areas. The whole set of planning instruments is involved: zoning, planning permissions.

However, the State reserves these prerogatives to itself in the case of:

- planning coastal and mountain areas;
- protecting the outstanding natural heritage;
- protecting the outstanding built heritage.

With reference to the law of 7 January 1983 on decentralisation, which emphasises the shared responsibility of public authorities for the protection and enhancement of the national territory, one may remark that **in France today, planning is an activity based on partnership** and negotiation between the different actors: local authorities, the State, planners and builders both public and private, not forgetting the residents of the cities. The current legal position in France tries to create the minimum conditions allowing residents to become involved in planning their living environment.

Participation - meaning the establishment of a certain balance between public authorities and residents - can only be achieved if, parallel to the growth in the powers of elected representatives, arrangements are put in place for respecting the basic rights of residents and establishing countervailing powers:

- the right to ownership of property is a basic freedom in the planning process, even though the exercise of this right remains subordinate to the public interest. Hence the importance which is attached to public enquiries before the implementation of planning operations. Massive opposition to a project by residents may lead to its rejection.

- The countervailing powers generally take the form of associations formed to defend local community interests, such as the historical heritage of towns or the environment.

MEASURES IN FAVOUR OF FRENCH TOWNS

French towns and cities are increasingly seeking a **public identity** which brings together the prestige of their historical past, the quality of their contemporary projects, and the enhancement of existing features of the environment, whether natural or built.

The State assists local authorities through a contractual policy of partnership either directly with the towns, or in the form of planning contracts lasting several years, involving the department or the region. This policy largely takes account of environmental concerns.

In France today, a national environment plan is in place. This plan proposes that French towns should set out their overall environmental policies in municipal plans.

There are two main aims in a municipal plan for the environment:

- to prepare an action plan covering several years, based on a comprehensive diagnosis;

- to facilitate a dialogue, following the preparation of this plan, between the municipal authorities and all the partners concerned.

THE METHOD IS RELATIVELY LIGHT

The whole range of available information is taken into account:

- data on the areas involved;

- social data on the perception of the environment;

- institutional data on the organisation of public services in the environmental area;

- data on the prospects for economic development.

The method proposed starts out with a diagnostic exercise based on all the data already collected by the competent services of the town and the State, without forgetting any specific studies done by university researchers or local associations.

This method implies a joint process with the main actors involved in the environment: political leaders and technical services of the towns, representatives of the residents, private and public planning bodies, local services of the State.

The diagnostic process makes it possible to identify the strong points and the weak points of the town, the actions to be planned and the partners to be mobilised. It informs the elected representatives about the main issues at stake, and introduces them to the various possible strategies. On the basis of their choices, the municipal plan for the environment will be drawn up, in a period of between six and twelve months.

The diagnostic phase is led by an external team, having a general competence in environmental matters, in close liaison with the elected representatives and the services of the Environment Ministry.

During the period of launching the first municipal plans for the environment, the Quality of Life Office contributes methodological follow-up and specific financing.

In this type of approach, the State plays an important educational role through:

- the mobilisation of the competences of all actors within the life of the town to **form teams,** organise **the dissemination of information** and encourage **the exchange of experiences** of an innovative and original kind between townspeople and environmental professionals;

- the observation of urban phenomena in drawing up strategies and actions in the medium and longer term (taking account of the time factors involved in a method based on **"prospects-planning-programming"**).

The actions defined in this way are taken over naturally into the instruments of town planning.

The zoning plan is the main town planning document which regulates land usage. It must compulsorily include the environmental objectives of towns with a view to:

- organising urban development;

- protecting natural spaces;

- reserving the necessary plots for the provision of public facilities;

- defining clearly the rights and obligations of each portion of land.

The environment is taken into account throughout the preparation of the zoning plan.

During the phase of preliminary studies, this is done through a specific environmental study which tries:

- to understand the municipal area, its functioning and its probable development;

- to prioritise the issues at stake in a medium-term and long-term development perspective;

- to identify the issues which must be incorporated in the zoning plan - for example: open space; energy saving; architectural guidelines; natural and urban landscape; historic monuments; noise levels. This list can be very long, depending on the complexity of individual cases.

The zoning plan becomes the subject of a public enquiry, and all citizens are legally entitled to oppose it. Once it has been approved, it remains in force without any time-limit. It is generally admitted that it has to be replaced once it is no longer suited to the development of the local situation (after 5 or 10 years). But it can be modified at any time. The procedure here is quite simple, so long as no damage is done to the general economy and **designated woodlands and natural sites are not reduced.**

This note only sets forth the very broad outlines of the French approach to taking account of environmental concerns in the town planning process.

Practical examples of French towns which have achieved a higher quality and better balanced management of their development could complete this contribution.

THE DETERIORATION OF THE ENVIRONMENT

KEY FACTORS FOR A SOCIAL CONTRACT

José Quintero

Huelva, one of the fifty Spanish provinces, is located in the far south-western tip of Spain. It has an area of 10,085 square kilometres and is bounded by the provinces of Badajoz to the north and Seville to the east, by the Atlantic Ocean to the south and Portugal to the west. It is under the administrative authority of the Autonomous Community of Andalusia, and in 1989 its population totalled 404,000.

Its capital, also called Huelva, is on the coastal fringe at the confluence of the rivers Tinto and Odiel. It has a population of 135,000, and a chemical-industry complex is sited in the town.

The province boasts the famous Riotinto mines which yield copper pyrites and which have been worked from ancient times. Relics of Tarshish, Roman and Arab occupation have come to light in the archaeological and mining work there. More recently the mining work was carried out on behalf of the Spanish Monarchy, until in 1873 the mines were sold to Matheson and Company, the forerunner of Río Tinto Company. In 1954 Compañia Española de Minas de Río Tinto purchased the land owned by Río Tinto Company. The province also contains the Tharsis mines purchased in 1866 by the Tharsis Sulphur and Copper Company.

These mines, and other smaller mines, are located on a pyrites deposit running across the province from east to west and into Portugal.

Throughout their ownership by the British companies, the minerals from these mines were shipped to the UK from the port of Huelva. Once the mines were bought back in 1954, the minerals had to be processed, mainly to produce sulphur dioxide, for use in the manufacture of sulphuric acid and copper through melting of the copper pyrites.

The capital, at the confluence of the Tinto and Odiel, had a natural harbour which, though of only shallow draught, offered possibilities of expansion. The chemical complex was developed via the fiscal and credit benefits allowed by the legislation covering Industrial Expansion Schedules. The site of the complex was selected on the basis of the location of the various industrial sites alongside the Odiel and the provision of moorings, as well as the existence nearby of the large marshy zone Las Marismas, suitable for dumping of the solid waste arising during roasting of the pyrites (and at a later date the gypsums produced in the manufacture of phosphated fertilisers), the favourable location of the port relative to the Bucraá mines and the oil pipelines, and the existence of various services (railway links, water supply, power supply, roads, etc.).

Whereas the Expansion Schedule indicated a growth in the economy and in the population above that of the national mean for the capital and its immediate environs in the 1960s and 1970s, the remainder of the province (like the rest of the country) recorded a substantial decrease in population. It was the labour potential offered by the town (especially during construction of the factories), in contrast with the poor opportunities for work in the agrarian sector, which caused this movement of the workforce.

Disordered expansion

With the arrival of the 1960s and the start of redevelopment of Spanish industry, the Government came to realise that further investment was required in depressed areas whose natural resources made them an important part of the national economy; in the case of Huelva this meant its rich mineral resources, from which sulphuric acid and copper in particular could be produced. In 1964 the Government therefore issued a decree establishing six Expansion Schedules, one of which was based on Huelva. These aimed at the provision of official aid to private industry and the establishment of a state-supported infrastructure.

Inefficient government at that time meant that the expansion turned into expansionism. The necessary infrastructure always lagged behind construction of the industrial complex. This had to be located at the Punta del Sebo, because of delay in construction of the bridge over the Tinto. The sulphuric and phosphoric acid industries were commissioned in the period between 1965 and 1969, whereas the bridge was not opened until 1970. This meant that there was a large conglomeration of highly polluting and potentially hazardous factories not more than 800 metres or so from an urban centre with 100,000 inhabitants.

As regards town planning, only provisional regulations covered planning of the sites under the Schedule, and industry mushroomed without proper town planning. Even today this area is called "non-scheduled land for urban development". The natural expansion of the seaside town has been throttled by these anomalies.

The situation as regards the environment deserves special mention. A lack of adequate legislation, failure to comply with the existing laws, and out-of-date technology, are compounded by employers aiming at quick profits without planning for the future, and a tolerant administration. As a result, in this area the surroundings have been transformed in the short space of ten years from a forested coastal zone with areas for bathing into a desolate, evil-smelling and highly contaminated locality. Twenty years of dumping 50,000 to 60,000 tonnes per year of sulphuric acid in the river have brought the pH value of the water to about 2. In the surroundings of the scheduled area, forming a 900-hectare belt extending virtually all round the town, 55, 15 and 2 million tonnes of phospho-gypsums, pyrites ash and slag respectively have been deposited.

The scheduled area has had very little influence on the province's economy, as it involves heavy basic industry and not manufacturing industry. The companies are large foreign firms taking their profits abroad, or local small and medium-sized enterprises having little or nothing to do with the foreign firms. The job situation in the province has not improved with the commencement of the Schedule. Thus in the secondary sector (mining and the manufacturing industries) employment fell from 38,000 in 1964, the date of introduction of the plan, to 25,000 in 1985, following a slight increase in the first few years due to the labour requirement for construction of the industries. Per capita income followed a similar and even more disturbing pattern: Huelva was ranked 35 in 1964 and 45 in 1985 in terms of the fifty Spanish provinces.

These trends, following the initial years of euphoria, demonstrate that the equilibrium has been affected by three factors: the loss of several thousand jobs on completion of the construction work, the oil crisis of 1973 where the industries based on cheap energy were the first to be affected by the economic and employment problems, and the advent of ecological awareness for the first time from 1980 onwards, have posed two fundamental questions. To all appearances there is no real redress for the economy/environment binomial, and citizens recognise the real deterioration suffered in such a short space of time.

The debate has begun, and from this moment on we see a rising curve whose point of inflection appears in the years 1986 and 1987; there is clear opposition to the Schedule, and the conditions are changing day by day.

Final Phase

The final phase of the present situation becomes clear when we analyse various factors. These are the confrontation between environmental and other economic sectors, protests whose intensity increases daily, and finally the steadily increasing conviction that the chemical industry will never adopt measures which would progressively reduce the harm it has caused. The main ongoing confrontation in recent years has been with the tourism sector, as Huelva is a town tailor-made for tourism.

Within this framework, under the PCV (plan controlling dumping into the river at Huelva), arranged by the Autonomous Community, which involves investment of approximately 90 million dollars, 60% of the investment will be by the firms themselves, on in-plant control and measures to exclude contamination, the remainder being paid by the administration for work on restoration and on the infrastructure of the area. This plan, unique in the history of Huelva, is designed as the final answer to this environmental problem which we can only describe as deplorable.

Paradoxically, the PCV, announced in September 1987, met with resistance from one section of the population, namely the zone of the province where it is intended to install the dump (the inert residues plant), putting an end to uncontrolled dumping in the river. The main hurdle to survival of the PCV will be overcome since from that time on and in this situation the PCV will cease to be exclusively a tool of the administration and will become an objective of all the province's political and social interests.

Because of this the PCV has been greatly expanded, as have its objectives, mainly in three directions:

a. the formulation of an air pollution control project,

b. the formulation of a project for the treatment of gypsum waste lagoons, and

c. a study of the treatment of the ash produced by the plants manufacturing sulphuric acid and other derivatives.

The administration is also meeting one of the main demands of a large proportion of the population and the priority aims of various local bodies, through the instigation of a study costing 350,000 dollars to determine the various ways in which certain industries can be moved from their current isolated position to one more in accord with the expansion of those activities, and to the use of more up-to-date technology.

These two tasks, the PCV and the study of possibilities for industrial change, are being handled as two distinct exercises but with the same investigators. The PCV monitors matters and checks the degree of consensus, the time scale and the commitment, while an initial progress report which we received in January 1990 indicates that we should have the final result of the study before the end of 1990. This progress report has already shown that any measure initiating change would require economic assistance from the Spanish Government and the European Economic Community.

One further major complication at present is the crisis which has arisen in the fertiliser sector of our industry; moreover, much of our industry is obsolescent because of the lack of renewal of production facilities over the last 20 years or so.

What, then, do we conclude from all this? So far, we can only think along the following lines:

The fact is that during 25 years of industrial production neither the firms nor the administration have undertaken any remedial measures such as those now being considered. As a result the zone has deteriorated progressively, and the various problems are now far more expensive to put right.

Because of this situation the growth of other economic sectors has been stifled: mainly tourism and other profitable activities. Another factor here, of course, is the need for growth in certain economic sectors before there can be any real chance of improving the environment to facilitate the spread of other activities.

What is absolutely certain is that the enormous effort we are now making here has been made possible through the existence in the zone concerned of the largest biological reserve in Europe, concentrated in the Doñana National Park, and the interest shown by the EC in preserving this asset.

Last but not least, concerted action is necessary in order to bring our plans to fruition, since clearly no single administration would ever be able to apply such complex measures without the agreement and collaboration of all concerned.

Location of Huelva in Spain   Location of Huelva in the province

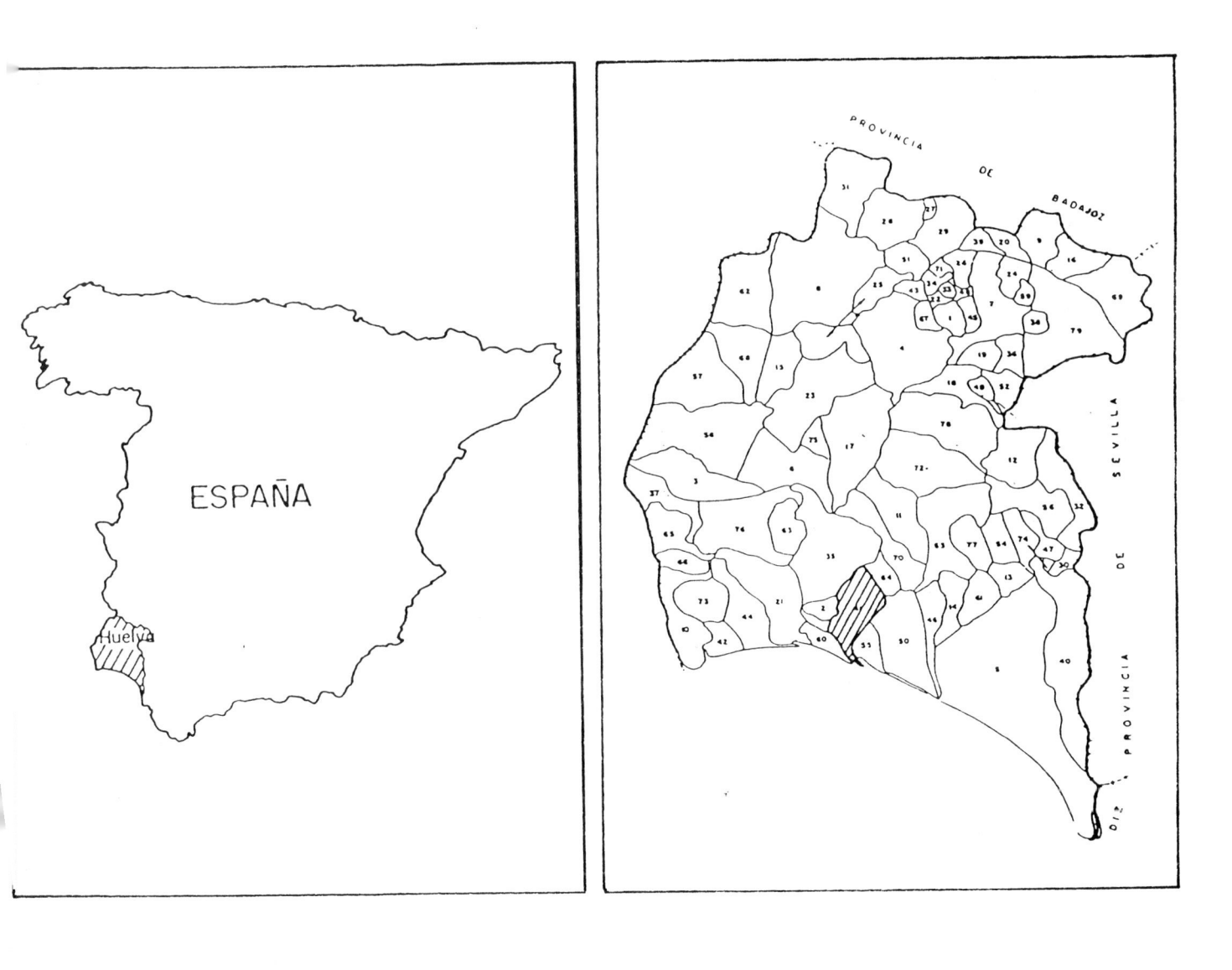

Site of industries in Huelva

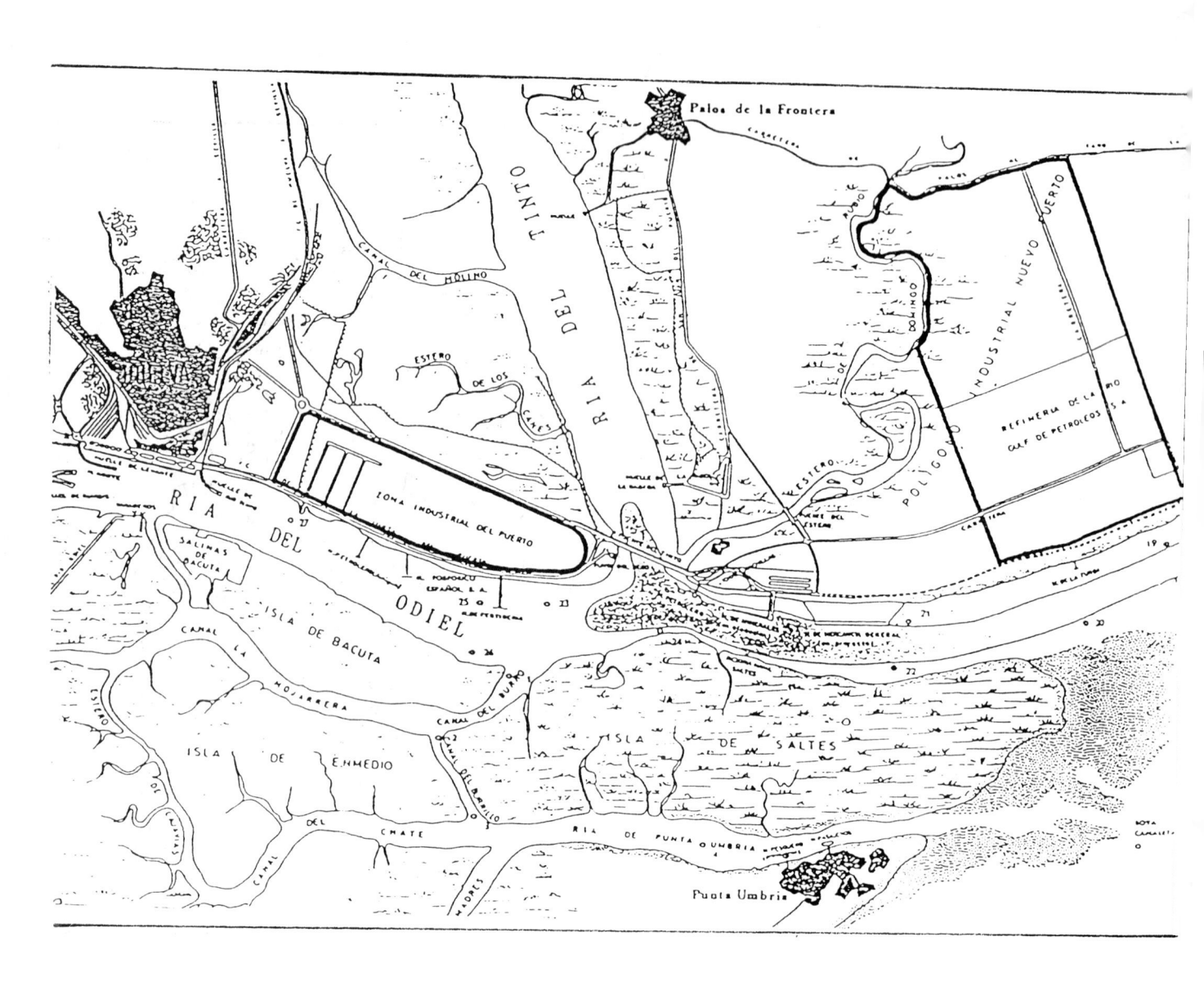

Annex

Distribution of employment in thousands of jobs per sector, in Huelva Province

Year	Primary sector	Secondary sector	Tertiary sector	Total
1955	66.4	33.2	29.2	128.8
1957	61.1	35.9	32.1	129.1
1960	57.0	34.1	36.3	127.4
1962	52.4	36.9	39.0	128.3
1964	49.5	37.9	38.8	126.2
1967	41.2	38.2	43.0	122.4
1969	41.0	39.9	45.2	126.1
1971	40.5	43.5	47.2	131.2
1973	39.5	41.7	47.5	128.7
1975	36.9	40.0	47.7	124.6
1977	34.1	40.4	46.6	121.1
1979	31.5	35.5	50.6	117.6
1981	27.5	32.5	47.9	107.9
1983	23.5	26.2	49.1	98.8
1985	21.0	25.3	51.1	97.4

Sources: Jesús Monteagudo Lopez-Menchero (1986): El entorno agroindustrial de Huelva (The Huelva agro-industrial complex); Huelva Official Chamber of Trade, Industry and Shipping.

Banco de Bilbao (1955-1985): Renta Nacional de España y su Distribución Provincial (Spanish national income and its distribution over the provinces); published biennially since 1955.

Annex

Economic indicators of Huelva Province

Listing relative to the fifty Spanish provinces

Year	Net production	Per capita income	Per capita available family income
1955	29	33	-
1957	34	34	-
1960	34	33	-
1962	35	37	-
1964	35	35	-
1967	35	37	38
1969	33	36	39
1971	33	37	38
1973	32	39	41
1975	24	31	31
1977	27	39	40
1979	31	42	46
1981	32	42	47
1983	35	44	45
1985	35	45	46

Sources: Banco de Bilbao (1955-1985): Renta Nacional de España y su Distribución Provincial (Spanish national income and its distribution over the provinces); published biennially since 1955.

Jesús Monteagudo Lopez-Menchero (1986): Comarcalización y organización del territorio de la provincia de Huelva (Commercial activity and organisation of Huelva Province territory); Huelva Official Chamber of Trade, Industry and Shipping.

José Maria Tejero Garcia (1981): El presente y el futuro de la economía onubense (The present and future of Huelva's economy); Revista Informativa de la FOE, Huelva.

Works	Company	Process and commissioning date Name	Year	Raw materials	Capacities x 1000 t/year Product	Quantity	Number employed Own	Contract	Sales distribution (%) Home	Abroad	Countries	General uses of products
Fesa Huelva Abonos	Fertilizantes Españoles SA	Sulphuric acid Phosphoric acid Ammonia, urea NPX complex fertilizer Mono- and diammonium phosphates	1965 1966 1966 1966 1969	Pyrites Phosphorite Urea	Sulphuric acid Phosphoric acid Urea Monoammonium phosphate Complex fertilizers	180 225 60	200 68 70 120 270	460	100	50	50	Venezuela, China, Cameroon, Turkey, Ghana, Ireland, Thailand, UK, Colombia, others	Agricultural fertilizers
Fesa Amoniaco Urea	Fertilizantes Españoles SA	Urea Ammonia	1975 1978	Ammonia Naptha LPG	Urea Ammonia	110.4 176.1 49.7	180 270	198	15	100	.		Agricultural fertilizers, fertilizer raw material
Aragonesas	Energia e Industrias Aragonesas SA	Chlorine/caustic soda Chloromethanes Sodium cyanide Ammonium sulphate Table salt	1973 1974 1978 1977 1977	Sodium chloride Methanol Refinery gas Ammonia	Salt Chlorine/caustic soda Chloromethanes Sodium cyanide Ammonium sulphate	150 9.7 2.8 18	170 170 21.5 6 42	320	21	85	15	Israel, USA, Portugal, South Africa, Cyprus, Korea, China, India, Ireland, Japan, Australia	Bleaching, disinfection, mining industry, solvents, pharmaceutical synthesis
Asland	Asland SA	First line Second line	1967 1970	Limestone clay slag Limestone	Cements Lime	615 260	400 130	173	.	100	.		Building construction, public works, environment, mining
Celulosas	Empresa Nacional de Celulosas SA	First line Expansion of first line Second line Bulk pulp Expansion of second line	1964 1967 1972 1979 1986	Timber Chlorine Chlorate Caustic soda Sulphuric acid	Bulk pulp	830 11 4.5 11 8	263	499	130	15	85	UK, USA, Switzerland, France, Germany, Italy, others	High-quality typing and printing paper
Central Termica C. Colon Cia. Sevillana	Cia. Sevillana de Electricidad SA	Group 1 Group 2 Group 3	1961 1983 1988	Fuel oil Water	Electricity GWh/year	700 200	3 329	149	Variable	100	.		Industrial and domestic electricity
Complejo Petrolifero de la Rabida	Ercros	Refinery and asphalt Petrochemicals Lubricants	1967 1970 1974	Crude oil	Fuels Asphalts Petrochemicals Lubricants	4 000	3 211	870	110	75	25	EEC, USA, Canada, Africa, others	Power, plastics, lubricants, fibres, asphalts
Ertisa	Ertisa SA	Methyl amines Derivatives Phenol acetone Cumene	1976 1976 1978 1979	Methanol Ammonia Methyl derivatives Benzene Propylene	Methyl amines Dimethyl acetamide Dimethyl formamide Phenol Acetone	14 4 7 83 46	10 3.5 3.5 87 54	185	22	25	75	France, Germany, USA, Netherlands, Japan, Belgium, Portugal, UK, Canada, Venezuela	Fibres, resins, fungicides, pharmacy, animal feeds, methyl methacrylate
Foret	Foret SA	Phosphoric acid Industrial phosphoric acid Polyphosphates Various phosphates Sulphuric acid	1968 1970 1969 1969 1962	Pyrites Phosphorite Caustic soda Sodium carbonate Additives	Phosphoric acid Polyphosphates Sulphuric acid	250 350 50 100 50	150 150 300	350	Variable	70	30	Areas of the Mediterranean and South America	Detergents, metallurgy, textile industry, ceramics industry
Fesa Fosforico	Fertilizantes Españoles SA	Sulphuric acid Phosphoric acid Mono- and diammonium phosphates Superphosphoric acid	69/75 69/75 69/74 1983	Pyrites Phosphorite Ammonia	Sulphuric acid Phosphoric acid Superphosphoric acid Monoammonium phosphate Diammonium phosphate	1 000 1 300 65	1 400 400 100 300 150	805	154	46	54	India, Indonesia, USSR, Turkey, Czechoslovakia, Ireland, France, UK, Portugal	Fertilizers, detergents, production of complex fertilizers
Lubrizol	Lubrizol SA	Lubricant additives Zinc dialkyl dithiophosphate	1969 1977	Intermediates preparation Mineral oil Amyl alcohol Isocyclic alcohol Phosphorus pentasulphide	Lubricant additives	18.5 1.2 0.5 0.1 0.8	20	23		100	.		Improvement of lubricants and fuels
Rio Rodano	Rio Rodano SA	TPP calcination 1 Phosphoric acid TPP atomization Special phosphates TPP calcination 2	1969 1969 1971 1974 1975	Phosphoric acid Caustic soda	Sodium tripolyphosphate (TPP)	120 70	60	170	10	85	15	Morocco, Portugal, Mexico, China, Egypt	Detergents

Works	Company	Process and commissioning rate		Capacities x 1000 t/year				Number employed		Sales Distribution (%)		General uses of products
		Name	Year	Raw materials	Quantity	Product	Quantity	Own	Contract	Home	Abroad / Countries	
Rio Tinto Minera	Rio Tinto Minera SA	Mamoda furnace fusion Copper refinery Sulphuric acid Flash furnace melting	1970 1970 1970 1975	Copper concentrates Blister or scrap-form copper	550 20	Copper cathodes Sulphuric acid Electrolysis sludge Slag	115 584 0.5	720	80	80	20 / UK, Italy, France, Portugal, Japan, Germany, Belgium	Copper wires, pipes and sheets, manufacture of fertilizers, gold and silver goods, abrasives, cement manufacture
SEO	Sociedad Española del Oxigeno SA	Oxygen, nitrogen and argon manufacture	1985	Air	500	Oxygen Nitrogen Argon	80 45 4	15	-	95	5 / Portugal	Oxidation, welding, oxygen cutting, investigation, inertization, oxygen-based therapy
Tioxide	Tioxide España SAP	Titanium dioxide Crystallization of ferrous sulphate Ferric sulphate	1978 1979 1985	Ilmenite Sulphuric acid Sodium hydroxide Iron scrap	120 190 12 12	Titanium pigments Ferrous sulphate Ferric sulphate	80 75 60	432	80	61	39 / USA, Portugal, South America, Canada, Morocco, France and 20 other countries	Paints, varnishes, inks, paper, synthetic fibres, rubber, glass, ceramics, soil and plant treatment, water treatment
Total for all companies					12 531		10 598	5 169	722	67.5	32.5	

SUMMARY OF DISCUSSION, RECOMMENDATIONS

Group 4 discussed ways and means to mobilise people towards environmentally sound behaviour.

It was concluded that a particular method must be followed at the European level (section 1).

Issues to be kept in mind are "ecological spirit", "responsibility" and "financing".

Characteristics of these three components are summarised in section 2.

This leads to a certain approach or vision (section 3) and recommendations for operationalisation (section 4).

1. METHOD

At the European level support should be provided to existing organisations to help them fulfil a function in the creation of environmental awareness. For this, a series of examples of good practice should be documented.

In this workshop examples were discussed from various regions (for instance Leicester, Berlin, the Netherlands, Spain) and from different organisations.

One should start from the viewpoint of the inhabitant in order to find ways for more environmentally sound behaviour.

A "state of the art" would be helpful as well as an analysis on how the perception of attitudes is used as an instrument of change. Perception is much more worthwhile as a starting point than systematic filing of demographic/sociological parameters or making enquiries by means of written forms.

2. ISSUES

The **spirit of ecology** must be reflected in all information given, in general and environmental education etc. This spirit can be used as an instrument for:

- changing attitudes,
- increasing awareness of ones own behaviour,
- explaining the connection between global issues and local problems,
- connecting the perception of the poor in environmentally impaired areas with general environmental policy issues,

- information on the basis of a dialogue (appealing to perceptions in order to gain a mirror of interests at the neighbourhood level, to be used in policies on the basis of which fields of participation can be identified).

Responsibility

The general attitude should change from "Not In My Backyard" (NIMBY) or "Not In My Task Of Office" (NIMTOO), to "IMBY" and "IMTOO": where pollution is produced, a solution should be found, by force or by care.

Thus global awareness will be transformed into local action.

Points to consider:

- the amount of pollution from the various urban actors determines their necessary participation in environmental protection policy. Their roles determine the prices they have to pay. The rich have a special responsibility.

- "ecology" is easier/more accessible for the rich (organic food, healthy housing etc.); they should thus take a lead in environmental protection.

- the authorities should allow/enable environmental pressure groups to develop. These groups are in many cases the "avant-garde" of this issue.

- the path of information and conscientiousness should be followed. Further participation of all urban groups concerned should be enabled.

Financing

The conventional "3 P's" (Polluter Pays Pollution) should be replaced by "5 P's" (Potential Polluter Pays Pollution Prevention). The "3 P's" leads to the impairment of disadvantaged areas because the poor will pay the price for the pollution/disruption which is replaced with money from the original polluter to areas already facing neglect.

3. VISION/APPROACH

The local community can act as a motivator for environmentally careful behaviour, providing good examples, because local networks can bring together members of the community (business, minorities and opinion leaders).

At the local level a meeting point/focal point for action will dynamise the process.

Such local points can function as knowledge base for local actions with global aspects, dealing with:

* products, chemicals,
* waste,
* energy,
* traffic, etc.

An incentive is needed. Process means should be made materially available.

A local focal point should be facilitated for instance, with:

* rooms, paper, telephone, etc.
* money,
* organisational help,
* knowledge (a good knowledge base is essential).

4. RECOMMENDATIONS FOR OPERATIONALISATION

Local authorities should take action to:

- set up a consumer advice service,

- do localised environmental audits, bringing experts into the community for "eco-counselling",

- set up models to bring together:

    * the business community,
    * minorities,
    * individuals,
    * pressure groups.

The European Community could assist in the above by:

- helping with methods of how to set up consumer advice services,
- helping with methods for auditing, and support focal points of local environmental expertise, as well as assist in developing "ecological labelling",
- conducting research into models of good practice on how to bring the various socio-economic actors together at the local level.

A knowledge base for this line of action should be developed.

Studies should be executed quickly by the appropriate methods.

- comprehensive, balanced studies of plans for local areas, in the field of:

    * urban ecology/environment,
    * urban design,
    * ecological/economical development,
    * social services, etc.

- studies of how to work with people, in both ways: demand driven and offering new insights/ideas/expertise. Questions to be researched would be:

    * how to link local action with global problems?
    * what do people think, how do they precisely perceive the local/global environment?
    * how are social networks composed, for instance which traditional social structures condition the daily life of minorities?

In large cities there is a danger that local groups, minorities in particular, will sense a loss of identity. It is important that when developing strategies for change in environmental attitudes and behaviour, social coherence is reinforced.

GROUP 5

URBAN PLANNING FOR THE 21ST CENTURY

Chairperson: Ms. Wendy O'CONGHAILE, European Foundation for the Improvement of Living and Working Conditions

Rapporteur: Professor Kai LEMBERG, Roskilde University

Participants:

Dr. Sten ENGELSTOFT, DG XII, FAST Programme, Commission of the EC

Mr. Sandro GIULIANELLI, Cabinet of Mr. Ripa di Meana, Commission of the EC

Mr. Richard HARTLEY, Council of Europe

Mr. Bernard LE MARCHAND, CLE

Mr. Jorge MARTINEZ CHAPA, Ministerio de Obras Públicas y Urbanismo, Madrid

Mr. Yannis POLYZOS, National Technical University of Athens

Mr. J.B. SARIS, Alderman, City of Amsterdam

Mr. René SCHOONBRODT, DG XI, Commission of the EC

Professor Jon WIERINGA, Royal Netherlands Meteorological Institute

ATHENS: A MEDITERRANEAN METROPOLIS UNDERGOING RADICAL CHANGE - CHARACTERISTICS AND FUTURE ROLE

Yannis Polyzos
Architect and Town Planner
Athens School of Architecture

All the famous cities which, up to the relatively recent past, were recognised either for their historic role or for their social and economic functions, now find their differences being blurred and their specific features being weakened. They fit increasingly into a network of exchanges at regional or international level, which they control very little, or very badly. Even capital cities do not escape this rule.

While it is clear, thus, that we are witnessing at the end of the twentieth century an accelerated transformation of the general structures of the European area - at least, for the foreseeable future, among the countries of western Europe - the question which is worth asking and debating is whether this trend towards integration leaves room for subtle differences, for a policy of enhancing individual features in the nature and function of cities. One must not be simplistic. This planned, rather than spontaneous, development cannot be achieved with all contestants coming first in the race. Between capitals and other "European cities" there will certainly be winners - meaning urban centres which are well placed in one or more integrated European urban networks.

For us, especially, in view of the developments which can be predicted for the beginning of the twenty-first century, the subject for discussion is the future role of Athens, in the double or perhaps triple geographical and human space surrounding it. On the one hand, Athens as a capital city is undeniably turned towards the European space to which Greece is linked by its membership of the European Communities, with the south-east Mediterranean as a favoured environment because it is "relatively intermediary" to the exchanges going on there. On the other hand it is a Balkan city. It should not be forgotten that Athens also belongs to this other space which has a precise geographic definition but less clearly defined social and economic boundaries; the Balkan peninsula. This is an entity with which Greece, in its recent history, has maintained close but sometimes hostile relations, and the political boundaries of which still remain undefined.

In this report, after taking a look at the recent socio-demographic behaviour of Athens, and the far-reaching spatial changes which are connected with it, we shall consider the development and future role of the Greek capital in two major directions: the one towards its national space, both as an overdeveloped human agglomerate and as a declining city centre, the other towards its neighbouring Mediterranean space. This approach would be incomplete if we did not deal, even briefly, with certain aspects of the town planning policy which is being followed, as well as recent measures on the environment aimed at improving living conditions.

1. THE PLACE OF ATHENS IN THE GREEK URBAN NETWORK

Up to the beginning of the 1980s, the Athenian agglomeration [1] has benefited from a very high rate of urban growth (37% between 1961-71 and 19% in the following decade), much higher than the rate of total urban growth in Greece (29% and 21% respectively) as well as the growth rate for the overall population (5% and 11%). This growth was not founded on rapid industrial development as in most western European countries, but on a process of organisation peculiar to Greece which, among other things, gave a dominant position to expansion in the services sector. The growth in the Athenian population took place in accord with the dominant economic strategy, which wished the capital city to be the main focus of growth, far ahead of Thessaloniki, which only has 700,000 inhabitants, and to the detriment of other medium-sized and small cities.

Even today, with a population which the official census of 1981 put at 3,027,000 inhabitants for the agglomeration (or 3,200,000 if one includes certain large municipalities on the outskirts which are structurally linked to the city but were separately enumerated), and with 3,500,000 today according to the lowest estimates, Athens maintains its predominant position in the Greek urban network, and is even strengthening this position in more than one sector of the economic and social life of the country. The relative importance of Athens is highlighted even further if one bears in mind that the total population of Greece does not exceed 10,000,000.

The speed of urbanisation during the last forty years reveals this growing role: between 1940 and 1981, Athens doubled its population as a percentage of the total Greek population, rising from 15% to 31% of the total. One in every three Greeks lives in Athens, and more than one city dweller in two is concentrated there.

Table 1: Development of population of Athens, 1920-1981

	Greece	Athens	% urban population	% total population
1920	5,016,889	453,037	37.9	9.0
1940	7,344,860	1,124,098	46.5	15.3
1961	8,388,553	1,852,709	51.1	22.1
1981	9,740,417	3,027,331	53.5	31.1

Without the emergence of any decentralisation policy or planning policy worthy of the name, we are witnessing a profound transformation in the urbanisation trend, and more particularly in the urban expansion of Athens. This is happening both at the level of the total agglomeration and in the two more restricted settings. The census of March 1991 should confirm this new development based on a number of indices, but which does not however appear to be a reversal of the situation. [2] The migration flows from country to city have not ceased, nor has the ration of urban to rural population stabilised.

2. SPATIAL REPERCUSSIONS OF RECENT SOCIO-DEMOGRAPHIC DEVELOPMENTS

The contrast which prevailed in the inter-war years, summed up in the clear differentiation between the bourgeois city within the walls, and the external districts inhabited by workers and refugees, which was replaced by an urban development at the same time selective and widespread, matching the large-scale growth in building during the 1960s and 1970s, is today re-emerging in the form of a new spatial contrast which appears under two main aspects. [3]

In the first place, we find a rapid shift in the population's centre of gravity in favour of the north-east and south-east districts, dynamic areas mainly covered by medium and high status housing. The areas dominated by the working class, most of which are situated on the west of the city, are losing ground to the east, and their population is at best stagnant (fig. 1). In the second place, we are finding a strong population shift towards the extended periphery, especially along the main access routes. This is the equivalent of the suburbanisation or deconcentration process, which according to Peter Hall is now found more or less universally in the population of western countries. [4] Thus,

Figure 1: The agglomeration of Athens. Population growth between 1971 and 1981 (average 19%)

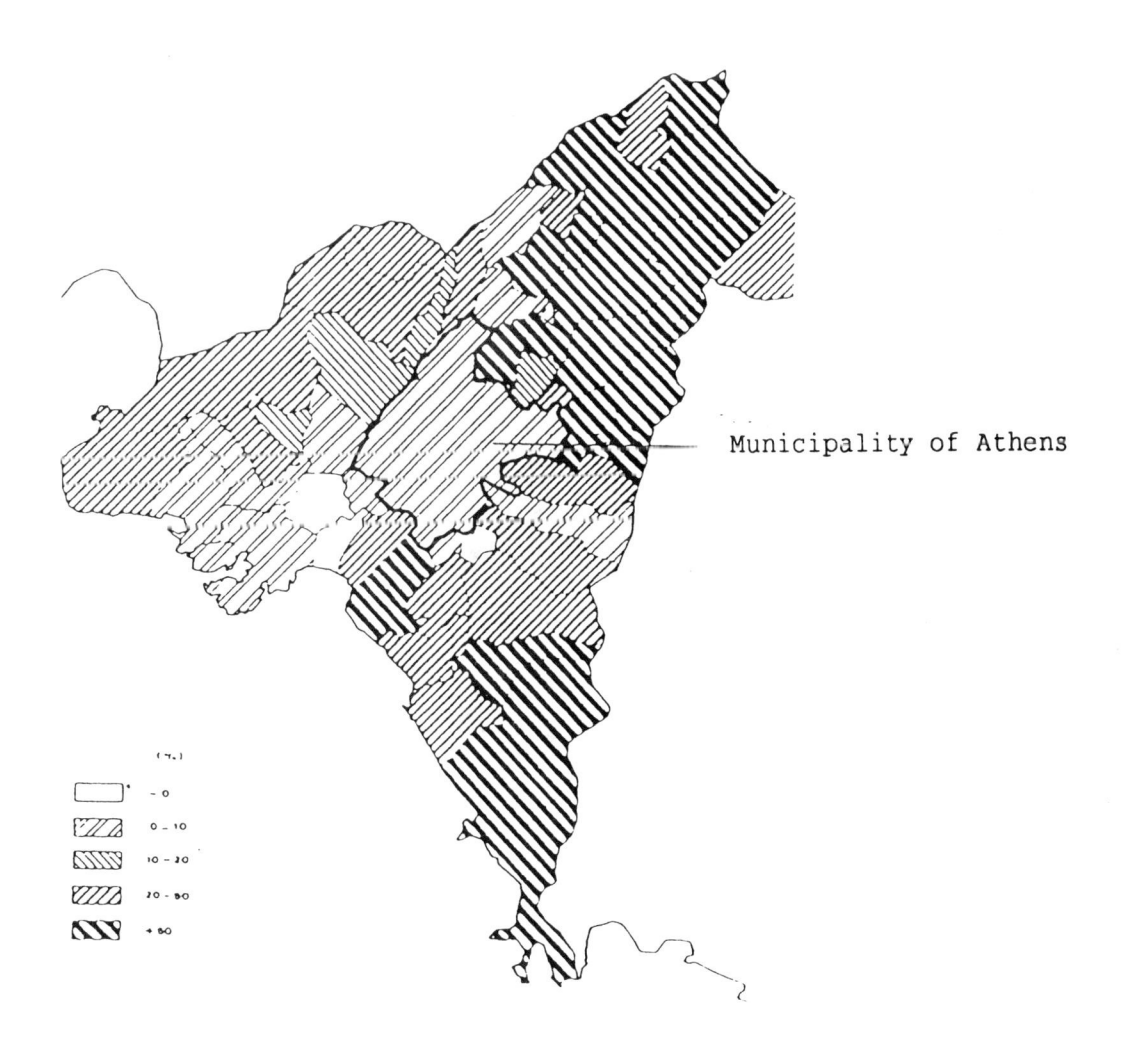

the two main municipalities, which up to now have been the "locomotives" of Athenian development - Athens and Piraeus - are losing their proportionate strength in people and in activities; they are showing respectively a 2% and a 5% increase as against 19% for the overall agglomeration, and in 1981 housed more than one Athenian in every three, as against more than double that proportion just twenty-five years ago.

But the point of convergence of this new demographic behaviour is the accelerated phenomenon of depopulation in the centre of the city. In particular, the district containing the historic and commercial centre of Athens (123,000 inhabitants in 1981 as against 166,000 in 1971) lost one-quarter of its population in ten years. In 1991, it is expected that only 89,000 inhabitants will be left. This "loss of substance", which is here expressed mostly in people rather than in activities, is taking place for the benefit of the tertiary sector and especially for the benefit of services. The inhabitants are moving away, prompted by the increasing pollution level and a deterioration in daily living conditions.

Figure 2: Municipality of Athens. Population growth between 1971 and 1981 by city district

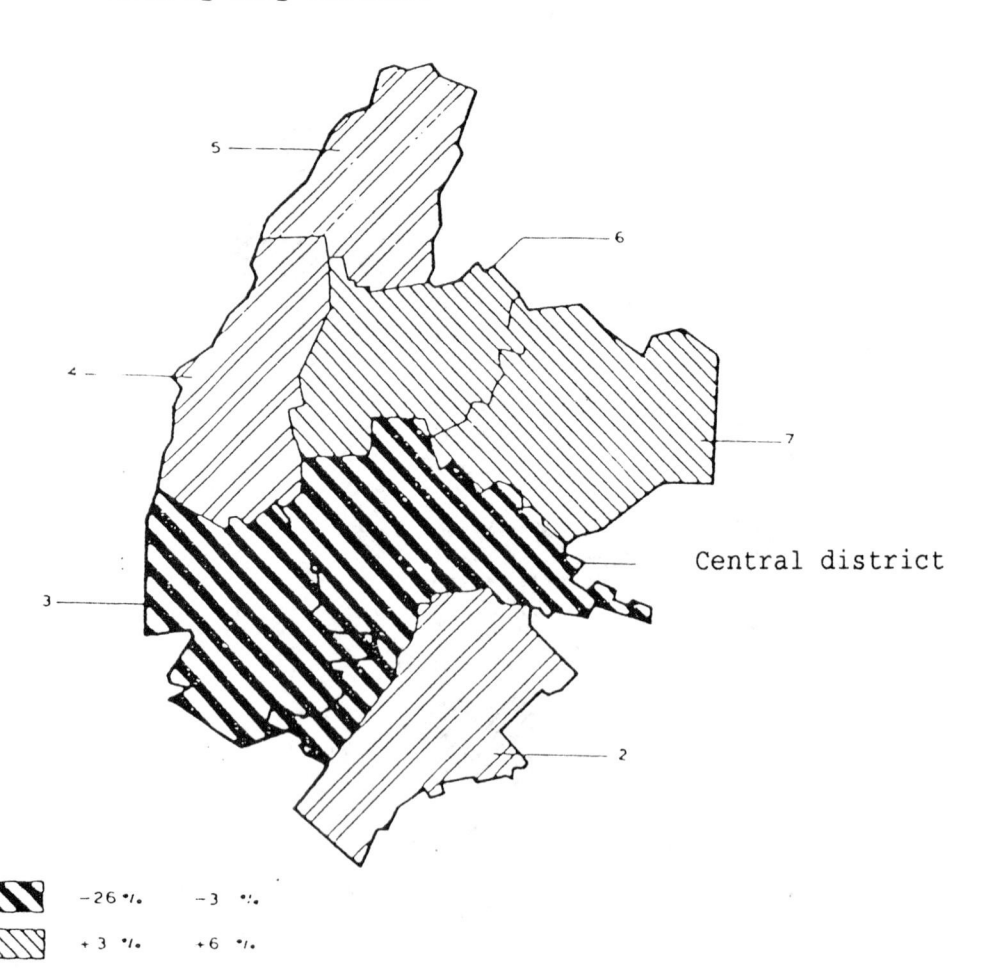

Ten-year average: 2.2%

In addition, the city is being affected by ageing, which has now extended over half the municipalities which make it up. In 1971 the agglomeration of Athens had only 9.3% of people aged over 65, but ten years later it had 11.5%, and today, according to certain estimates, it has 13% to 14%. Although this percentage does not yet match the example of other European capitals, it is still surprising, not only on account of its rate but also on account of the rapidity of its spread and its generalisation. Up to the preceding decade, Athens had had a rate of ageing lower than the national average, in keeping with its population make-up which included a high number of recent and relatively youthful immigrants. If one examines the situation in the city more closely, looking at the central district, the phenomenon is intensified, and takes on a more spectacular character: the percentage of elderly people grew from 11% in 1971 to 14.2% in 1981 and has grown even higher in the intervening years.

The profound social changes experienced by Greek society in the last fifteen years are having repercussions on the family, and have a direct effect on housing. In the first place, we may note a major decrease in the average size of households. Taking the whole Municipality of Athens, households shrank from 2.85 in 1971 to 2.59 in 1981, as against 2.93 for the whole agglomeration, while the number of households showed a 13% increase. Single-parent families are also increasing, as are people living on their own, while the large families are gradually disappearing. This does not necessarily lead to a lesser demand for housing, nor indeed for a demand for smaller-sized units: everybody wants a bigger home. This leads us to revise the standard which was commonly accepted up to now, of one person per room.

Lastly, the total absence of a demographic policy at national level, shown by the sharp and continuous decrease in the percentage of young people (29% in 1951 against 23% in 1981) and the doubling of elderly people during the same period, is linked to the inadequacies of policies on spatial planning, which ought to be flexible and diversified, in relation to the different socio-demographic categories encountered in the urban setting. Although this situation is not unique, in comparison to other metropolitan areas which have undergone or are undergoing similar developments, it deserves to be examined more closely.

3. THE FUTURE ROLE OF THE CAPITAL

The role of Athens at European level, or rather its lack of a role [5] - despite the major planning projects and other painstakingly assembled plans which try to prove the contrary - is brought out by a recent report by the French Delegation for Local Planning and Regional Action [Délégation Française à l'Aménagement du Territoire et à l'Action Régionale (DATAR) on "European" cities. [6] Leaving aside one's reservations (and there are many reservations) on the choices and indicators forming the basis of the study, it appears clearly that Athens is far from being competitive. This is not so much the case on account of the major multinational firms or large business establishments which have set up in Athens, but rather on account of its lack of infrastructure, telecommunications and research centres. These reception and "reputation" factors put Athens at the bottom of the European league table, often lower than Rome and Barcelona and at the same level as

Valencia, Genoa, Naples or Palermo. As for the "city profile" criterion (international relations, communications, economic power, research and technology, cultural function), here again Athens is disadvantaged: it appears among those capitals which are seen as "incomplete" because they present poor indices, with some rarer exceptions.

More importantly, the Greek capital does not lie along the axis of major European development (London, Benelux, Munich-Stuttgart-Frankfurt, Milan), nor in the more recent southerly sub-system reaching from northern Italy to Spain. The "remainder", as has been said, is the periphery of Europe, "reserve development space for tomorrow, but with serious employment problems today".

This problematic image, which is only partly due to the geographical distance of the country from the rest of the European Community, is aggravated by the lack of reliable communications networks and an inadequate transport infrastructure. Taking all these factors together,

Figure 3: The network of "European" cities in 1989 (Source: DATAR/RECLUS)

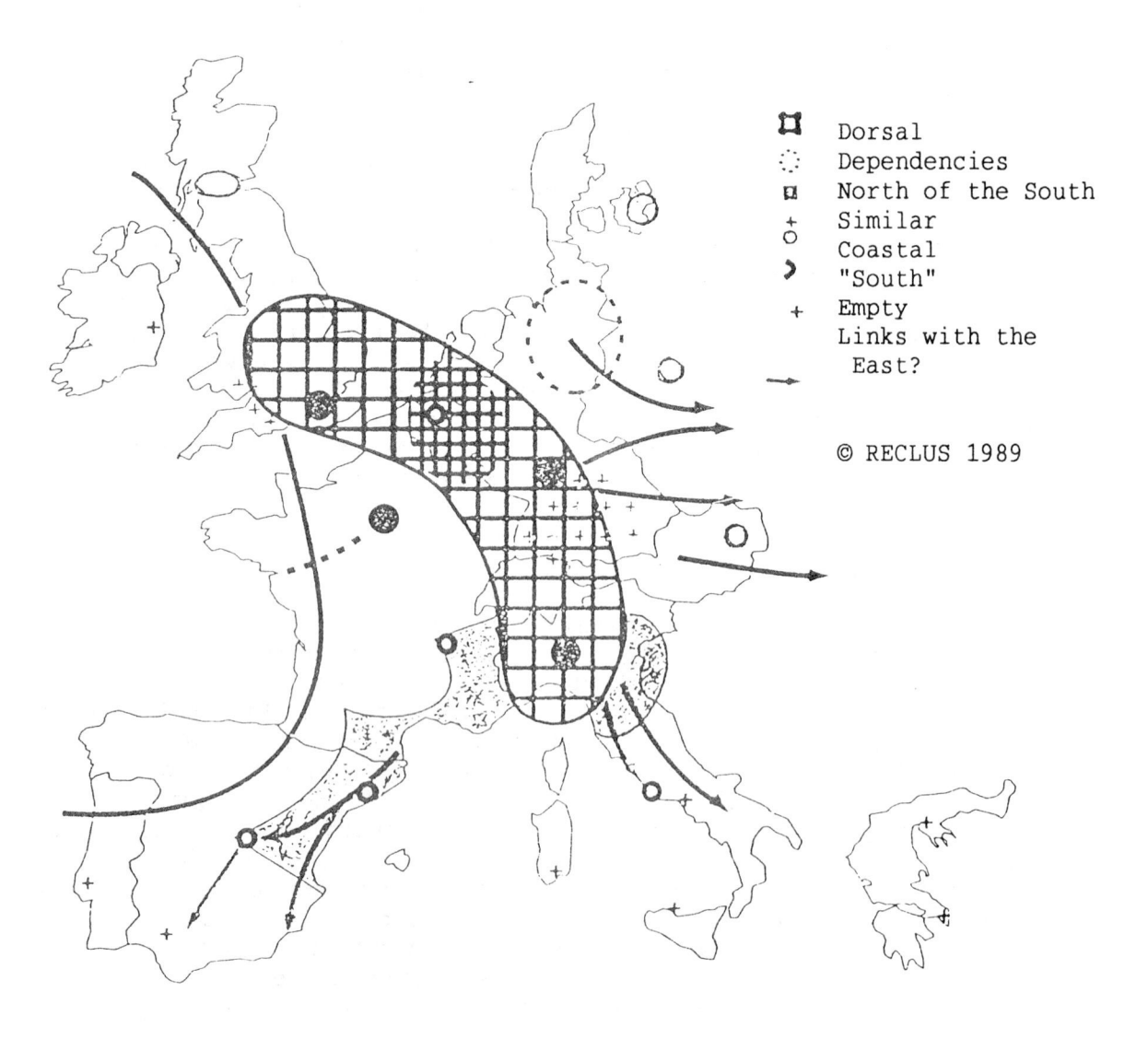

we become increasingly aware of the critical situation in which Athens finds itself as it faces the twenty-first century. This situation of isolation is made even more clear when one considers the new privilege relationships being set up, and new partnerships: Athens belongs neither to the club of "Eurocities", nor to the more recent club of "Eurometropolises". [7]

There is room, however, for a certain degree of optimism. As already noted, the numerical data provide a glimpse of a differentiation in the locomotive role played by the Athenian agglomeration for the rest of the Greek urban network - a differentiation in the sense of an undeniable weakening of its relative demographic importance. Without being fully aware of the extent of this spontaneous decentralisation, its features, or whether it affects other activities, one can certainly say that it does not yet constitute a reversal of the structural situation. Athens is still holding and even extending its position of absolute power, as a centralising megalopolis as regards services, the specialist tertiary sector and the cultural domain.

The question is whether this emerging phenomenon, which appears to be of greatest benefit to large-scale urban centres on the Athenian model, will recreate at regional level, or at a more local level this time, the same symptoms of excessive growth. What will be the long-term repercussions of the various Community programmes on the infrastructure such as the recently approved Mediterranean Action Plan? Indeed, it appears certain that the lack of a planning policy is being felt as keenly as the delay in establishing local and regional authorities with financial autonomy and greater decision-making powers - the only authority which could promote a different model of spatial organisation.

4. URBAN EXPANSION AND THE QUALITY OF LIFE

The lack of a policy to direct urban growth, already described, is accompanied by a laissez-faire situation in regard to the urban texture of Athens, as with other cities. In Greece, it is normal to have no control over the production of built space. It is difficult to use the term "town planning" in the sense of a technical intervention directed towards the built environment, managed by agents with a certain decision-making power within a social structure. The production of built spaces is a sector offering major profits, with investments which rapidly break even, while the urban texture is determined by property speculation which dictates its norms, localises its functions, and finally shapes the city.

The State, the only agency capable of regulating the market, only intervenes to a minor extent, in bursts of action following cycles of economic recessions and electoral results. Depending on the intensity of social or sectoral claims, faced with extreme cases or problems arising from natural factors, the State legislates in a sporadic way, and indeed spends considerable sums of money under different headings, but it does not impose a real control on the production of buildings. There are laws, decrees and plans in force which are worth closer examination, but these do not yet amount to a different policy, a consistent overall policy. Urban space still remains one of the best places for the creation of profit, and housing has a preferential exchange value.

This description of the urban texture, which is itself problematic at several points, although less so than is found in some other large towns (segregation, marginalisation, violence), is matched by a new negative element: atmospheric pollution. The incidence of pollution is invasive and constraining for the daily life of the population and its activities: the circulation of private cars according to the even or odd numbers of their number-plates in the inner city area, for ten months of the year, and the same constraint over shorter periods in the outer circle, together with periodic stoppages of a large number of industries. This pollution, composed both of nitrogen dioxide and carbon monoxide, often exceeding official limits, [8] according to official data is attributable to motor vehicles (75% to 80%, with 75% of these being private cars, 15% being two -wheeled vehicles and 5% to 10% being lorries and buses), to industry (15% to 20%) and to badly run collective heating systems (about 5%).

The fight against atmospheric pollution in Athens - and today Thessaloniki is also affected - is taken very seriously by the population, as shown in opinion surveys, and takes pride of place in official declarations issued on various occasions since the 1980s. As already mentioned, certain measures have been taken, and a large number of other measures have been announced several times, but everyday reality proves that we are far from having solved this problem which remains strikingly topical. In fact, January 1991 is to see extra measures being approved, such as the circulation only of cars with catalytic converters from 1993, the improvement of motor fuels, and the gradual replacement of the present buses by new ones which cause less pollution.

These new measures, which bear the name of the current Greek Minister for the Environment and Planning, are in our opinion quite inadequate, and are even a step backwards in relation to certain commonly accepted priorities. The whole effectiveness of these measures is based on the private car - a sort of "dream" as the price is still difficult to bear - while forgetting the other components of the "atmospheric pollution problem", which are the bad urban structure of the city due to the over-concentration of activities and the excessive population density, the lack of public or private green spaces, and the inadequacy of public transport.

This brief glance at the structural features of the urban formation of Athens, and on the dialogue now taking place on pollution, may perhaps allow us to achieve a better understanding of the "problem case of Athens" which Henri Lefebvre deals with in "Le droit à la ville", and in particular may lead us to adopt, in the years to come, a more precise position on urban policy.

The topic of the urban environment in general (working conditions, young people, elderly people), constitutes one of the axes of various comparative European research projects [9] and is preoccupying Community institutions. Globally, however, it has not been exhausted. The quality of life can and must be improved. Moreover, we believe that it is of paramount importance, within a sustained policy for revitalising the European city - the centre as well as the periphery - to reflect in terms of an urban society - a new model of urban life - without segregations or exclusions, and to accentuate our effort on the improvement of the physical and human environment of the urban setting.

REFERENCES

[1] A purely administrative entity containing 57 municipalities and communes, including about 85% to 90% of the population of the Athens area.

[2] A research project which we are doing on this topic, the preliminary report of which will shortly be available, has as its main aim a better definition of these indices, while relating them more closely to a detailed analysis of recent statistical data. "Development of the population and of functions within the Athenian agglomeration. Character and prospects of the centre city." Athens School of Architecture - General Secretariat for Research and Technology - Municipality of Athens.

[3] Cf. Y. Polyzos, "Conséquences de l'évolution sociodémographique récente sur l'agglomération athénienne," Seminar on current demographic trends and ways of life in Europe, Council of Europe, Strasbourg, 18-20 September 1990 and 17th UIA Congress, Montreal, 27 May - 1 June 1990.

[4] "Population and planning of major cities in developed countries," International conference on population and the future of cities, Barcelona, 19-22 May 1986.

[5] According to a guiding blueprint for the planning of the Athenian agglomeration (Rythmistiko 1983, p.13), the role of Athens at international level is described as "metropolis of the Balkans, of the Mediterranean, of Southern Europe, and as an international centre between Europe, the Middle East and East Africa," while the contributions from the Municipality of Athens (1988, p.5) reinforce its role by naming it as "capital of Hellenism and international business and commercial centre".

[6] DATAR/RECLUS, "Les villes européennes," Paris, Documentation Française, 1989.

[7] By Eurocities we mean the seven super-regional metropolises: Frankfurt, Rotterdam, Hamburg, Munich, Milan, Lyon and Barcelona. The club of twenty Eurometropolises, Antwerp, Birmingham, Rotterdam, Amsterdam, Glasgow, Manchester, Frankfurt, Stuttgart, Munich, Hamburg, Leipzig, Milan, Turin, Barcelona, Oporto, Marseille, Lyon, Lille, Bordeaux and Toulouse, has set itself the mission of "facilitating the exchange of information and experience, studies and expertise" and "setting up bilateral or multilateral common actions, either within or outside Europe, in the areas of industry, tertiary activities, universities and research, transport and communications".
Le Monde, 4-5 December 1990.

[8] A good image of this situation is an example taken at random: on 26 November 1990, nitrogen dioxide stood at 316 mg/m^3, whereas the alert threshold was 200, and carbon monoxide stood at 16.7 mg/m^3, as against a threshold of 15.

[9] See OECD, "Les villes en mutation. Vol. 1. Politiques et Finances", Paris 1983, and European Foundation for the Improvement of Living and Working Conditions, "Living Conditions in European Cities", Dublin 1989.

TECHNOLOGY, CITIES AND PLANNING FOR THE 21ST CENTURY

Sten Engelstoft
University of Copenhagen
presently affiliated to the FAST programme (CCE/DG XII/H/3)
as research fellow

The information and viewpoints expressed in the present paper do not necessarily express the views of the Commission.

1. ABSTRACT

The present paper attempts to elucidate some points relating to **science, technology and the future of European cities**. The contribution has **four key elements**: (1) to evaluate the renewed and increasing interest in urban problems, (2) to specify this concern within the context of the Commission of the European Communities, (3) to evaluate the possible links between science, technology and cities and finally, within this framework, (4) to establish some main trends and problems associated with the future function of our cities.

2. REVIVAL OF URBAN CONSCIOUSNESS

In the developed industrial world, cities are both the place where social demand is generated and managed and where, in an increasingly global scientific and technological context, new modes of industrialisation, new transport, information, communication and technology-based services are being created. **The effects of the Single European Act** will serve to accentuate these phenomena by offering cities **new perspectives** and generating **new problems**. It is expected that the more technology and the economy internationalise and globalise, the more cities will recuperate both a **local and global** function as the importance of the national economy is constrained and reduced.

After experiencing years of decline European cities have entered a new historic phase of development, apparently revitalised by economic restructuring, new technologies and other transformation processes. Despite these tendencies it can be argued that **many cities remain in crisis**. The problems they face are very different from those of 20 years ago; city managers are grappling not only with the **new pressures of growth** but also with **the legacies of the recent past**, for example, traffic congestion, social deprivation, concentrations of ethnic minorities, environmental pollution etc.

Cities are also having to brace themselves to meet the new challenges expected in the 1990s, for example:

* triple challenge of international competition, Europe without internal trade barriers in 1993 and the globalisation of the economy;

* population ageing and international migration;
* geo-political change in central and eastern Europe;
* multi-level institutional structures;
* impact of new technologies and innovations.

It will be an important challenge to city, national and European institutions to alleviate the problems and adjust to **meet the new challenges and opportunities**. Only then will cities be able to play a full part in the inexorable movement towards adaptation and European integration. At the moment the spirit of collaboration that is required between cities is often overshadowed by survival strategies based on perceptions that cities are actually competing with each other in a zero-sum game.

Such perception, the legacy of recent transformation problems and the new challenges and adaptations will undoubtedly influence the sustainability of our cities as well as their creative and innovative potential.

3. THE CATCHWORDS

Urban places, Cities, Towns, Metropolitan areas, all these concepts, have very much become catchwords in recent years[1]. This is particularly true in connection with **wishes for economic and industrial growth** and the ideas of **science-parks and technopolis', teleports** and so on, as well as the whole range of problems often associated with cities such as pollution, traffic congestion, crime, delinquency and social problems etc. Urban problems and solutions to these problems, as well as urban potentials for growth and development are continuously and increasingly attracting the attention of politicians and researchers. For instance in **1988 in France, the prime minister created a special committee on urban problems, a "Délégation à la Ville"**. Only this year in March the **Danish parliament** "Folketinget" had a whole day's debate on the **possibilities of strengthening** Copenhagen and the Copenhagen region to the possible benefit of the whole nation; and the **British "House of Commons"** has recently had a vigorous debate on future investments in **traffic solutions in London** in order to improve the functionality of this city.

The growing interest in urban problems can also be detected within the work of various national organisations and agencies. Recently, for instance, a new section of urban development has been set up as part of the Dutch TNO institute ("Netherlands Organisation of Applied Technology

---

[1] The actual content and meaning of an urban concept is highly problematic: it often seems to be dependent on the context in which it is used (Drewett & Engelstoft 1990). In the present paper however, a city is (implicitly) regarded as an administrative body represented by decision makers or actors; it is a local region of particular "power" depending to a large extent on the political set up.

Research") in order to improve the future possibilities for strategic actions of individual cities. In Italy this year's triennial conference in Milan ("Triennale di Milano") was dedicated to the future of European cities.

At the same time **the work of international organisations** also reflects **the increasing interest in urban problems**. At **OECD** in Paris, for instance, the **"Group of Urban Affairs"** has within their new framework programme of "Urban Affairs" launched a programme on "Urban Impacts of Technological and Socio-Demographic Change", a programme particularly concerned with possible spatial consequences of new technologies, and only in November this year OECD has co-organised an international conference on "Cities and New Technology". Another example is a recent conference, organised by the **Council of Europe**, bringing persons (politicians, civil servants, planners and private entrepreneurs) together, who are in one way or the other, responsible for urban development. The purpose being to determine, on the basis of concrete examples, the courses followed by major towns in Europe in order to develop urban strategies and achieve innovative programmes. Furthermore the conference formed part of the Council of Europe to **prepare an "URBAN CHARTER"**. All these efforts, as well as the present workshop, are a part of a vast number of activities related to the increasing interest in urban problems.

Also **the individual cities themselves have become more aware** of themselves as important actors within all kinds of activities and in recent years several networks of cities have been established for different purposes. The **"EUROCITIES"** are such an example: started and run by the cities themselves in order to accomplish **the desire of a certain number of large European cities to promote the interests and European conceptions of cities in Community institutions and the national governments** (EC newsletter, 1990), it is thus clearly a political instrument created in order to **influence policy making**. Two conferences (Barcelona, April 1989 and Lyon, May 1990) have so far been organised by the EUROCITY founder group[2]. Another example is the **R.O.M.E.-network**[3] which is a European network of metropolitan "observers". The network is independent and self-financing although it was originally initiated by the Commission of the European Communities as an instrument to comment and advise on a specific research programme[4] (R.O.M.E.-newsletter, 1990).

---

[2] The founder group of EUROCITIES are the cities of Barcelona, Birmingham, Frankfurt, Lyon, Milan and Rotterdam.

[3] R.O.M.E. is a French acronym meaning: Reseau des Observatoires Metropolitaines en Europe.

[4] FAST (Forecasting and Assessment in Science and Technology) prospective dossier n° 4: The Future of Urban Societies: The Role of Science and Technology (DG XII/H/3).

4. URBAN RESEARCH

Within the Commission of the European Communities the increasing interest in "urban problems" can be detected by the **expanding number of programmes dealing with various urban related problems**, which are currently underway. At least four DG's are presently involved in major programmes concerned with problems associated with, or focusing on urban areas or "urban problems" of some sort i.e.:

* **DG V** (General Directorate on Employment, Social Affairs and Education) are running a programme entitled **Employment and Insertion for the Strengthening of Economic and Social Cohesion in Urban Areas** (ELISE, 1989; CCE 1990a).
* **DG XI** (General Directorate on Environment, Consumer Protection and Nuclear Safety) has recently finalised the so-called **Green Book of the Urban Environment** (CCE, 1990b).
* **DG XII** (General Directorate on Science and Research) is running a programme on **The Future of European Cities: The Role of Science and Technology** (CCE, 1989; Drewett, 1990; Drewett & Engelstoft, 1990).
* **DG XVI** (General Directorate on Regional Policies) has just launched a programme concerning **Urbanisation and the Functions of Cities in the European Community** (Parkinson, 1990).

Other research relevant to the urban areas[5] is supported by the Commission; the research carried out in connection with the four DG's mentioned have one thing in common: it takes **the urban "setting" or urban problems as a starting point and frame of reference.** The research carried out within the framework of DG XII, the FAST prospective dossier n° 4 are the point of departure for the present paper. Prior to a further discussion of the future urban development however, let us have a brief look at the concept of technology and cities.

5. SCIENCE TECHNOLOGY AND CITIES

The **previous FAST programmes** have identified three priorities on the issue of the interplay between science, technology and society (FAST, 1989). Firstly, that human resources are the core of future growth and innovative capability; secondly, that new dimensions exist in innovation and competition[6] and thirdly, that European science and technology

---

[5] Examples would be parts of large programmes like ESPRIT II (European Strategic Programme for Research in Information Technologies) and RACE (Research and Development in Advanced Communications Technologies for Europe) but also the newly established EURET-programme (European Research in Transportation) could be mentioned.

[6] By new dimensions of innovations is meant the study of innovations by usage and within different kinds of modes.

operate within an emerging global economy. Furthermore it was stressed that **the innovative capability of Europe is crucial** to its future competitiveness and economic integration. It is thus argued that this capability is dependent, other things being equal, on the degree of anthropocentricity[7] of technological changes as well as immaterial investments based on new forms of integration between technologies, skills and organisational factors. It is recognised that "knowledge" inputs are crucial, particularly as knowledge content in goods as well as services is increasing. Consequently there is a growing interest in how and where these knowledge components are produced, distributed and consumed; and whether the "milieux" necessary to sustain these activities are likely to develop in the future.

As **cities are usually considered to be the principal centres of innovation and diffusion** as well as **nuclei of knowledge resources**, it is conceivable to regard "cities" as key "actors" in science and technology. Not only do **the cities "produce" new science and technology**, they **also constitute major "consumers"**. They provide intellectual and physical infrastructure for knowledge- (or **brain-) workers** (Gixycky, 1988), but also **the cultural and social environment** for their personal needs. **The necessary framework for innovations** should thus not be regarded as purely technological; and consequently cities are centres of many different kinds of innovations in addition to the technological ones: social, cultural, institutional, morphological etc. The latter, however, often interact to give expression to and to add a new quality to technological change, but they may also serve to constrain it. It is therefore important to understand how the urban "milieux" can provide for the innovation flux and maintain the quality of the urban living (human) environment. The outcomes will affect not only the competitive position and quality of life of individual cities, but of European society as a whole.

6. MAIN TRENDS AND PROBLEMS WITHIN RECENT URBAN DEVELOPMENT

The inherent diversity that exists in the European urban system makes it **difficult to generalise about development trends**. Nevertheless cross-national comparative urban research has identified mutual evolutionary trends that exist despite varying national contexts; **what varies is the level of development that each national urban system has reached** (Hall & Hay, 1980; Cheshire & Hay, 1988).

---

[7] An anthropocentric quality of any technology is related to the way it is linked to the human faculties brought into play in the labour process. For a technology to acquire an anthropocentric quality, work has to be organised accordingly. A technical system may thus be called anthropocentric if it facilitates human work processes by its very use and in conjunction with the other working conditions. The concept is further developed in a FAST-report of "European Competitiveness in the 21st Century" dealing with integration of work, culture and technology (Cooley, 1989).

Whatever the level, post-war Europe has experienced dramatic changes within its urban systems as well as within the structure of the individual cities. **All countries of Western Europe have had to face some form of urban expansion.** A development trajectory of Northwest Europe[8] illustrates some key aspects. In the 1970s due to rapidly increasing incomes, rising standards of living and booming car ownership (combined with decreasing quality of life in the traditional major cities) **the areas surrounding the larger cities** went through a **remarkable period of "growth".** This growth took place in population and later in employment and economic activities outside the traditional city areas. It was a growth associated with economic transformation expressed through decline of traditional urban manufacturing industries and associated with decay and urban obsolescence of inner city areas. Tertiarisation, diversification and rationalisation of the industries took the form of an "economic **suburbanisation**"[9], by some researchers it was even referred to as **disuburbanisation** and this stage of modern urban development is sometimes even described as a period of "antimetropolism" (Vonk, 1989). The period was dominated by policy ideas on general decentralisation, self (local) government, and "city-social" problems such as better quality housing, urban renewal, etc., i.e. problems relating to the sphere of reproduction. During this period one might generally talk of a comparatively large scale of public involvement, such as attempts within various types of planning in the social and economic processes in general.

In the 1980s however, the trends have given rise to considerable debate because of uncertainties resulting from **lack of sufficient empirical evidence.** Certainly one view is that the above mentioned 1970 pattern has consolidated itself with only one important new dimension: the core areas of the urban networks had started to revitalise. The period may be described under the headings of **"reurbanisation"** and "urban revitalisation". The cities of Europe have shown a **most astonishing revival of their older inner cities.** Obsolescent physical structures of the earlier years have been demolished and replaced by new ones: some of

---

[8] Some aspects of the developments described in the following can also be identified in southern, central and eastern European cities although it has been argued that the underlying mechanisms are culturally determined and therefore the relevance of transferability of experience has been called into question (Leontidou, 1990).

[9] This expressed itself through a growth of small and medium sized subdominant cities. The result became a network of dominant and subdominant cities emerging as a result of technological innovations within transport and communication. From a research point of view this development led to an urban systems perspective on urban structures rather than the earlier focus on individual cities.

the most striking examples are the transformation old of harbour related industrial areas such as the **London Docklands.** The examples are numerous, it is typical however, that the bulk of projects have come into existence through some kind of **public/private ventures** rather than as ordinary, publicly planned developments.

The urban changes of **the 1980s,** contrary to the changes of the 1970s, have been dominated by **a complete restructuring of the urban economy.** Within this period most larger towns have experienced a further **decrease of jobs in traditional manufacturing industries** and a **simultaneous growth** in what could be described as "business-related **tertiary employment";** this latter has become relatively more important because of general industrial decline. The changes have been carried out and financed primarily by **private investments** (banks, insurance companies, pension funds etc.). Due to central government retrenchment, this development has furthermore been characterised by **privatisation.** These developments are often referred to as **urban revitalisation** and it is characteristic that the growth essentially has taken place within the sphere of production.

Simultaneously with industrial restructuring, the cities have seen **the rise of completely new lifestyles** associated with the people engaged in the new activities. An influx of **new well-to-do groups**[10] has lead to **widespread gentrification,** and the increasing importance of **business and leisure trip visitors** has resulted in a massive increase in demand for various cultural facilities, goods and services. In fact the rising demand for various cultural events has been used as a feature or instrument in the revitalisation process.

7. URBAN TRENDS AND PROBLEMS OF THE FUTURE

Today we are thus confronted with a series of problems associated with urban restructuring in the western world; it is comparatively easy to describe and explain the present situation. Similarly it is easy to speculate in the future as long as the present trends are taken for granted; the problem is **which tendencies will remain, which will change and which new ones will arise?** Furthermore the identified tendencies are often conflicting and it is hard to establish which of them are going to be dominant in the future. There is little doubt however, that the following list of problems or issues will prove important to the future of urban Europe:

---

[10] The academic literature is rich in new words invented to describe these groups: YUPpies (Young Urban Professionals), SINKies (Single No Kids) and DINKies (Double Income Nanny and Kids).

(1) Urban social tensions and associated potential conflicts
The size of the total population is relatively stable but the composition of the urban population is changing rapidly. This is true demographically as well as ethnically. The future urban population will thus be highly polarised. On the one hand we will experience an ageing population and at the same time a growth in the number and size of ethnic groups (partly due to migration and partly due to higher fertility). On the other hand industrial restructuring will create an increasing group of well educated, high salary new urban professionals. The hitherto equalising effect of a growing middle class, which has been so characteristic in the post war period, now seems to be surpassed by new social dividing lines and a so-called **two thirds society** is appearing; associated with this development increasing social tensions will inevitably emerge as an increasing number of **social conflicts**.

(2) Structural unemployment due to continuing restructuring of urban industries
The change in the type of economic activities associated with cities, is transforming the locational pattern of these activities; in turn demand and type of qualifications needed is altered. This development will result in increasing structural unemployment: lack of skilled personnel within the new urban industries and at the same time growing unemployment within the unskilled labour force. The problem could be described as an emerging **urban skill-gap.**

(3) Increasing environmental problems and a deterioration of the urban environment
The environmental consequences of economic growth have manifested themselves very conclusively during the last decade. Size as well as complexity of the problems has made environmental problems a central political issue which implies large investments, if significant improvements are to be achieved. Increasing urban pollution due to an expanding number of cars, rise in solid as well as fluid waste etc. seems to be the inevitable result, and a declining urban **environmental quality** is to be feared.

(4) Urban economic crises relating to a lack of correspondence between the function and form of urban areas
Within many countries of the western world (particularly the so-called welfare states) the problem of how to fight unemployment and inflation while at the same time ensuring competitiveness and the balance of payments, has turned into a major dilemma. The changes in the composition of the urban population will inevitably lead to increasing expenditures for social and unemployment benefits. Unless new systems are designed in order to share the economic burdens of urban restructuring there is no doubt that an increasing number of urban **fiscal crises** will emerge, often closely related to the afore mentioned social conflicts.

The trends mentioned so far are all characterised by being tied to developments and restructuring processes which have already taken place or which are currently in progress. There are other important new tendencies however; they may be easy to identify but it is certainly difficult to evaluate their full impact.

(5) **The restructuring of Europe and the position of individual cities under these new conditions**
Two superordinate events tend to influence and alter the regional preconditions in Europe completely. These are the Single European Act[11] and the crumbling of old regimes in Eastern Europe. Few people have doubts that the creation of a huge common European market, and eventually a single currency, will ultimately lead to a "Europe of Regions". No doubt this in turn will diminish the importance of the national state and simultaneously increase the importance of the individual regions. This development will undoubtedly change the "position" and possibilities of a number of regional capitals such as Milan, Barcelona or Hamburg. These cities will probably improve their possibilities as individual actors, whereas the advantages hitherto enjoyed by national capitals such as Copenhagen, Dublin or Lisbon might be at stake. Yet again, for cities such as Copenhagen or Berlin the recent developments in Eastern Europe will influence their hinterlands, and thus their possibilities in the emerging new Europe.

(6) **Uncertainty about intra-governmental decisions above the local (urban) level as well as inter regional (urban) competition.**
For the cities, which may be regarded as local areas or regions (though of a special kind and with specific problems), decision making at the national or sectorial level poses particular problems. Such decisions often restrict the scope of action available for the individual city. One typical example might be new national industrial legislation and labour market regulations, another would be new environmental directives. Inter-regional competition illustrates some of the paradoxes embedded in future urban development: Regional development often promotes fruitless competition between cities that ought to co-operate in order to obtain comparative advantages by specialisation.

(7) **Decreasing public resources (internationally (EC) as well as nationally).**
The changing world economy (and particularly in its present stage) has reduced the availability of public funds. In general this is true nationally as well as internationally. Reunification of Germany and the democratisation of Eastern Europe will no doubt increase the competition for the available international funding. Within the EC,

---

[11] The expression "Single European Act" refers to the legislative framework of the Commission of the European Communities which have been designed in order to ensure the free movement of capital, goods, services and people within the Community. This is to be achieved by 1st January 1993.

support has already been reserved for Eastern Europe. Presently the actual resources are comparatively limited, but there is hardly any doubt that a further development in Eastern Europe and closer ties to the EC will change this. Concerning EC funding from an urban point of view, it is further worthwhile to remember that presently it is not possible to direct Community aid to cities as such. Aid from the regional funds may be given to regions eligible according to certain objectives. However, in many cases such areas are heavily urbanised, for instance "objective-2" regions which are regions with specific industrial problems. Particular **urban** aid would require a community policy for urban areas, and such a policy does not exist at the moment.

(8) Increasing public-private ambiguity (i.e. the increasing importance of the private sector)
Privatisation is one of the most important megatrends in social development within the western world. To some people this means that the welfare state, at least the Scandinavian model, is in crisis. If this is true it will certainly lead to the most acute problems in the bigger cities with their concentration of underprivileged groups. Basically however, it is undeniable that tendencies are turning away from cost intensive public engagements and towards strengthening the responsibilities and possibilities of individuals as well as of private and semi-private bodies, often through quasi-governmental institutions (QUANGO's). It is furthermore obvious that decreasing public funding increases the demand for private capital. This will typically be provided by financial institutions aiming for long term investments, such as pension funds. There is a definite danger associated with this development, however, i.e. the possible lack of democratic control. The "efficiency" of private or semi-private engagements though, are closely related to their ability and freedom to act[12]. There is little doubt however, that future success within urban development will be closely related to the ability to create a "market based **managed** competition".

(9) Increasing international spatial (urban) competitiveness and co-operation
Seen from outside Europe, there has been a distinct fear as to whether developments concerning the Single European Act will lead towards increasing European protectionism. Several firms outside the EC have thus expanded their commitments in Europe and invested

---

[12] At a recent conference a representative from the London Dockland Development Corporation (LDDC, a typical QUANGO) expressed the view that public involvement in planning as much as possible ought to be "laissez faire". Furthermore he suggested that the LDDC had the advantage to local administrations that they were able to take "unpopular" decisions as they had no future elections to fear(!).

heavily in EC countries[13]. There is no reason to believe that these investments will decrease in the future, and the intra urban competition for investments will undoubtedly increase. In this competitive game, the individual cities, through "image creation", will all attempt to emerge as attractive **international centres of economy, commerce, culture etc.** The success of the individual city in future Europe, however, will be closely related to its ability to find (and use) its specificity: i.e to use locally rooted skills and traditions. Cities have to find their niche in the emerging new European urban system. Furthermore the ability of individual cities to co-operate with each other seems to become crucial. Cities that exclude themselves from the various networks of co-operation will find it hard to sustain their development.

8. CONCLUDING REMARKS

In the evaluation of the urban future and related problems, one has to **distinguish between the general trends in the development of the urban system (mega-trends** or general opportunities) **and the individuality of a particular city** (the so-called **heritage**). The **general opportunities** are constituted from factors which are related to common (global or **international) tendencies** within population dynamics, economic restructuring and social differentiation etc. Contrary to the general opportunities, the **heritage** is something much more difficult to define. It is connected to history and culture, and is thus a variety of factors specifically related to a given locality. It is **tradition and conventions as well as lifestyle and many other things embedded in the local population,** it is a legacy. There is a very close connection between the idea of a heritage embedded in a given society and the concept of a cohesion founded in a promotion of social and cultural differences[14]. Heritage is thus **an expression of a "diversity of**

---

[13] This is true regarding Swedish, Norwegian and Finnish investments and certainly concerning Japanese capital. In particular the Japanese have been very politically conscious in this respect and are currently introducing a new car "for a country called Europe".

[14] The concept of economic and social cohesion is obviously of great concern within all work carried out in the Commission. Major efforts have been made to reduce differences between regions in the Community. Within the FAST-Programme particularly, the prospective dossier n° 1 on "Science Technology and Social and Economic Cohesion in the European Community" is of interest. In this dossier it is argued that a Community that strengthens its economic and social cohesion is a Community promoting cultural, social and economic inter-linkages between the regions and territories that constitute its diversity. In that in a more cohesive Community, the scientific and technological innovation will thus reach a higher level of excellence as it innovates by confronting a diversity of modes (using new technologies and knowledge) in co-operation and exchange (Hingel, 1990). It is worthwhile noticing that the cohesion concept is fundamentally different from the prevailing American "melting pot" philosophy.

modes" of doing, and the heritage is extremely important to innovators who are actually working in the specific environment.

Technology many certainly help us to improve the urban setting (milieu), it is highly important however, to stress that **technology is a means and not an end in itself.** Technology may provide us with invaluable skills and possibilities in our attempts to create better cities. New technologies though, **may also create new differences and conflicts** within the urban setting. If we introduce new technologies because of their inherent, absolute qualities rather than within the specific social context in which it should be used we risk creating **a new urban barbarism based on individual differences** in the ability to employ the new technology and social alienation will be the inevitable result.

The city, with its highly developed **urban culture,** being **the very essence of contemporary society** and **a highly condensed image of societal processes, multidimensional in time and space,** is the perfect place to develop the intricate relations between research and development (particularly with respect to growth through technology) as well as the ramifications of a private/public infrastructure. The framework of **(urban) problems** as well as the **(urban) possibilities** mentioned above, makes it highly important though, that we support and **develop the whole spectre of "urban attributes"** and that we do **not restrict ourselves to a sectoral search** for economic or technical solutions aiming to ensure the highest possible economic growth.

REFERENCES

CCE (1990a): The City - Integration - Employment: Summary report by the Steering Group on Employment and Integration for the Strengthening of Economic and Social Cohesion in the Urban Environment. Commission of the European Communities, DG V, Brussels.

CCE (1990b): Green Paper of the Urban Environment. Commission of the European Communities, DG XI, Brussels.

CCE (1989): Information Package MONITOR Programme (1989-1992). Commission of the European Communities, DG XII, Brussels.

Cheshire, P.C. & D.G. Hay (1988): Urban Problems in Western Europe: An Economic Analysis. London.

Drewett, Roy (1990): FAST prospective dossier n° 4: The Future of Urban Societies. The Role of Science and Technology. Research Programme. The London School of Economics. Department of Geography. London.

Drewett, Roy & Sten Engelstoft (1990): Science and Technology. Cities and the Human Dimension. FAST Occasional Papers n° 220. Commission of the European Communities, Brussels. (Forthcoming).

EUROCITIES. EC-newsletter (February 1990), Areas de Salut Pública. Ajuntament de Barcelona.

FAST (1989): The FAST II Programme (1984-1987). Results and Recommendations: vol. 1. A Synthesis Report: Science, Technology and Society: European Priorities. (A report from the FAST-Programme of the Commission of the European Communities), Brussels.

Gizycky, R. von & W. Ulrici (1988): The Brainworkers (A Report from the FAST-Programme CCE). R. Oldenburg Verlag, München.

Hall, P. & D. Hay (1980): Growth Centres in the European Urban System. London.

Hingel, Anders J. (1990): Diversity, Equality and Community Cohesion. FAST working paper "PD 1/01". Commission of the European Communities, DG XII/H/3 (FAST), Brussels.

Leontitidu, Lila (1990): The Mediterranean City in Transition. Social Change and Urban Development. Cambridge.

R.O.M.E. (July, 1990): Newsletter, Comissionat per al Pla Estratègic. Ajuntament de Barcelona.

Parkinson, Michael (1990): Urbanisation and the Function of Cities in the European Community. A Research Proposal to the Commission of the European Communities (DG VI). Centre for Urban Studies. University of Liverpool.

Vonk, Frans P.M.: The New Urban Development (1989). In: Knight, Richard V. & Gary Gappert: Cities in a Global Society. Urban Affairs Annual Review, vol. 35.

ACTIVITIES OF THE WORLD METEOROLOGICAL ORGANISATION IN THE AREA OF URBAN CLIMATOLOGY

Jon Wieringa
Royal Netherlands Meteorological Institute
De Bilt
The Netherlands
Department of Applied Physics
University of Technology
The Netherlands

On behalf of the World Meteorological Organisation

ABSTRACT

The World Meteorological Organisation (WMO) has long been active in the area of Urban and Building Climatology (UBC). This is done by publishing and updating guidance material and reviews, by education and training, by preparing databases in co-operation with the National Meteorological Services, and by co-operation with research activities of the worldwide meteorological community.

Some practical problems are reviewed in the area of urban climatology, describing the influence of the built-up environment on the climatological situation. Some goals are outlined for up-to-date application of building climatology, the art of defining the atmospheric influence on buildings. In particular, attention is required for objective estimation of climatic parameters at locations where standard meteorological observations are not available. The magnitude and impact of possible changes in climate and climate variability on building is discussed.

INTRODUCTION

The World Meteorological Organisation (WMO) was initiated in 1872 and is nowadays an agency of the United Nations. Compared to other U.N. agencies it is a small and non political organisation, essentially consisting of a 240-person secretariat in Geneva financed jointly by the 160 member states. Its primary task is to maintain the lifeline of meteorology, continuous worldwide exchange of weather data observed according to agreed standards. Moreover it co-ordinates and stimulates research in meteorology and related subjects, and plays an important role in meteorological training, education and technical co-operation. In the actual execution of these tasks WMO co-operates very closely with the member states.

In other words, WMO is the global authority co-ordinating the National Meteorological Services (NMS), which do the actual operational work of data collection, forecasting and climatological surveys. Tasks of research and education in meteorology are shared between NMS's, specialised institutes and (relatively few) universities. The latter have a separate organisation nucleus in the International Association of Meteorology and Atmospheric Processes (IAMAP), which is dedicated to scientific research and plays no part in operational meteorology.

The WMO has a long record of activities in the area of Urban and Building Climatology (UBC) as well as in the related area of Climate and Human Health (CHH). The co-ordination between the projects related to CHH and those of UBC is ensured by the WMO Commission for Climatology (CCI), and in particular by its Rapporteur on Building Climatology within the Working Group on Climate Applications.

Numerous meetings have been organised by WMO on topics related to UBC and CHH. Of major importance were the WMO/WHO Symposium on Urban Climates and Building Climatology, held in Brussels in 1968 [1, 2], and the WMO/WHO Technical Conference on Urban Climatology and its Applications with Special Regard to Tropical Areas, held in Mexico in 1984 [10]. In addition to conferences for purposes of scientific and operational planning, several regional WMO training seminars have been arranged for purposes of education and training in the UBC and CHH areas.

Below, a review is given of meteorological aspects of city environmental problems. This is concluded with a survey of some relevant WMO actions.

URBAN CLIMATOLOGY AND ITS INFORMATION PROBLEM

Formally defined, urban climatology deals with the influence which a large built-up area has on the local climate and how it relates to the atmosphere. Building climatology, to be discussed further below, considers rather the impact of the overall atmosphere situation on a building and its immediate environment.

Essentially, urban climatology studies apply general principles of atmospheric physics (fluid dynamics, thermodynamics) to the highly irregular surface situation of a city. Significant features of such a surface are its high heat storage capacity, its dry surface and large variations in surface orientation with respect to solar radiation. A special problem is the rough, obstacle-studded nature of the surface and the fact, that we are interested in airflow and air temperature between those obstacles. Usual meteorological descriptions of vertical fluxes of heat and momentum have been developed for rather homogeneous open-country situations and need only to consider change in the vertical direction. We cannot use those relations safely in cities, where we have to analyse three-dimensionally. This makes urban climatology rather intractable; for a review, Landsberg [15] and Oke [16] can be recommended.

However, one aspect should be discussed here, namely the usefulness of meteorological observations in urban situations. Everybody should be aware that observations in the city itself are not usually even representative for the immediate surroundings without difficult azimuth-dependent corrections for the nearness of warm and flow-obstructing buildings. The alternative is using wind and temperature observations in more homogeneous surroundings outside the city (often at an airport), and deriving from these the corresponding atmospheric situation at some reference height well above average city roof level. The next step, obtaining the situation below between the buildings, is difficult, but more reliable than using low-level observations.

Long-term climatological information in urbanised regions, however, tends to suffer from the gradual encroachment of buildings everywhere, even around airports. Figure 1 [17] shows clearly, how the urbanisation of Japan in the sixties led to sizeable decreases of the maximum annually observed wind speed at most weather stations. For wind date a correction of such effects is possible by using gust observations at the considered stations [18], but urbanisation corrections for temperature will be highly subjective. Application of such corrections is still mandatory - homogeneity of climatological data series cannot ever be assumed safely in urbanised regions.

Figure 1: **The yearly variations of annual maximum windspeed and building density ration averaged overall in Japan [17]**

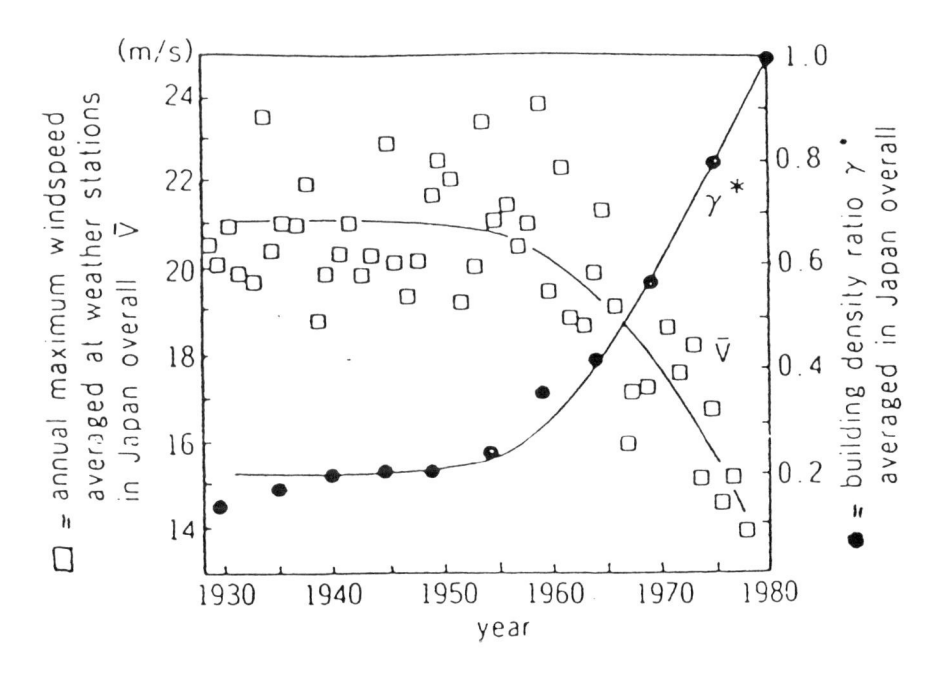

Use of a well-derived urban climate description in city planning is manifold. Its content ought to be considered in deciding on street orientation and width, amount of green space, storm-water routing, admissible building height and height variability, preferable building materials, and siting of pollutant sources - both height and place of simple chimneys as related to their buildings, and location of emission-prone industry relative to the city. It is not sufficient to use only "climatological averages" of e.g. temperature, precipitation, winds, etcetera - we also must consider typical diurnal and annual variation ranges, as well as the frequency of occurrence or "risks" of specific dangerous extreme conditions.

For example, the influence of buildings on their surroundings is usually underrated. It is well known, that a solitary high building can easily triple the windspeeds occurring at ground level, making the entrances of the building itself quite dangerous for use in moderately windy situations [16, 19, 20]. This particular problem can be solved by extending the ground floor of the building in all directions, or else planting a dense treescape at the foot of the building. Another climate-related example is the possibility of optimal orientation of buildings towards the sun, with purposes varying from good use of windows in the interior heat balance to provision of well-slanted roofs for solar boilers. A good climate-dependent review of this is given by Givoni [11, vol. 1, p. 259].

BUILDING CLIMATOLOGY - INDOOR/OUTDOOR CLIMATE

It should be obvious, that environmental conditions around a building have a strong influence on aspects related both to construction and to operation of a "healthy building". The reasons for building "in harmony with the environment" may be manifold - e.g. aesthetics, comfort, energy saving, choice of material etcetera - but they always relate to the economy of using the building. Cost-effective housing depends to a high degree on climate (see Figure 2). It is important that the building remains sound, and that the structure withstands the physical strain of wind and weather (e.g. snow load) and that building materials do not deteriorate too early.

Figure 2: A "Healthy Building" has to be designed and built in harmony with the climatic conditions and the actual needs of its occupants

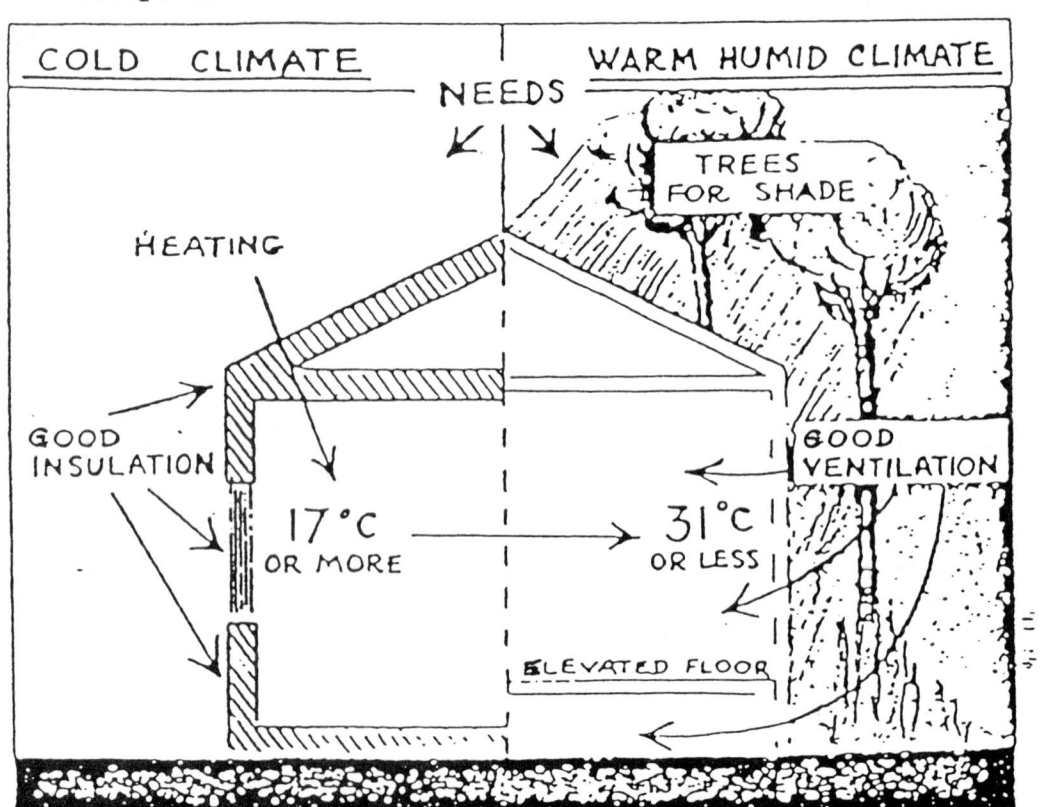

It may be of even greater importance that the indoor climate be kept within reasonable bounds at a reasonable cost. Comfort for indoor activities is a relative measure, and e.g. the range of acceptable temperature variations depends on clothing and activity. An indication of the tolerance range is, that heating "degree days" are measured relative to 18°C; apparently, heating becomes for many people an interesting proposition at lower temperatures. On the other hand, U.S. cities do keep riot police on stand-by if temperatures rise above ~ 30°C. According to bioclimatic mapping [9], the thermal tolerance range of a lightly clothed healthy person is about 14°C; obviously it would be absurdly extravagant to maintain the indoor climate in all buildings during all seasons and worldwide in the middle of this range, say at temperatures of 22°C to 23°C, accompanied by a relative humidity of 50-60%. Good choice of clothing can extend the range appreciably, especially on the cool side. Strictly controlled indoor climates are only required for some purposes, e.g. hospitals, laboratories, precision equipment, etcetera. In very polluted city centres, extra expenses may be needed for maintaining indoor environmental conditions at acceptable levels through ventilation, filtering systems etcetera.

The planning problem is that for the builders the cost of climate-optimised building construction (see Figure 2) is often slightly higher than the cost of erecting just one more apartment house in so-called "international" style, with cheap glass walls and little insulation or inherent ventilation. The builder is therefore tempted to keep the initial scale costs of his product low in this manner, and to leave the high continuing costs of adjustment to the prevailing weather (by heating or air-conditioning) to the occupants. This is a perverse form of mock economy, which can only be beaten by good and strictly applied building regulations.

In order to be economic regarding construction costs as well as costs of living and upkeep, it is preferable to have the active involvement of a building climatologist during planning and design. His or her input should not be restricted just to providing climatological tables for evaluation of a cut-and-dried design.

THE IMPACT OF CLIMATE CHANGE AND VARIABILITY ON BUILDING

Humanity seems to have woken up to the fact that we are modifying our limited amount of atmosphere in a significant manner by adding CO_2, methane, chlorofluorocarbons (CFC), nitrous oxides and pollutants in non-negligible amounts. The worst danger would be to induce noxious irreversible climate changes of long duration, and we have already an obvious example that such changes are possible, namely the ozone hole over Antarctica, generated by CFC's.

The average temperature of the Earth has varied by less than 2°C over the past 10,000 years. There is clear evidence of a continuous increase of the so-called "greenhouse gases", such as CO_2 and methane. It is estimated that this will induce changes of the same order of magnitude in this global average temperature in the next 50-100 years (the same length of time that might be the lifetime of a building). The results of the most recent numerical model experiments show, that global mean temperatures could increase by anything between 1°C and 5°C in 100 years, depending on model assumptions. These results must be considered as our best present guess for the future. It is obvious that such a change would have a serious impact on society, not the least on the urban environment.

Our understanding of long-term climate fluctuations is still far from complete, and factors that are still unknown or not clearly understood may enhance or counteract the greenhouse effect, both globally and regionally. There is a need to focus research on improving tools used to forecast the occurrence of future climates, and to make it possible to evaluate existing data sets which cannot be studied now for lack of manpower. Even so, the possibilities of man-induced changes and long-term fluctuations warrant close attention in view of their potential impact on socio-economic activities, including that of building, and on options for society to deal with potential negative effects and to take advantage of possible positive changes.

Obviously, any change in climate of some magnitude will not occur evenly throughout the globe, but will rather lead to a distortion of the whole climate system. Certain regions will get drastically warmer and drier, others will get wetter, and frequencies of severe storms may increase or decrease regionally. A globally-occurring change may be due to the adjustment of the sea level, as the temperature of the ocean surface waters increases. Due to expansion of the water, and to melting of the icecaps, this is expected to lead to sea-level rises of about 0.5m to 0.8m in 100 years, while the rise in the last century has been only c. 0.2m. This would exert a serious threat to some coastal areas and to lowlands of the Earth, especially if gales increase in frequency or in strength.

Regionally, and particularly locally, climate has already been altered much more than that which the global projections call for. The urban heat island, i.e. the influence of building and urbanisation on the temperature climate, might be the most well-known impact, but there are many other influences which need to be considered in the planning, design and operation of buildings. In an urban area many of the climatic parameters, e.g. wind, precipitation, insulation etc, are altered compared to what would have been "natural values". Changing land-use, e.g. opening up forest areas for farming, have altered climates in entire regions.

Naturally all these changes of climatic conditions, whether planned or inadvertent, need to be accounted for in the planning, design and operation of "healthy buildings" in an optimal way. In a relatively short time, less than 100 years, e.g. less than the expected "life" of many constructions, at any one location the value of a structure and its use may deteriorate significantly due to either increased pollution or to local climate change.

WMO ACTIONS IN CLIMATOLOGICAL INFORMATION APPLICATION TO THE URBAN ENVIRONMENT

Within the various WMO/UBC projects a major effort is directed towards development and application of knowledge of the physical climate-related processes, which need to be considered in urban planning and building in tropical and sub-tropical regions. A breakthrough in UBC was achieved at the 1984 Conference on Urban Climatology, held in Mexico [10]. The Conclusions and Recommendations of this Conference provide a framework for the further development of the WMO programme in UBC. Guidelines for urban design in various climates are being prepared and the feasibility of applying existing UBC methods and models are being investigated.

Guidance material and reviews have been published by WMO [e.g. 3, 4, 5, 6, 7, 8, 9, 10, 11, 12, 13, 14]. Moreover, WMO regularly has published extensive bibliographies of urban climate, compiled by T.J. Chandler and T.R. Oke. In the present WMO Second Long-term Plan, priority is given to the development of new or updated sets of guidance material. A first action was a data base called Climate Applications Referral System (CARS), subject-centred summaries of climatological reports, compilations and other material available in WMO countries. Moreover, efforts are being made to develop reliable climatological databases, which can be used for applications in urban planning and building. This involves both improved climatological observations and implementation of computerised data handling.

The CLICOM project of the WMO World Climate Programme is designed to deliver micro-computer hardware, software and training as a standardised package for comprehensive climate data management and user services to all countries which need assistance. The first phase of CLICOM will enable NMS's to provide users with standard data, and to produce various climatological statistics: normals, means, extremes and averages; daily, monthly and annual summaries (tables); graphical output such as time-series plot of one or more parameter values, special plots of data values on a base map, computation of selected probabilities, etcetera. In the second phase of CLICOM, specialised application modules will enable NMS's to produce outputs in a user-oriented way, e.g. for application in building design. In the development of these specialised application modules, close collaboration between meteorologists and the various users, e.g. architects, building and construction engineers, is of course vital. More than 100 NMS's are expected to have CLICOM systems installed in the near future.

At the Mexico '84 Conference, the Tropical Urban Climate Experiment (TRUCE) was initiated. The reason for this undertaking is the severe scarcity of urban climate studies done in the tropics. Less than 10% of such investigations are related to tropical cities, and most of those studies are descriptive only and done by local individuals without support of foreign expertise. It is proposed to run extensive experiments in selected large cities in the tropics, including education of local teams to ensure future development of urban meteorology in the involved countries. The plan will be finalised by WMO in 1991 in close co-operation with other organisations such as CIB, WHO and IGU.

The overall purpose of this and other WMO actions is the attainment of quantified applicable meteorological knowledge about cities in all possible climates, not only moderate but also humid tropical, dry desert and polar climates. Too often yet the evaluation of air pollution dispersion, of thermal discomfort, or of various impacts of extreme weather conditions must be done by unconvincing application of relations describing average mid-latitude climate.

REFERENCES

[1] WMO (1970): "Urban Climates". Volume I of Proc. of WHO/WMO Symposium on Urban Climates and Building Climatology (Brussels, October 1968). WMO No. 254, Techn. Note No. 108.

[2] WMO (1970): "Building Climatology". Volume II of Proc. of WHO/WMO Symposium on Urban Climates and Building Climatology (Brussels, October 1968). WMO No. 255, Techn. Note No. 109.

[3] WMO (1971): "Selected papers on Meteorology as related to the Human Environment". WMO No. 312, Special Environment Report No. 2.

[4] H.E. Landsberg (1972): "The Assessment of Human Bioclimate". WMO No. 331, Techn. Note No. 123.

[5] H.E. Landsberg (1976): "Weather, Climate and Human Settlements". WMO No. 448, Special Environment Report No. 7.

[6] J.K. Page (1976): "Appreciation of Building Climatology to the Problems of Housing and Building for Human Settlements". WMO No. 441, Techn. Note No. 150.

[7] T.J. Chandler (1976): "Urban Climatology and its relevance to Urban Design". WMO No. 438, Techn. Note No. 149.

[8] WMO (1981): "Meteorological Aspects of the Utilisation of Solar Radiation as an Energy Source". WMO No. 557, Techn. Note No. 172.

[9] V. Loftness (1982): "Climate/Energy Graphics: Climate Data Applications in Architecture". WMO/WCP-30.

[10] WMO (1986): "Urban Climatology and its Applications with special regard to Tropical Areas". Proc. Techn. Conf., Mexico City, 26-30 November 1984. WMO No. 652.

[11] WMO (1987): "Climate and Human Health", Vols. I & II. Proc. Techn. Conf., Leningrad, 22-26 September 1986. WMO/WCAP Nos. 1 and 2.

[12] WMO (1988): "Report of the first session of the CCI Working Group on Climate and Urban Areas including Building and other aspects (and some related papers by E. Jauregui and Shen Jianzhu)". WMO/WCAP No. 8.

[13] B. Giovoni (1989): "Urban design in different climates". WMO/WCAP No. 10.

[14]   WMO/IFHP/CIB (1989): Conference on "Urban Climate, Planning and Building", Kyoto, Japan.

[15]   H.E. Landsberg (1981): "The urban climate". Publ. Academic Press.

[16]   T.R. Oke (1987): "Boundary layer climates" (2nd ed.). Publ. Methuen.

[17]   Y. Tamura, K. Suda (1987): "Correction of annual maximum windspeed considering yearly variation of the ground roughness in Japan." Proc. 7th Internat. Conf. Wind Engin. (Aachen) Vol. 1, 31-40.

[18]   A.C.M. Beljaars (1987): "The measurement of gusts at routine wind stations - a review". WMO/CIMO Instr. Obs. meth. Rep. 31 (KNMI-WR-87-11).

[19]   J. Gandemer, A. Guyot (1976): "Intégration du phénomène vent dans la conception du milieu bâti". Publ. Centre Scientifique et Technique du Bâtiment, Nantes, France.

[20]   A.D. Penwarden, A.F.E. Wise (1975): "Wind environment around buildings". Publ. Building Research Est., U.K.

Acknowledgements: For information support I thank Lars E. Olsson (WMO, Geneva) and the Rapporteur on Building Climatology, dr. Roger Taesler (SMHI, Sweden).

EUROPEAN WORKSHOP ON CITIES AND THE GLOBAL ENVIRONMENT

Related Work of the Council of Europe

Richard Hartley

Secretariat of the Council of Europe's
Standing Conference of Local and
Regional Authorities of Europe
(CLRAE)

INTRODUCTION

The Council of Europe's work on urban questions is conducted by its **Standing Conference of Local and Regional Authorities of Europe** and, particularly, its Committee on the Natural and Built Environment (present Chairman, Mr Alexander Tchernoff, the Netherlands).

The Standing Conference of Local and Regional Authorities of Europe is the body within the Council of Europe which brings together regularly elected representatives at the local and regional level within the 24 member countries, to discuss and, if possible, reach consensus on matters of common concern and interest for this tier of authority.

It meets once a year in Plenary Session in Strasbourg. Its five specialised Committees (1) meet at regular intervals.

It organises ad hoc colloquies, hearings, conferences; prepares reports and, based upon them, Resolutions addressed to the Committee of Ministers of the Council of Europe; to other international organisations, both governmental and non-governmental, and to municipalities and regions in Europe.

It has a responsibility within the Council of Europe of keeping the committee of Ministers informed on matters relating to the interests of local and regional authorities; helping to ensure that such authorities are aware of the current topical issues involved in European intergovernmental co-operation; above all, conducting a programme of intermunicipal exchange between member countries.

---

(1) The five specialised Committees are:

    Committee on Regional Problems and Development
    Committee on Structures, Finance and Management
    Committee on the Natural and Built Environment
    Committee on Culture, Education and the Media
    Committee on Social Affairs and Health

A. SOME RECENT EXAMPLES OF WORK ON THE URBAN ENVIRONMENT

This work is inspired very much by the principles of the earlier Council of Europe Campaign on Urban Renaissance (1980-1982) - a European-wide focus on urban policies designed to emphasise the "human dimension" in towns, for public authorities and the public as a whole.

This tradition of concentrating upon policies for "a better life in towns" (the slogan of the Urban Renaissance Campaign) has been continued through attention being directed at environmental improvement, social cohesion, cultural development, physical quality etc. in urban areas.

The main characteristics of this work are an exchange of information and experience between local leaders and professionals in Europe and co-operation with specialised non-governmental organisations.

1. The Reduction of Urban Insecurity

This work has concentrated particularly on the way in which crime levels in cities can be reduced via changes in the physical and social urban environment (community and neighbourhood development, better sport and leisure activities, architectural preservation, the role of police in prevention policies, positive policies for dealing with drug abuse).

This activity has been characterised by the organisation of major international conferences (Strasbourg 1986, Barcelona 1987, Montreal 1989); the stimulation of the creation of the Forum of Local and Regional Authorities in Europe for Urban Safety and, most recently, the organisation of an international Hearing on 14 November 1990, for mayors from North America, Canada and Europe to assess the problems arising from the incidence of the cocaine-derivative "crack" in northern America and European cities.

The Council of Europe will also be involved in the organisation of the Conference in Paris, 18-20 November 1991, on "Urban Safety and Crime Prevention".

2. Health in Towns

This programme has been organised in collaboration with the WHO "Healthy Cities" programme, looking particularly at the way in which urban development favours - or the opposite - good health (Conference in Vienna and specialised working groups).

A report on this subject and a Resolution has been adopted by the Standing Conference at its March 1989 Session.

3. Historic Towns

The Standing Conference, over the years, has developed a series of international symposia on the problems affecting historic centres in

Europe. The first of these Symposia was held in Split in Yugoslavia in 1971, the most recent having been held in Cambridge, September 1989, looking at the impact, positive or negative, of tourism on historic centres.

4. North/South

The Standing Conference, in a general sense, has contributed to the organisation of the Council of Europe's European public Campaign on North/South Interdependence and Solidarity, particularly through the stimulation and involvement of local and regional authorities and in the development of the fourth plank of North/South co-operation (governments; parliaments; non-governmental organisations, and local and regional authorities).

The Standing Conference continues to express its commitment to this subject via a close involvement in the body established by the Council of Europe to ensure the follow-up to the Campaign, i.e. the North/South Centre in Lisbon.

In particular, the CLRAE has organised in Lisbon in October 1989 a Conference on "Managing urban development: North/South solidarity", looking at the way in which European experience can help understand and deal with some of the problems faced by major towns in developing countries.

5. Architectural development in cities

Parallel to the Council of Europe's work on the protection of the historical heritage in Europe, the CLRAE has developed programmes concerned with the physical rehabilitation of buildings; the improvement of contemporary architecture; policies for in-fill; policies and strategies for public open space; an analysis of the relationship between the municipality, architects, promoters, developers and the community as a whole.

Much of this work is carried out in collaboration with specialist, non-governmental organisations, such as the International Union of Architects and the International Society of City and Regional Planners.

The CLRAE is currently co-ordinating a questionnaire procedure on architecture of the 20th century ("Art Nouveau"), with a view to the establishment of a network of towns possessing outstanding examples of such architecture.

6. Regeneration of Industrial Towns and Regions

This activity has concentrated particularly upon the way in which environmental, social, cultural and, particularly, conservation policies can act as a catalyst in economic revival of towns and regions which have lost their traditional industrial base.

Conferences on this subject have been held in Lille; Dortmund and, most recently, at Halifax, United Kingdom (1989), which looked particularly at the way in which the industrial heritage of the 19th century can be used in achieving successful urban regeneration.

Through these activities, the Standing Conference has been instrumental in bringing about the creation of the European Association of Regions of Industrial Tradition (RETI).

The above work has been drawn together by the CLRAE in three ways:

a. The preparation of a series of reports and Resolutions on most of the above activities at its Plenary Session in March 1989.

b. The organisation of a "review" conference in Strasbourg in June 1990, entitled "European Towns: Strategies and Programmes" which, apart from acting as a vehicle for a review of some of the above activities, also concentrated upon an analysis of some recent phenomena such as increased international co-operation between cities in Europe and the municipality as a vector in its own economy over and above traditional roles of provision of infrastructure - a subject to be further explored at a future Conference to be held in Blackpool (United Kingdom) in May 1991 on "Local and Regional Economic Development Policies".

c. The preparation of a European Urban Charter, which will summarise the essence of the findings of most of the above activities and, with the help of specialised consultants, will constitute a comprehensive guide to good urban practice and management.

d. The preparation of a report for the 1991 Plenary Session on Towns in Europe - a report which will also include as one of its components an Opinion of the CLRAE on the EC "Green Paper" on the urban environment.

B. RECENT EXAMPLES OF WORK ON THE NATURAL ENVIRONMENT

1. Mountain Regions

The CLRAE, at a Conference on Mountain Regions in Trento in May 1988, reviewed the problems facing mountain regions throughout Europe, described and assessed the effectiveness of the action taken, prepared policy recommendations to national and international agencies and administrations and called for a European Charter for Mountain Regions.

2. Energy, Pollution, Traffic

Activities of the CLRAE on these subjects have included:

a. a Forum on Energy and Towns, held in Geneva in November 1988, examining problems relating to energy conservation and re-use of waste and the possibilities of renewable energy sources;

b. a Conference on Local Authorities and Air Pollution, held in Winterthur in October 1988, where an evaluation was made of the achievements of medium-sized European towns in combating air pollution. Particular emphasis was laid on the problems created by motor transport in towns;

c. a Seminar on Transalpine Traffic and the Environment in Innsbruck in May 1990 (in collaboration with the Parliamentary Assembly), examining the impact, particularly on Alpine countries, of long-distance trunk routes and encouraging the creation of a High Authority for transalpine traffic regulations;

d. a Conference on Improving Traffic and Quality of Life in Metropolitan Areas, held in Gothenburg in June 1990, the Conclusions of which will be drawn into a report on the same subject, to be prepared by the Standing Conference for its 1991 Session.

3. Rural questions

In addition to having initiated and contributed to the Council of Europe's Campaign for the Countryside, the Standing Conference has organised a number of ad hoc events, for example, a Colloquy at Vial Real (Portugal) in May 1989. This Colloquy looked particularly at the role of territorial authorities in mitigating the socio-economic difficulties of rural areas and on possibilities for promoting rural development particularly through better management and inter-municipal co-operation.

4. Tourism and the Environment

In 1989, a Seminar on Tourism and Integrated Planning Policy was held in Limassol (Cyprus), looking at the environmental impact of tourism, particularly the reduction of adverse environmental impact by selective and positive visitor management, and the promotion of tourism in cities and large towns as a counterbalance to coastal tourism.

A future strand of this activity will concern a comparison of policies in Europe at a local level for the creation of "Greenways".

5. Drinking water quality and control

The CLRAE Committee on the Natural and Built Environment is embarking upon a comparative study of the problems faced by local authorities in ensuring an adequate supply of good quality drinking water. Based upon information supplied directly by the municipal authorities in response to a questionnaire, the report will be prepared in 1991.

6. Flood control

Following its Resolution of flood control measures, adopted at the 1990 Session of the CLRAE, the Committee will be gathering material on problems and suggested policies concerning the responsibilities of local and regional authorities, particularly in upland areas, to take measures to avoid flooding further downstream.

7. The responsibilities of local and regional authorities for the environment in Europe

The Standing Conference is embarking upon a questionnaire procedure designed to elicit information from local and regional authorities in Europe on their responsibilities for the environment.

There is, as yet, no international picture of these responsibilities, which vary from country to country.

Some of the subjects covered by the questionnaire include ground water protection, disposal of toxic waste, protection of air quality, noise abatement, use of environmentally friendly materials, environmental control of the business and commercial communities. In terms of **mechanisms**, the report will also look at the existence of integrated planning mechanisms for environmental education in schools and , significantly, policies for raising public awareness about the environment, e.g. publication of the Brundtland report, use of TV and the media, etc.

The material arising from such an investigation will also be used as the basis for national monographs on municipal and regional environment policy in member countries.

8. Local and regional authority measures for reducing the pollution of lakes and rivers

Following recent examples of such co-operation, e.g. within the Danube Basin, organised by the Standing Conference of Yugoslav Towns; steps towards co-operation in the Rhine region, developed by the Union of Dutch River Communities, the Standing Conference will be organising a series of activities, colloquies, designed to compare such co-operative ventures and develop others.

9. Local authorities and the "greenhouse effect"

Comparative material is being drawn together, under the aegis of the CLRAE Committee on the Natural and Built Environment, on the role of local authorities in dealing with the problems caused by climatic change.

C. CO-OPERATION WITH CENTRAL AND EASTERN EUROPEAN COUNTRIES

The recent admission of Hungary as a full member of the Council of Europe (November 1990); applications for membership by Poland, the Federation of Czech and Slovak Republics and Yugoslavia; and increasing contacts at all levels with some other Central and Eastern European countries, have given the Council of Europe a significant role in co-operation within a wider family of European nations, particularly in the creation of democratic structures at national, regional and local level.

Such collaboration, however, is not limited to questions relating to democracy and human rights but also extends into other areas, including the natural and built environment.

The Standing Conference is therefore discussing with representatives of newly-created national associations of municipalities in Hungary, Poland, the Federation of Czech and Slovak Republics and Yugoslavia, the organisation of specific activities.

These activities will hinge initially upon the organisation of fact-finding missions, specific colloquies of an information nature and dealing with ad hoc requests made by the newly-elected municipal authorities in the countries in question.

MAN AND CITY ENVIRONMENT IN DEVELOPING COUNTRIES

K. Khosh-Chashm
World Health Organisation/EMRO

SUMMARY

Since the Second World War, for many complex and interrelated reasons in the developing world, cities have developed a powerful gravity force. This self-perpetuating magnetism attracts people, jobs, services, interests and opportunities. This city attraction in the recent decades has resulted in an unprecedented growth of urban populations. In the developing countries the inability of the authorities to respond to rapid urbanisation and to provide adequate environmental health and other services, is detrimental to a congenial and healthy living environment. The plight of the urban poor deserves special and urgent attention.

Environmental health conditions in many cities are severely stretched; air, industrial and noise pollution as well as hazards are increasing. Sewerage, drainage and solid wastes collection and disposal facilities are deficient. Hurriedly built housing and rapid growth of cities are unplanned and largely inappropriate, resulting in the disintegration of neighbourhoods, traditional community bonds and social support systems. People are not involved in improvement measures, while the activities of municipal agencies are not properly co-ordinated. Moreover, both municipal and government agencies lack manpower and other resources to halt and counteract the deterioration of environmental conditions in cities.

The city is influenced by certain fundamental elements. These are Humanity, Environment, Time, Space and Form. Humanity is the most influential of all factors and its impact on the city and vice versa could be seen in two facets. The individual, his/her rights, dreams, privacy, etc. and the group of individuals as the community including politics, institutions, locality, social environment, etc. Environment in this relation refers to the physical setting, ecology and biological and chemical systems. Time is the link with the forces and events outside the city and the country. Space is the room for physical, social and spiritual expression and forms are architectural and historical marks.

In the cities of the developing world humanity is the predominant force, environment and ecology is disturbed, life quality in terms of health and financial well-being is not ideal. However, social support systems facilitate relatively good bonds with others. The historical and shape and architecture, which historically have developed in harmony with other elements, are badly threatened. There is unsightliness and disharmony as the result of haphazard physical growth.

For improved action people must be involved and people be made more aware to attain a better quality of life.

The "urban living" in the developed world, especially with the life-style of the disadvantaged dictated by poverty, is disturbing the global natural, social and political ecology. It is essential for the rich cities in the developed world to assist the developing cities. Twinning arrangements through the Healthy City Programme is a good opportunity. Technical and financial support is needed to enhance city leadership and strengthen urban institutions for action.

1. INTRODUCTION

Since the Second World War, for many complex and interrelated reasons in the developing world, cities have developed a powerful gravity force. This self-perpetuating magnetism attracts people, jobs, services, interests and opportunities. This city attraction in the recent decades have resulted in an unprecedented growth of urban populations. In the developing countries the inability of the authorities to respond to rapid urbanisation and to provide adequate environmental health and other services, is detrimental to a congenial and healthy living environment. The plight of the urban poor deserves special and urgent attention.

Environmental health conditions in many cities are severely stretched; air, industrial and noise pollution as well as hazards are increasing. Sewerage, drainage and solid wastes collection and disposal facilities are deficient. Hurriedly built housing and rapid growth of cities are unplanned and largely inappropriate, resulting in the disintegration of neighbourhoods, traditional community bonds and social support systems. People are not involved in improvement measures, while the activities of municipal agencies are not properly coordinated. Moreover, both municipal and government agencies lack manpower and other resources to halt and counteract the deterioration of environmental conditions in cities.

This exposé is an attempt to review briefly the population growth pattern, essential physical, social and environmental elements that make a city. Also the impact of "city living" on human health and well being as well as the natural ecology in the developing world will be discussed.

2. POPULATION

Population is one the basic features in "urbanisation" and can indicate the extent of urban expansion.

As population growth in the industrialised countries has levelled off, most of the increase is in Third World cities. Average annual urban population growth rates of 3.5% have not been uncommon in developing countries and annual increases of more than 3% are expected over the next 40 years. The rates of urban growth 2-3 times those experienced by industrialised countries in the past - may be even faster over the next four decades (1).

The megalopolis has become a developing country phenomenon. Of the 26 cities of 5 million or more in 1980, 16 were in developing countries. By region, the increase in cities of more than 5 million population is forecast to change as follows:

REGION	1970	2000
Africa	0	2
East Asia (Excluding Japan)	4	8
Latin America	4	9
Middle East	1	4
South-East Asia	2	12
Europe (including USSR)	4	6
Japan	2	2
North America	3	3
Total	20	47

Further, 11 cities in the developing world are likely to have populations in the 20-30 million range (Mexico City, Sao Paulo, Lagos, Cairo, Karachi, Delhi, Bombay, Calcutta, Dhaka, Shanghai and Jakarta). In all, it is estimated that, by 2025, one-third of all urban dwellers will live in cities of more than 4 million population, the majority of them residing in smaller conurbations (1).

For the Eastern Mediterranean Region, Figure 1 shows the population growth pattern in the urban areas.

3. CITY

A city is not a mere geographical location; it is not simply a collection of buildings, shops and streets. It is the embodiment of its inhabitants' social and physical environment, the mark of their particular architectural forms and past expression, a place of human bonding, cultural and spiritual heritage.

3.1 City Elements

In the case of the Eastern Mediterranean Region, before rapid population growth, it appears that the historical development and evolution of cities are governed by certain human, ecological, physical, spiritual, social and economical systems. These systems and the order, within which they relate to each other, allow the city to be thought of as a **"bio-social"** organism. To expand on this, the following systems or co-ordinates shape and make a city:

(1) Humanity

Humanity is the single most influential of all parameters in shaping the physical setting and the life of the city. The individual's interaction with the environment, time, space and form is the reality of the city as a habitat.

Figure 1: Population growth pattern in the region

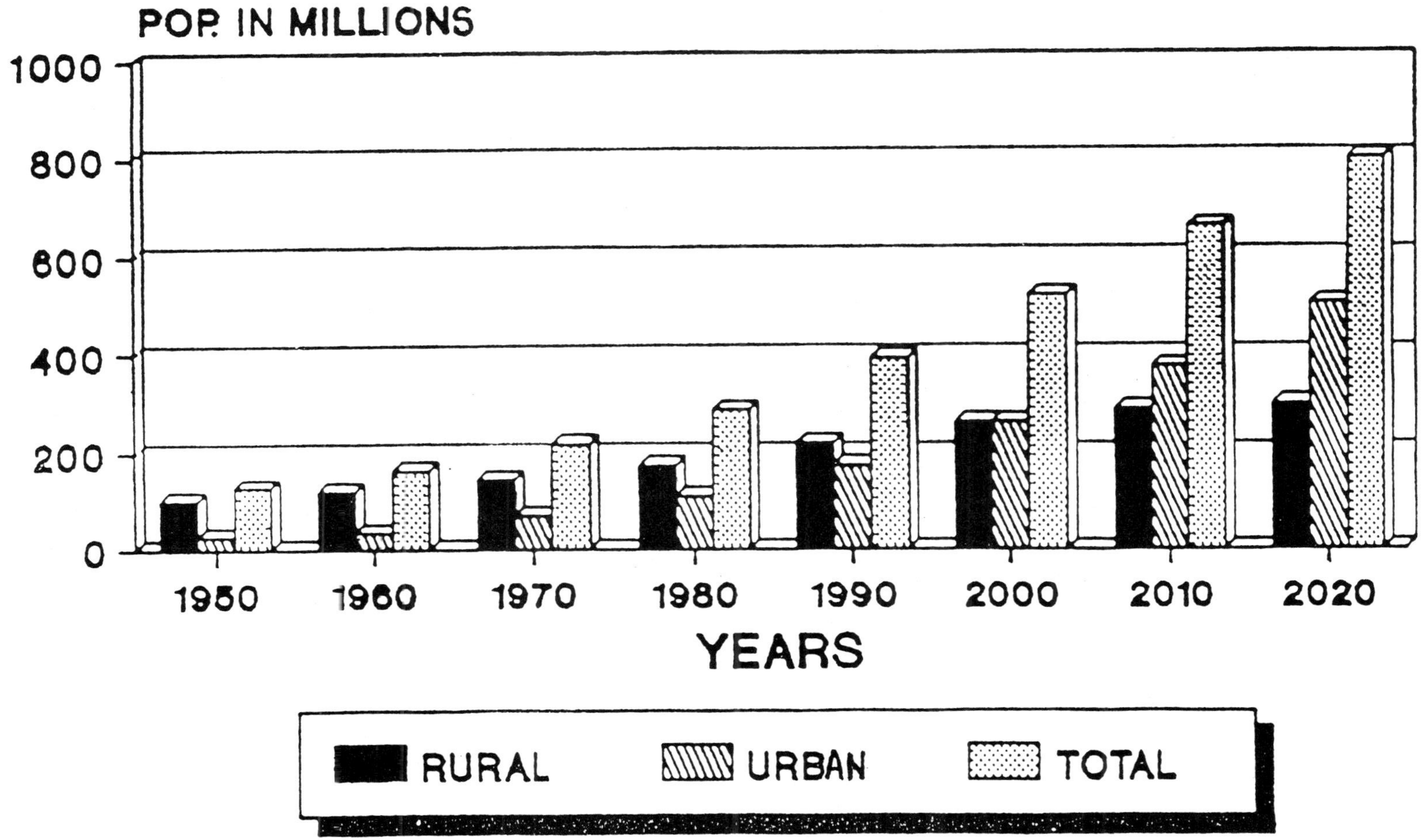

The relationship between people and the city has two facets: people as individuals, and the group of individuals as the community.

The factors for individuals include: personal needs, safety, privacy, hopes, dreams, individuality, etc.

Community factors are: power, politics, economy, beliefs, institutions, groups, locality, social environment, etc.

(2) Environment

Environment in this context encompasses physical settings and the natural ecology. Physical features include: location and landscape. The natural ecology consists of water, vegetation, climate and biological and chemical systems.

(3) Time

Time is the link between the city and the influences outside, i.e., technological advances, architecture and style in the developed world and their impact on the cities of the developing world.

(4) Space and Form

Space means room for physical, social and spiritual expressions, while form is the mark of people's interaction with their surroundings. Together, space and form manifest: access, shape, architecture, historical and cultural sketches.

The above is illustrated graphically in Figure 2.

4. ECOLOGICAL, SOCIAL AND SPECIAL CONDITIONS OF THE MAJOR CITIES IN THE DEVELOPING WORLD

4.1 Legal and Political Issues

The legal framework to protect human health, well being and environment in the cities is neither properly defined nor adequate. Many political, social and economic reasons prevent city administrations from forcefully enforcing even rudimentary regulations. Urban elites and economic pressure groups somehow manage to bypass building regulations and zoning reactions. The industries located in the cities do not comply with the standards, and under the cloak of "economic necessities" authorities look the other way to industrial pollution. The money and the land and housing market squash all codes and standards.

Safety regulations for roads, houses, workplace, etc, are not observed. One of the most fundamental detriments to the environment and the city's health is the lack of a proper legal framework and the ability of the system to safeguard the rights, safety and wellbeing of their citizens.

Figure 2

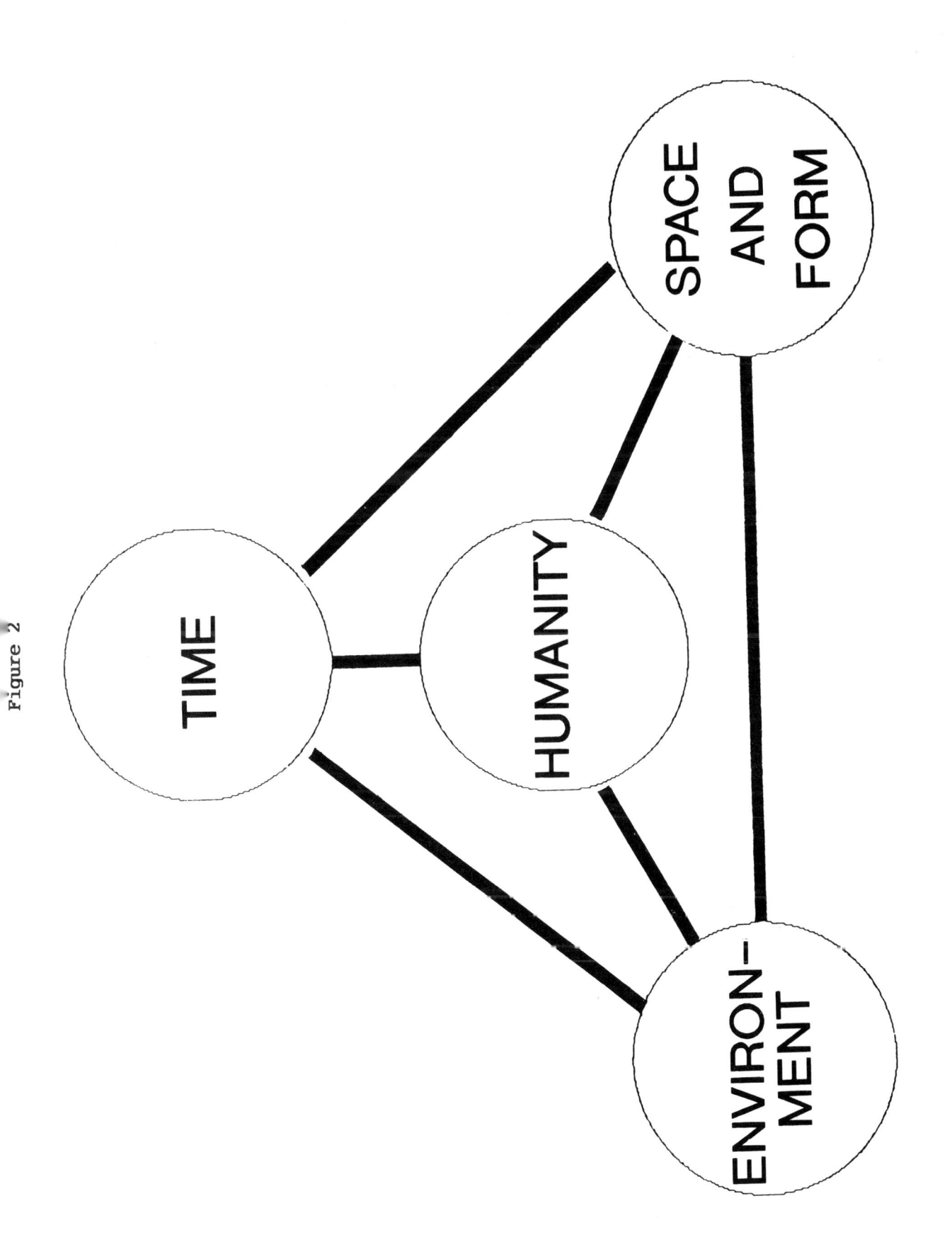

4.2 Economy - Poverty

In major cities of the developing world, there are high rates of unemployment and underemployment as urban labour markets are unable to absorb the expanding numbers of those seeking jobs. Despite these, and the problems of jobs, insufficient housing, inadequate services and other shortcomings, migration to urban areas continues. This is partly because declining mortality rates in rural areas are not matched with declining fertility rates. The resulting natural increase in population cannot be sustained by stagnating rural economies and it is the urban areas that are perceived to offer better economic opportunities (3).

Poverty has probably much more adverse impact on environment and health than any other factor. To alter people's self-esteem and, consequently the betterment of their life and environmental quality, the major task for 1990's will be to create enough jobs to employ billions of new workers throughout the developing world (3).

In the Eastern Mediterranean Region, for example, urban areas are the centres of national economy (see Figure 3). This has come about with the rapid decline of rural economy and agriculture, especially in the oil-producing countries.

In many instances, the growth patterns are not necessarily according to the national long-term economic development plans. This ad hoc characteristic has created severe gyration vis-à-vis employment and housing services and has caused serious physical and social disharmonies in urban areas.

5. HEALTH

A draft paper has been prepared for the World Health Organisation's Commission on Health and Environment. This paper entitled, "A review of the health impacts of environmental problems in urban areas of developing countries" (Carolyn Stephens, Trudy Harpham, David Bradely and Sandy Carincross, September 1990). The paper, after examining hundreds of studies, concludes:

> "Urban populations in developing countries are suffering the 'worst of both worlds' in their mortality profile."

> "There are several studies linking water quality and access to it to infant mortality from communicable diseases. Access to an individual 'water supply' emerges as an important variable."

> "Some studies perceive that the health outcomes in urban areas are ultimately from socio-economic, not physical environment".

> "Evidence of intra-urban differentials in nutritional status is plentiful, with poorer groups (particularly women and children) being at a distinct disadvantage."

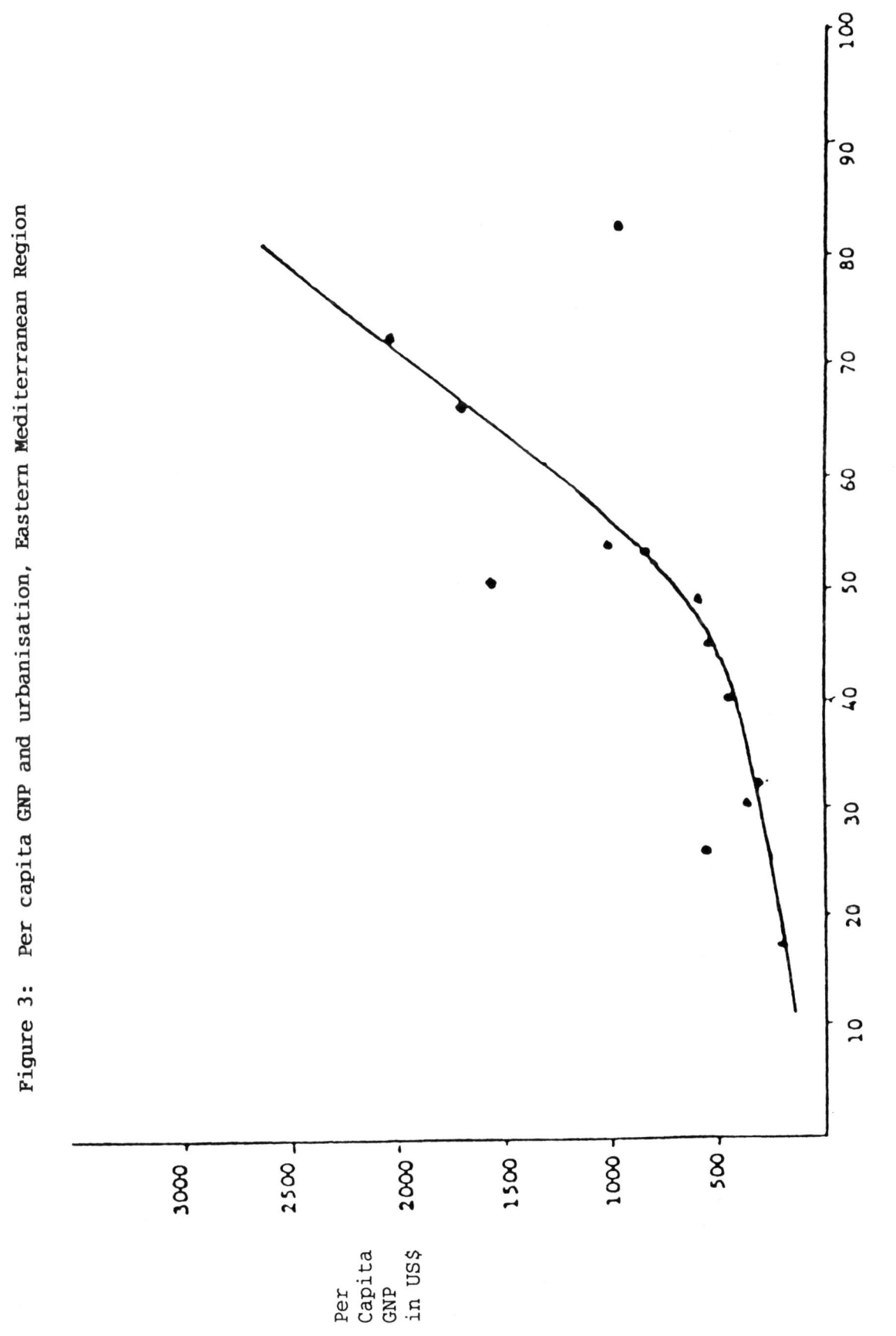

Figure 3: Per capita GNP and urbanisation, Eastern Mediterranean Region

"Poverty, as a composite index of deprivation extending command over economic resources, access to education, social support, and self-esteem, the housing and physical environment quality, remains the most significant predicator of urban morbidity and mortality."

For the Eastern Mediterranean Region, Figure 4 shows the relationship between infant mortality and percentage of total population in urban areas in different countries.

6. ECOLOGY/ENVIRONMENT CONDITION

In the developing countries, the capabilities of the cities to safeguard the physical, chemical and biological environments are limited. As a result, air, water and noise pollution as well as chemicals and human contacts with them, the health hazards of urban dwellers have increased. The cities lack proper urban development framework, housing policy, pollution control and monitoring, sanitary services, food safety, etc. Also, the industries have grown in or around the cities without proper zoning or planned pattern. As a result, in addition to social disharmony that such a growth may cause, it has increased the exposure and risk to chemical accidents. Also, in the dry areas, i.e., Middle East, in some towns, urban growth has devoured arable land and the traditional green areas around cities. These have resulted in disturbance of ecosystem, turning the congenial natural surroundings into unsightly concrete disharmony.

In more specific terms, the environmental health problems of developing cities could be listed as:

- air pollution in the cities and larger towns;
- inadequate solid waste management, especially in the secondary towns;
- development of industries in and around cities;
- inadequate housing, especially in low-income sections;
- lack of adequate water supply in some cities;
- absence of sewerage and proper drainage in many cities;
- lack of adequate roads, compounded with traffic congestion and haphazard growth in major cities;
- lack of green space, sport and social facilities in many cities;
- absence of adequate food safety in public eating places and food markets as well as abundance of street vendors;
- noise pollution;
- water pollution.

6.1 Environmental management

Resources to deal with these environmental problems are grossly insufficient, and it is vital that the resources, whatever are made available, be used to best effect. Environmental improvement efforts in urban development are usually focused solely on water supply, or housing or transportation, or waste disposal or other issues, such as air quality, but then often fail to consider how a solution to one problem may help or hinder solutions to other problems. The result is that

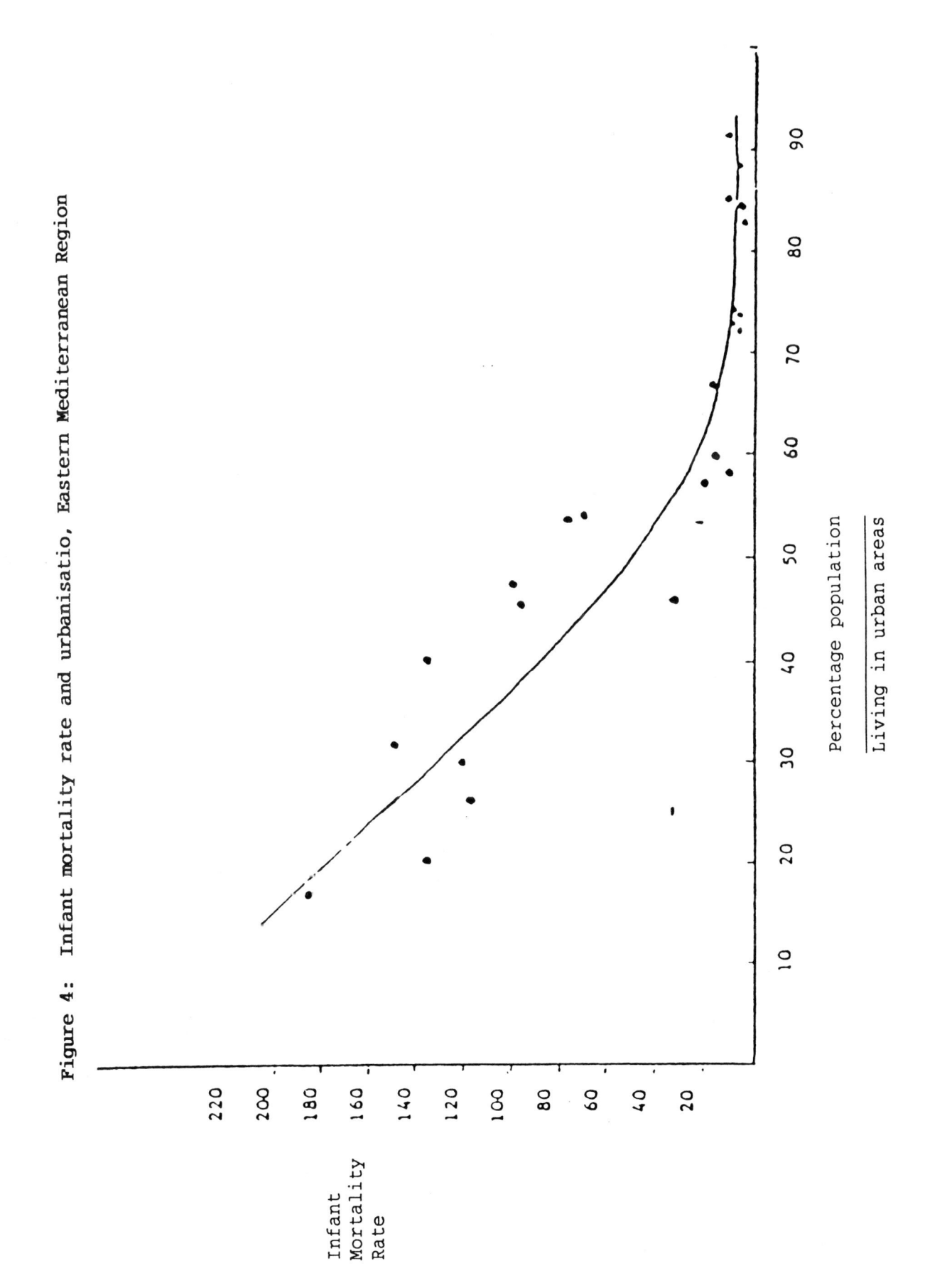

Figure 4: Infant mortality rate and urbanisatio, Eastern Mediterranean Region

individual efforts do not produce the full desired benefits, available resources are not used in the most efficient way, some improvements are neglected, and sometimes the effort is even counterproductive.

7. SOCIAL ENVIRONMENT AND THE URBAN POOR

In view of rapid urbanisation and the result in physical change and with many new arrivals in towns, traditional social and neighbourhoods bonds have weakened. City authorities cannot establish appropriate associations including ward councils, etc., to address, in an informal way, the problems of families and individuals. In the absence of traditional social care, people in big cities tend to feel more and more isolated.

Also, physical growth in many instances is not in harmony with people's cultural heritage and their religious and spiritual conditioning. This, too, has caused a certain social disruption. However, in the cities of the Middle East, at least, there are much lower rates of crime and drug abuse than in the West; this could be attributed to strong religious beliefs and bonds.

Also, because of the prevailing economic conditions, the urban fringes of some of the big cities are occupied by poorer sections of society; they are also usually the landing ground for rural migrants. These fringes have a negative impact on shaping the life-styles and attitudes of the newcomers which is detrimental to cities' environments.

8. THE WITHERING OF PHYSICAL AND VISUAL VALUES OF SETTLEMENTS

The following statement for the Eastern Mediterranean Region describes the issues and the emotions involved.

> "Cities in the Region are rich with their cultural, religious, organisational and imageable architectural heritage. They are distinctly identifiable in old streets, market places, squares, mosques and social institutions. Most of the quarters which contain this valuable heritage (some quarters are huge open air museums) are deteriorating and suffer from congestion, conflict and neglect. They cannot accommodate the pressures of the technological age, soaring traffic volumes, or the rising complexities of communal needs. Their pattern is simply incapable of meeting the contradictory demands of today's urban movement and functions. It is indeed unfortunate that authorities in their rush for modernisation have adopted imported architectural cliches, slum clearance in historic quarters, urban renewal stereotypes, foreign solutions and irrelevant building codes. The blind trust in imported know-how and finished products have corrupted local values and replaced them with symbolistic expressways, skyscrapers and kaleidoscopic panoramas of conflicting images, colours and patterns, as well as fallacious forms that are

divorced from environmental dictates. The new additions lack a sense of belonging and identification. They tend to supercede and insult, rather than complement and pay homage to the shaping forces of the local urban environment (4)."

9. STRATEGIES FOR IMPROVEMENT ACTION

The strategic approaches for urban improvement, while needing an idealistic touch, must be pragmatic and sober. The undesirable conditions existing in the major cities cannot be radically changed in a short time.

Cities' agencies in many instances do not have the capacity to cope with the immense urban problems. Therefore, a new look and approach for mobilisation and utilisation of resources are needed.

9.1 Resources

With the above in mind, the resources could be viewed under the following headings:

   (1) Leadership
   (2) People
   (3) Institutions
   (4) Technology

(1) **Leaders** may be drawn from municipal or national political fora, the media, academia, concerned citizens, etc.

(2) **People** are the foundation of actions. They should be made aware of their rights, so that they demand both services and a better life quality. They should participate and be active in building political and legal bases for improvement.

   People's lifestyles could be responsible for many of the cities' maladies. They can either minimise problems or add to them. Therefore, for any approach, the challenge is how to involve people and how to influence their lifestyles to be more co-operative and less waste- and problem-generating.

(3) For City **Institutions**, several issues are at stake. They need basic strengthening; they need realignment; they need more skilled manpower; they need co-ordination - the classic prescription for institutional ills. However, without a major political and social push, no managerial or technocratic action is enough to resolve institutional problems.

   If people are made aware and brought into the main stream of activities, the inertia of their actions will streamline institutions and make them more responsive to people's needs.

(4) The **Technologies/Methodologies** are known, but they need to be adapted to suit institutional capabilities.

9.2 Guiding principles for action

As a strategic approach, certain guiding principles should be established. Considering the conditions of the cities in the Region and the need for action, these guiding principles are:

(1) enhancing leadership;
(2) increasing awareness, facilitating dialogue and bringing urban issues to public notice;
(3) mobilising people and positive resources;
(4) developing co-operative and positive attitudes.

The relationships between these guiding principles and institutional action and technology are shown graphically in Figure 5.

9.3 Strengthening of institutions and technology

To improve urban environmental conditions, the institutional and technological competence of the responsible city agencies should be strengthened. To achieve this, the following classic measures should be undertaken:

(a) establishment of an urban development planning framework;
(b) strengthening of institutions' infrastructure, legal and financial frameworks and administration and management;
(c) ensuring intersectoral action;
(d) development of human resources;
(e) improving technical management and arranging for technology transfer;
(f) strengthening research and information.

These are as comprehensive as they are vague and can only mean something tangible when all involved sit together to specify and define them.

9.4 Policy basis

To facilitate the application of the above technological tools in addition to the guiding principles, a certain policy basis and matching legal frameworks are also needed. Here, care should be taken to bring such policies as close to the people and streets as is possible. Some examples are given below:

(1) Population policy
(2) Land Use Policy
(3) Housing Policy
(4) Environmental Policy

Figure 5: Guiding principles and institutional actions

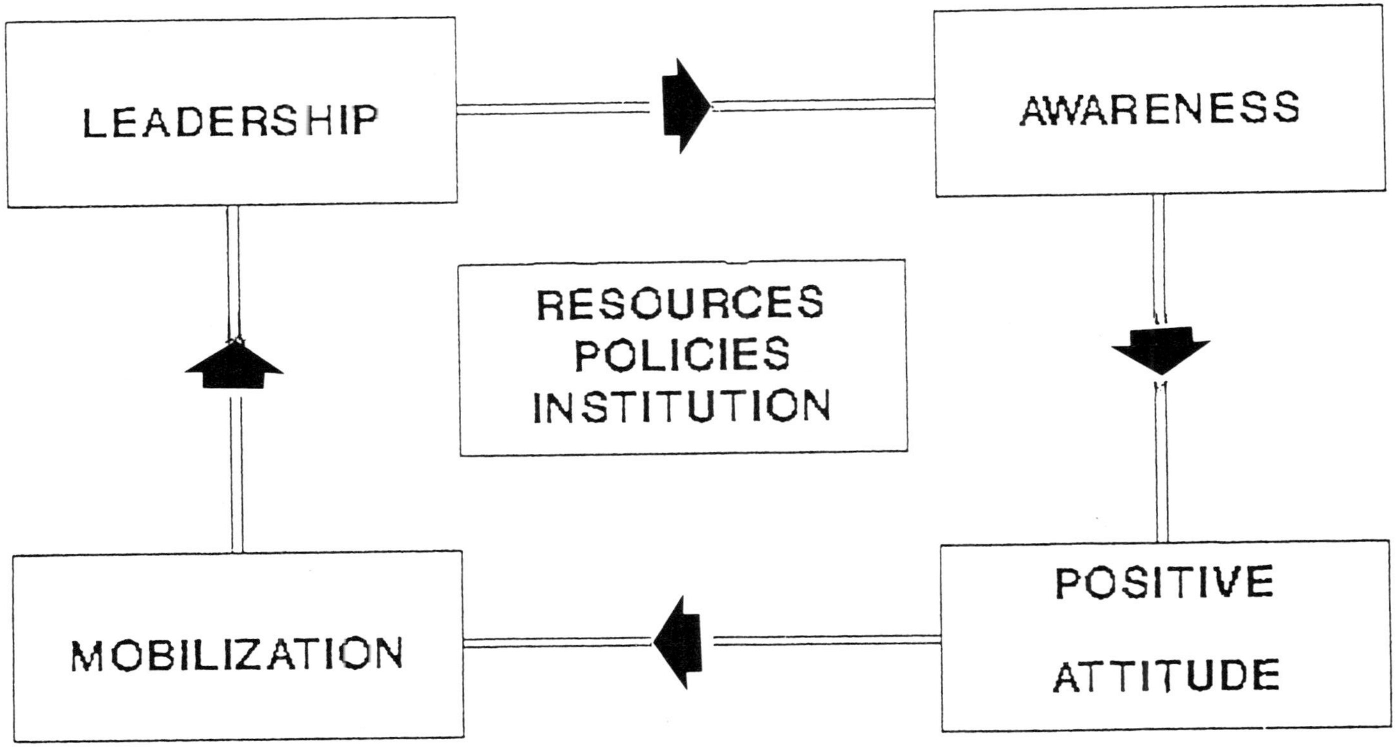

10. HEALTHY CITIES CONCEPT

The Healthy City concept which has been promoted by the European Region of the World Health Organisation has an emotional appeal; it has a positive message and stirs pride in people to "stand up for" their cities. Its systems and methodologies are very much in harmony with the **Strategic Approaches, Guiding Principles and Policy Basis** mentioned in the previous section.

The Healthy Cities message injects these Approaches, Principles and Policies with warm blood and brings them to life for action.

11. CONCLUSIONS AND RECOMMENDATIONS

(1) It has been said that the ecological debt in the developing world has far more severe consequences than the economic one. Rapid urban growth accelerates over-population, decentrification, over-extension of water resources, loss of green areas to cities (especially in the arid region) and the decline of agriculture. Also, poverty and its proliferation in the urban areas induces unhealthy lifestyles which are detrimental to global health and environment.

(2) From a geo-political and social point of view, urban slums could be breeding grounds for crime, drug abuse, violence and upheavals.

(3) Not only because of the moral imperatives, but for ecological, social and political benefits, the fortunate rich cities in the developed world should assist the cities of the developing world. Attempts must be made to have a direct contact and avoid as much as possible the cumbersome bureaucracy and red-tape of country to country actions. Twinning of cities through the Healthy City Programme and networks is a good venue.

(4) City authorities and Government cannot do everything; people have to be mobilised to participate in improvement measures. Improvement of life quality cannot be provided as a service; it must be attained by people. It is a continuous process rather than a product.

(5) Collective action must be promoted to alleviate poverty and to foster income-generation opportunities. Also, activities should aim at encouraging positive lifestyles and attitudes. These must start in schools; children's education should be adapted to enable them relate to their environment and train them to generate positive improvement actions.

(6) In the developing World power and authority have had a profound impact on the shape, if not the **mind** of the city. But rapid growth has weakened authority in the cities. Strong leadership needs to be enhanced to challenge the problem. Therefore, there should be a "Dual Focus Approach": strong leadership based on community participation.

(7) The international and bilateral donor agencies should provide funding support for improvement of environmental health conditions of the cities. Specific projects and programmes need to be developed and co-ordinated. These are needed to support the Healthy City concept.

(8) External support is needed to preserve the cultural heritage and traditional architectural and monuments in the developing world. The standard of the civilised world dictates a moral and educational imperative to safeguard the historical art and culture of different regions. Help is urgently needed. Poverty and urban crisis have already caused serious damage, but the threat must be arrested.

REFERENCES

1. **Protecting and Promoting Health in the Urban Environment:** Concepts and Strategic Approaches, Morris Schaefer, D.P.A.

2. **The Environmental Health Challenge of Urbanisation,** K. Khoshchashm, Regional Adviser, WHO/EMRO, Inter-country Seminar on Health in Housing and Urban Environment: Criteria, Methods and Strategies, Damascus, Syria, November 1990.

3. **Coping with the Urban Crisis in the Third World: Mechanisms for Creating Healthy Communities by Strengthening Urban Management and Planning at the Municipal Government Level,** Fritz Wagner, College of Urban and Public Affairs, University of New Orleans, USA.

4. **The Physical, Socio-Economic and Cultural Considerations for a Harmonious Urban Environment,** Mohsen M. Zahran, University of Alexandria, Egypt.

5. **Housing, Health and Well-Being: An International Prospective,** G. Goldstein, R. Novick and M. Schaefer.

6. **Urbanisation; Strategic Approaches for Environmental Health Action in the Eastern Mediterranean Region,** K. Khoshchashm, Regional Adviser Environmental Health WHO/EMRO.

7. **World Population Prospectus,** 1988, United Nations.

8. **The Mind of the City - The Context for Urban Life,** Len Duhl, University of California Berkeley, USA.

9. **Health and the City,** Len Duhl, World Health Magazine.

SUMMARY OF DISCUSSION, RECOMMENDATIONS

With many examples from European Cities the group discussed current planning and development problems in (primarily metropolitan) cities, related to global phenomena within demography, energy, pollution, the greenhouse effect, climate change, social contacts and conflicts, urban and suburban transportation, housing problems and urban renewal.

The problems are different in different cities, but with **many common characteristics.** Differences are due to climatic conditions, cultural identity, stage of economic development, political structure, etc. All cities go through certain stages/phases of an **urbanisation process**: central urbanisation-sub-urbanisation - deurbanisation - reurbanisation. But shorter and longer **time-lags** exist between the development of different cities. The problems and efforts toward their solution depend on the interaction between different population classes and groups.

Those **population groups interact** in different ways of which some can be productive and stimulating (love, co-operation, conflict), while others are destructive (alienation, anomie). The possibility of getting through with claims and wishes depends on the **position of the groups in the economic and political power structure.**

Their respective attitudes may be illustrated in a simplified way in a politological diagram of **2 fundamental types of opposites**: right wing versus left wing policies and economic growth policies versus "green policies". Both are combined and present a wide range of attitudes from strong principles to pragmatic compromises.

The discussion within group 5 identified a number of **"worst planning problems"** within cities and urban agglomerations. The following were stressed by the participants:

- Rising land prices in central city areas
- Transportation, especially by car
- Air pollution and noise (stemming from motor vehicle traffic, energy production, heating and industries)
- Large old and unmodern housing stock
- Obsolete areas, left by old heavy industries, harbours, railways
- Lack of cross-sectoral co-ordination

A number of proposals were mentioned and discussed, but the group did not succeed in selecting a few of those proposals for detailed study and presentation in a more elaborate form.

So, instead, the "blocks" of proposals discussed are mentioned here.

Proposal at city/region level:

1. Establish **a list of relevant city needs,** short term as well as long term.

2. Private/public co-operation in preparing some sort of **general land-use plan for well-defined obsolete areas,** and for **subsequent implementation and financing** of the plan through a strong position of land ownership and planning powers.

3. **Public transport improvements** combined with (and partly financed by) **introduction of a fee on cars used during daytime in a defined inner city area** (cp. Singapore and Stockholm).

4. **New approaches for residential urban renewal** with the **active participation and decision-making by the local tenants, shopkeepers, etc.,** in the area defined for that purpose. Decentralisation of public administrative management into the local area (cp. Amsterdam and Rotterdam).

5. Grants to some **local grassroot and professional group** to plan, design and (maybe) build **an "Ecological House"** on some vacant land.

Proposals at European Community level:

6. Establish in different European regions an ad hoc **"Urban Plan and Design Centre",** collecting information from cities on problems, good practices, costs, etc. - analysing and disseminating the information, making recommendations and proposing grants from EC funds.

7. More **thematic workshops** by the Foundation for the Improvement of Living and Working Conditions like this one, but concentrated on one specific theme, such as "Obsolete areas", "Ecological building".

8. Organise a **co-ordinating meeting** between international organisations on their work within urban problems. Participants could, for instance, be:

   The European Foundation for the Improvement of Living and Working Conditions and other EC agencies,
   OECD (Urban Affairs Group),
   ECE (Housing & Planning Section),
   Council of Europe,
   WHO.

   Participants should define current areas of work, make a programme in order to avoid duplication or squeezing out of useful work and agree on division of work, co-ordination and mutual information.

The diagrams drawn by the rapporteur K. Lemberg visualise some of the issues discussed.

The Stages of the Urbanisation Process

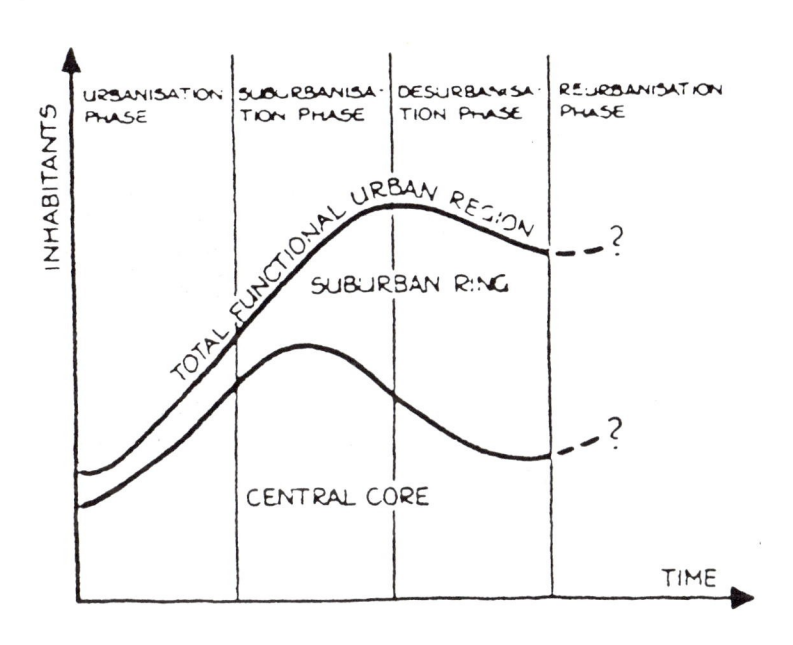

Main Types of Social Interaction

LOVE

COOPERATION

ALIENATION

CONFLICT

ANOMIE

Kai Lemberg

The Power Structure in Physical Planning

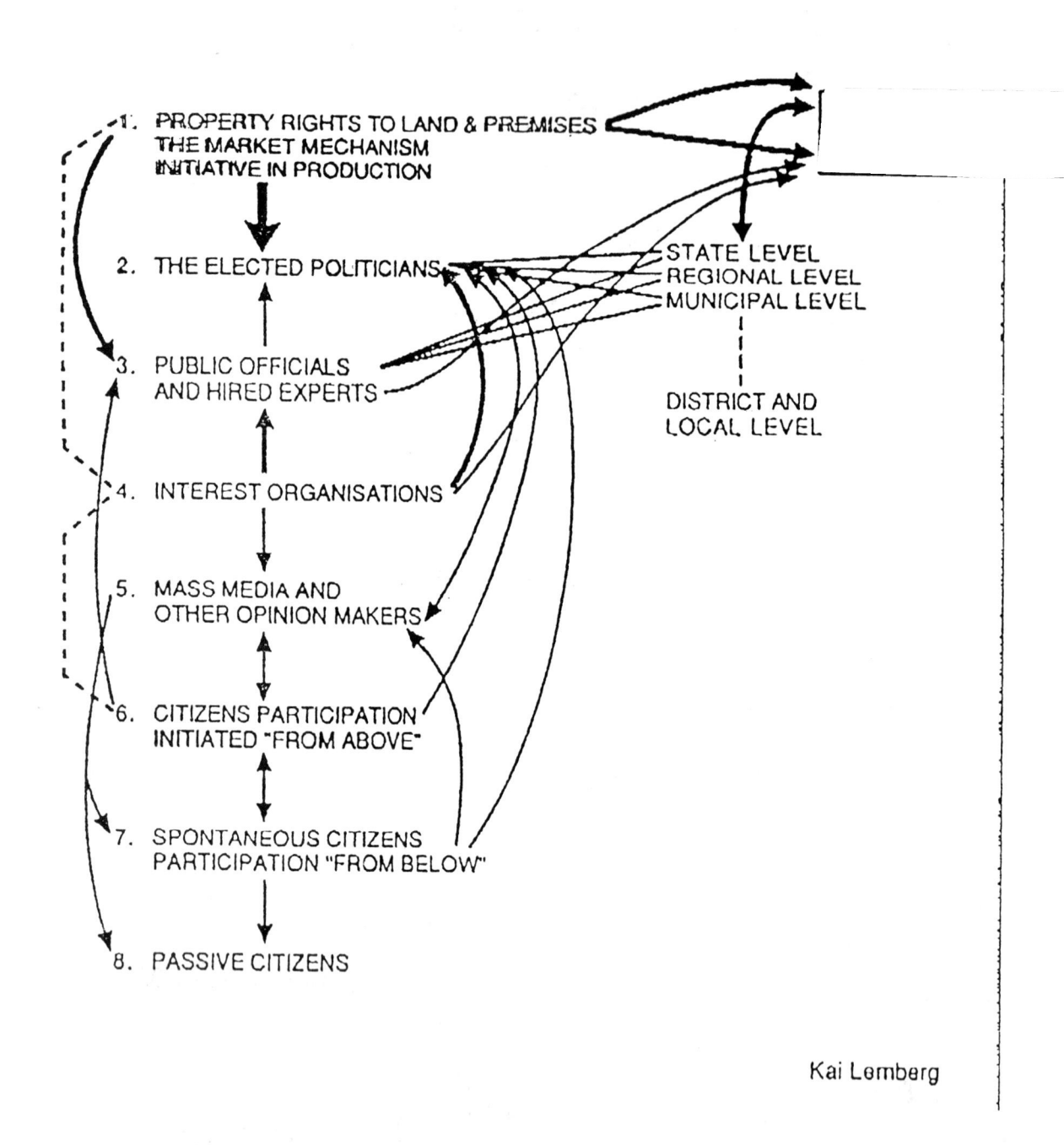

1. PROPERTY RIGHTS TO LAND & PREMISES
   THE MARKET MECHANISM
   INITIATIVE IN PRODUCTION

2. THE ELECTED POLITICIANS

3. PUBLIC OFFICIALS AND HIRED EXPERTS

4. INTEREST ORGANISATIONS

5. MASS MEDIA AND OTHER OPINION MAKERS

6. CITIZENS PARTICIPATION INITIATED "FROM ABOVE"

7. SPONTANEOUS CITIZENS PARTICIPATION "FROM BELOW"

8. PASSIVE CITIZENS

STATE LEVEL
REGIONAL LEVEL
MUNICIPAL LEVEL

DISTRICT AND LOCAL LEVEL

Kai Lemberg

The Two-Dimensional Politological Diagram

KIT LEMBERG: THE TWO-DIMENSIONAL POLITOLOGICAL DIAGRAM

ECONOMIC GROWTH POLICIES:

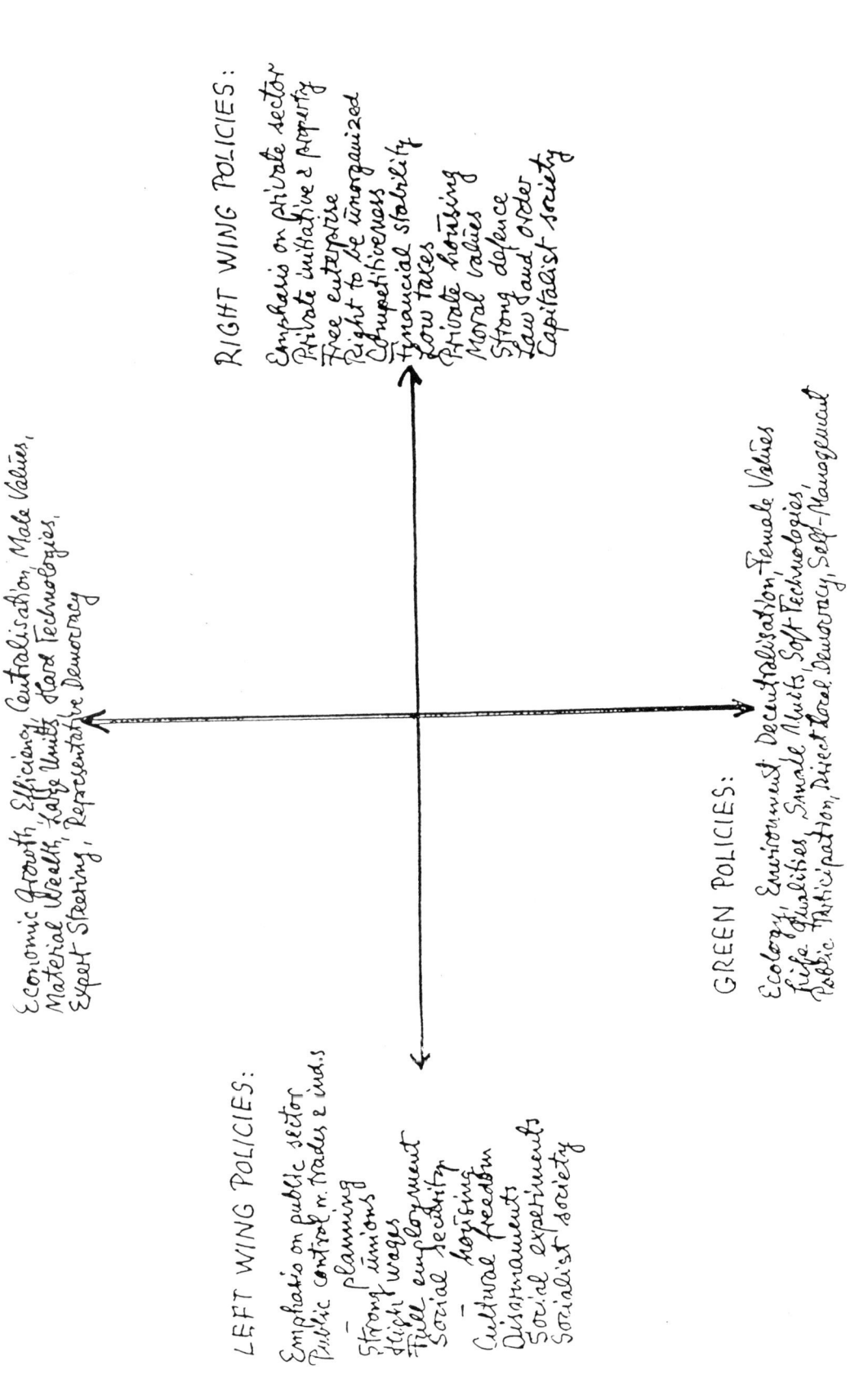

Economic Growth, Efficiency, Centralisation, Male Values, Material Wealth, Large Units, Hard Technologies, Export Steering, Representative Democracy

RIGHT WING POLICIES:

Emphasis on private sector, Private initiative & property, Free enterprise, Right to be unorganized, Competitiveness, Financial stability, Low taxes, Private housing, Moral values, Strong defence, Law and order, Capitalist society

LEFT WING POLICIES:

Emphasis on public sector, Public control m. trades & inds., Planning, Strong unions, High wages, Full employment, Social security, Housing, Cultural freedom, Disarmaments, Social experiments, Socialist society

GREEN POLICIES:

Ecology, Environment, Decentralisation, Female Values, Life Qualities, Small Units, Soft-Technologies, Public Participation, Direct Local Democracy, Self-Management

CONCLUSIONS AND SUGGESTIONS EMERGING FROM THE WORKSHOP

Tjeerd Deelstra
Director of the International Institute for the Urban Environment
Delft
The Netherlands

The discussions in the Workshop have focused on a wide range of themes. It is my impression that local environmental problems, such as traffic or waste, were not always explicitly related to global issues such as climate change, the depletion of the ozone layer or the reduction of biodiversity.

A major local cause of global climate change is the combustion of fossil fuels in industry and traffic, but also the heating and cooling of housing, incineration of waste and the generation of electricity.

Reduction of biodiversity on the "global commons" such as the oceans and vulnerable rainforests, is related to the over-fishing, the intensive use of timber in construction, and raw materials and food from tropical countries in European cities, and to the dissemination of chemical wastes from cities.

In Europe the majority of people nowadays live and work in cities. In several papers it is discussed which problems occur on the European scene since some cities face growth, others decline, and many European cities are entering a period of transformation and change, with all kinds of environmental problems related to that. Outside Europe cities grow quickly. Particular environmental problems occurring in relation to growth in developing countries were also touched upon in the workshop.

It is generally recognised nowadays that the global environment is being disrupted by cities, with increased dangers for the cities themselves.

Cities in Southern Europe for instance are expected to suffer more in the future from heat waves and droughts (as a consequence of climate change). Medicine production and the production of food for urban inhabitants becomes dangerously dependent on a diminishing number of biogenetic reservoirs.

Participants of the workshop reviewed a selection of European local policies and projects, that can help to reverse trends towards environmental disruption and to prevent dangerous global environmental impacts.

General principles of these policies and projects are:

- Reduction in the level of consumption of energy and resources.
- Making urban systems more efficient, thus conserving energy and resources (for instance using public transport instead of cars).

- Being more selective in the type of energy and resources used (renewable versus fossil energy resources).
- Reduction in streams of toxic wastes through changing processes of production and consumption, through recycling, reuse and recuperation.
- Using more locally available resources, and local markets (shorter distances for transportation; greater self-reliance).
- Making the use of energy and resources more visible (in the pocket and to the eyes). This will lead to the coupling of decentralised supply and waste management systems with centrally organised systems at urban level.
- Involvement of all parties that live and work in the city in energy and resource management. It requires information and visual design of energy and resource use in architecture and in the layout of neighbourhoods and the city as a whole.

Participants recommended that parallel to conventional administrative tools such as permits, financial "punishments", surveillance and control, city administrations should be aware of the global dimensions of local activities and play an innovative role in this respect.

The city could for instance look at itself as a household that should be properly managed. City offices should set an example in its architecture (to minimise energy for heating and cooling), in its urban setting (reducing the need of car use through convenient allocation of public transport systems), and in the ways resources (material as well as human) are used.

The city is also important in land-use planning and building control. A long term view on the function and form of the city, the management of green spaces and infrastructures will help to direct investments into a more conserving direction.

The city could act as animator, bringing local actors together, stimulating co-operating in environmentally sound activities. A local focal point, facilitated with people and equipment is an important means to this end. Incentives are needed. A local centre could for instance accommodate an "eco-councillor".

In addition, the city administration could give information to industry, commerce and inhabitants on how to reduce global environmental impacts in various sectors. Such information could help and support all the urban actors that are prepared to behave in an environmentally friendly manner.

Moreover: a framework could be developed by the Town Hall for more environmentally sound production, transport and consumption in the private sector. The city's administration should address the parties involved and indicate available ways and means to reduce the global impacts of local activities.

Cities could then start a dialogue with industry, for instance with the car, timber and packing industries (as well as citizens) stressing the necessity of recognising their responsibilities in global environmental issues. The 5 P's principle could be practised: the Potential Polluter Pays for Pollution Prevention. Chambers of commerce can plan an active role in propagating these principles.

When the public and private sector is mobilised in the above mentioned ways, a new "ecological" set of demands will be created.

It is expected that cities will play a stronger political and economic role in the near future. Now that national frontiers in Europe begin to lose their importance cities will compete more, but will also be more willing to co-operate.

The role of the Commission of the European Communities with respect to cities and the global environment could be to assist in the exchange of local experiences that can serve as examples of good practice, thus widening its applicabilities. In addition the Commission could help to create a number of pilot projects. Research and accumulation of knowledge (and making this knowledge accessible) is of equal importance.

The European Foundation for the Improvement of Living and Working Conditions could help by providing information on innovative approaches. And the Foundation could play a particular role - considering its focus on the social dimensions of the European environment - in indicating means and tools for citizens and their organisations that enable participation in the development of sustainable urban environments in which people can express (in life and work) their personal care for the global environment.

APPENDIX

EUROPEAN WORKSHOP

ON

CITIES AND THE GLOBAL ENVIRONMENT

The Hague, 5-7 December 1990

FINAL LIST OF PARTICIPANTS

J. G. M. ALDERS							Minister for the Environment
								The Netherlands

René VLAANDEREN						Alderman for the Environment, Quality
								of Life and Public Relations
								The Hague

Sandro GIULIANELLI						Cabinet of Mr. Carlo Ripa di Meana
								Commission of the European Communities

Jean ALEGRE							Commission of the European Communities
								Directorate-General for Employment,
								Social Affairs and Education (DG V)
								Rue de la Loi, 200
								(A 1 05/23)
								B-1049 Brussels
								Belgium
								Tel : 2-2351071
								Fax : 2-2350129/2356507

Ariel ALEXANDRE						OECD
								Urban Affairs Division
								2, rue André-Pascal
								F-75775 Paris Cedex 16
								France
								Tel : 1-45249745
								Fax : 1-45247876

Inés AYALA							Union General de Trabajadores de
								España (UGT)
								Hortaleza 88
								E-28004 Madrid
								Spain
								Tel : 1634-1-5897600
								Fax : 1634-1-5897603

Michael J. BANNON						The Service Industries' Research
								Centre
								Department of Regional and Urban
								Planning
								University College Dublin
								Richview, Clonskeagh
								Dublin 14
								Ireland
								Tel : 1-693244, ext. 2718
								Fax : 1-837009

Daniel BEGUIN   Agence Nationale pour la Récupération
                           et l'Elimination des Déchets (ANRED)
                           B.P. 406
                           F-49004 Angers Cedex
                           France
                           Tel : 41204132
                           Fax : 41872350

Edith BRICKWELL   Ministry for Urban Development and
                           Environmental Protection
                           Lindenstraße 20-25
                           D-1000 Berlin West 61
                           Germany
                           Tel : 30-25860
                           Fax : 30-25862211

Enrique CALDERON   ETSI Caminos
                           Ciudad Universitaria
                           E-28040 Madrid
                           Spain
                           Tel : 1-3366000(switch);
                                 1-3366694/5(direct)
                           Fax : 1-5492289

Michael COOKE   Environmental Health Department
                           Leicester City Council
                           New Walk Centre
                           Welford Place
                           Leicester LE1 6ZG
                           U.K.
                           Tel : 553-526303
                           Fax : 553-548954

Tjeerd DEELSTRA   International Institute for the Urban
                           Environment
                           Nickersteeg 5
                           NL-2611 EK Delft
                           The Netherlands
                           Tel : 15-623279
                           Fax : 15-624873

Sten ENGELSTOFT   Commission of the European Communities
                           Directorate-General for Science,
                           Research and Development (DG XII -
                           FAST)
                           Rue de la Loi, 200
                           (ARTS-LUX 3/28)
                           B-1049 Brussels
                           Belgium
                           Tel : 2-2350658
                           Fax : 2-2364299

Bjørn ERIKSON   Norwegian Confederation of Trade
                                 Unions
                                 Youngsgata 11
                                 N-0181 Oslo 1
                                 Norway
                                 Tel : 2-401723
                                 Fax : 2-401743/401100

Ricardo GARCIA HERRERA   Gobierno Vasco
                                 Duque de Wellington, 2
                                 E-01011 Vitoria-Gasteiz
                                 Spain
                                 Tel : 45-246000
                                 Fax : 45-225358

J. GOEDMAN   National Physical Planning Agency
                                 Ministry of Housing, Physical Planning
                                 and Environment
                                 Postbus 450
                                 NL-2060 MB Leidschendam
                                 The Netherlands
                                 Tel : 70-3174717
                                 Fax : 70-3174722

Jake GOMILNY   European Local Environmental
                                 Information Clearinghouse (ELEICh)
                                 393 Corn Exchange Building
                                 Manchester M4 3HN
                                 U.K.
                                 Tel : 61-8391589
                                 Fax : 61-8344674

Jupp HAMACHER   Commission of the European Communities
                                 Directorate-General for Energy (DG
                                 XVII)
                                 Rue de la Loi, 200
                                 (TERV 03/22)
                                 B-1049 Brussels
                                 Belgium
                                 Tel : 2-2352555
                                 Fax : 2-2350150

Richard HARTLEY   Council of Europe
                                 B.P. 431 R6
                                 F-67006 Strasbourg Cedex
                                 France
                                 Tel : 88412241
                                 Fax : 88412784

Richard HILTON	Department of the Environment Room C14/01 2 Marsham Street London SW1P 3EB United Kingdom Tel : 71-2766708 Fax : 71-2763936
Michael R. JACOBSEN	Aarhus Municipality Orla Lehmanns Allé 3 Postbox 539 DK-8100 Aarhus C Denmark Tel : 86132000, ext. 2340 Fax : 86132619
Wigand KAHL	Stadtdirektor Landeshauptstadt München Umweltschutzreferat Bayerstraße 28 a D-8000 Munich 2 Federal Republic of Germany Tel : 89-2336000 Fax : 89-2337724
Willem J. KAKEBEEKE	Hoofd afdeling Internationale Milieuzaken Directoraat-generaal voor de Milieuhygiëne Ministerie van V.R.O.M. Postbus 450 NL-2060 MB Leidschendam The Netherlands Tel : 70-3174174 Fax : 70-3174722
Serge KEMPENEERS	Institut Bruxellois pour la Gestion de l'Environnement Avenue Louise 149, Bte. 1B B-1050 Brussels Belgium Tel : 2-5389922 Fax : 2-5382033
Henny KETELAAR	International Institute for the Urban Environment Nickersteeg 5 NL-2611 EK Delft The Netherlands Tel : 15-623279 Fax : 15-624873

Kawmars KHOSH-CHASHM   World Health Organisation
                              E.M.R.O.
                              P.O.Box 1517
                              21511 Alexandria
                              Egypt
                              Tel: 3-4830090/4820223/
                                   4820224 (home:857423)
                              Fax: 3-4838916

Claude LAMURE   Institut National de Recherche sur les
                              Transport et leur Sécurité (INRETS)
                              109, Avenue Salvador Allende
                              Case 24
                              F-69675 Bron Cédex
                              France
                              Tel : 72362315
                              Fax : 72378424

Bernard LE MARCHAND   CLE
                              76, Avenue V. Gilsoul
                              B-1200 Brussels
                              Belgium
                              Tel : 2-7715871
                              Fax : 2-7627506

Kai LEMBERG   Sundvænget 9
                              DK-2900 Hellerup
                              Denmark
                              Tel : 31620032

Heather MACDONALD   World Health Organisation
                              Scherfigsvej 8
                              DK-2100 Copenhagen
                              Denmark
                              Tel : 31290111
                              Fax : 31292940

Ann McGUINNESS   Department of the Environment
                              Custom House
                              Dublin 1
                              Ireland
                              Tel : 1-728153
                              Fax : 1-742710

Aughi MARKOPOULOU   Municipality of Athens
                              10, Praxitoulos St.
                              GR-10561 Athens
                              Greece
                              Tel : 1-3236380/3248508/7227957

Jorge MARTINEZ CHAPA	Head of Service of Urban Studies ITUR Ministerio de Obras Públicas y Urbanismo Paseo de la Castellana, 67 E-28071 Madrid Spain Tel : 1-5535600, ext. 2724 Fax : 1-5538595
Voula MEGA	European Foundation for the Improvement of Living and Working Conditions Loughlinstown House Shankill, Co. Dublin Ireland Tel : 1-826888 Fax : 1-826456
Jacqueline MILLER	Institut de Sociologie Université Libre de Bruxelles Avenue Jeanne 44 B-1050 Brussels Belgium Tel : 2-6503183 Fax : 2-6503521
Michel MILLER	European Trades Union Congress Rue Montagne aux Herbes Potagères, 37 B-1000 Brussels Belgium Tel : 2-2183100 Fax : 2-2183566
David MORRIS	Institute for Local Self-Reliance 2425, 18th Street NW Washington DC 20009 U.S.A. Tel : 202-232-4108 Fax : 202-332-0463
or	220, West King Street Saint Paul Minnesota 55107 U.S.A. Tel : 612-228-1875 Fax : 612-292-9007

Neil MORTON	Director of Environmental Health and Consumer Affairs Rotherham Metropolitan Borough Council Elm Bank House 73 Alma Road Rotherham South Yorkshire S60 2BU United Kingdom Tel : 709-823100 Fax : 709-823183
Peter NIJKAMP	Faculty of Economics and Econometrics Free University of Amsterdam De Boelelaan 1105 NL-1081 HV Amsterdam The Netherlands Tel : 20-5484930 Fax : 20-462645
Bríd NOLAN	European Foundation for the Improvement of Living and Working Conditions Loughlinstown House Shankill, Co. Dublin Ireland Tel : 1-826888 Fax : 1-826456
C. J. NYQVIST	Streekvervoer Nederland Kantoorgebouw "Janssoenborch" Godebaldkwartier 355 Postbus 19222 NL-3501 DE Utrecht The Netherlands Tel : 30-306800 Fax : 30-341449
Wendy O'CONGHAILE	European Foundation for the Improvement of Living and Working Conditions Loughlinstown House Shankill, Co. Dublin Ireland Tel : 1-826888 Fax : 1-826456
Jørn PEDERSEN	European Foundation for the Improvement of Living and Working Conditions Loughlinstown House Shankill, Co. Dublin Ireland Tel : 1-826888 Fax : 1-826456

A. H. PERRELS   Faculty of Economics and Econometrics
                                 Free University of Amsterdam
                                 De Boelelaan 1105
                                 NL-1081 HV Amsterdam
                                 The Netherlands
                                 Tel : 20-5484930
                                 Fax : 20-462645

Stephen PLOWDEN   69 Albert Street
                                 London NW1 7LX
                                 United Kingdom
                                 Tel : 71-3873944

Yannis POLYZOS   School of Architecture
                                 Department of Planning
                                 National Technical University of
                                  Athens
                                 42, Patission Street
                                 GR-10682 Athens
                                 Greece
                                 Tel : 1-3613810/3691290
                                 Fax : 1-3619288

D. W. PURCHON   Director of Health and Consumer
                                 Services
                                 Town Hall Chambers
                                 1 Barkers Pool
                                 Sheffield S1 1EM
                                 U.K.
                                 Tel : 742-734614
                                 Fax : 742-736464

Clive PURKISS   Director
                                 European Foundation for the
                                 Improvement of Living and
                                 Working Conditions
                                 Loughlinstown House
                                 Shankill, Co. Dublin
                                 Ireland
                                 Tel : 1-826888
                                 Fax : 1-826456

José QUINTERO GARCIA   Izquierda Unida
                                 Ayuntamiento de Huelva
                                 Avda. Adoratrices
                                 Edificio Luis Cernuda 5º-A
                                 E-21004 Huelva
                                 Spain
                                 Tel : 55-249744/210138
                                 Fax : 55-250588

René SCHOONBRODT	Commission of the European Communities Directorate-General for the Environment, Nuclear Safety and Civil Protection (DG XI) Rue de la Loi, 200 (BREY 10/200) B-1040 Brussels Belgium Tel : 2-2358716 Fax : 2-2350144
Laurent SELLES	Commission of the European Communities Directorate-General for Information Market and Innovation (DG XIII) DRIVE Programme Rue de Trèves, 61 (TR61 06/5) B-1040 Brussels Belgium Tel : 2-2363469 Fax : 2-2362391
Carmen SERRANO GOMEZ	Secretaria General Medio Ambiente Ministerio de Obras Públicas y Urbanismo Paseo de la Castellana 67, 4ª Planta E-28071 Madrid Spain Tel : 1-2535600, ext. 3118 Fax : 1-5537811
Jack SHORT	European Conference of Ministers of Transport 19, rue de Franqueville F-75775 Paris Cedex 16 France Tel : 1-45249721 Fax : 1-45249742
Juraj SILVAN	URBION - The State Institute for Town and Country Planning Hanulova Str. No. 9/A 844-40 Bratislava CSFR Tel : 7-383967/369924 Fax : 7-382683

Sybren SINGELSMA   International Union of Local
                                 Authorities
                                P.O.Box 90646
                                NL-2509 LP The Hague
                                The Netherlands
                                Tel : 70-3244032
                                Fax : 70-3246916

Nédialka SOUGAREVA   Ministère de l'environnement -
                                Délégation à la qualité de la vie
                                14, Boulevard du Général Leclerc
                                F-92534 Neuilly sur Seine Cedex
                                France
                                Tel : 1-47581212, ext. 2491
                                Fax : 1-47572605

Mr. SPREEKMEESTER   Directorate-General for Housing
                                Ministry of Housing, Physical Planning
                                and Environment
                                Postbus 450
                                NL-2060 MB Leidschendam
                                The Netherlands
                                Tel : 70-3174717
                                Fax : 70-3174722

H. W. STRUBEN   International Society of City and
                                Regional Planners
                                Mauritskade 23
                                NL-2514 HD The Hague
                                The Netherlands
                                Tel : 70-3462664
                                Fax : 70-3617909

Karola TASCHNER   BEE
                                Maison européenne de l'environnement
                                20, rue de Luxembourg
                                B-1040 Brussels
                                Belgium
                                Tel : 2-5141432
                                Fax : 2-5140937

Eric VERBORGH   Deputy Director
                                European Foundation for the
                                Improvement of Living and
                                Working Conditions
                                Loughlinstown House
                                Shankill, Co. Dublin
                                Ireland
                                Tel : 1-826888
                                Fax : 1-826456

Harry WALS   Director
                              Department of Parks and
                              Environmental Education
                              Huygenspark 39
                              NL-2515 BA The Hague
                              The Netherlands
                              Tel : 70-3889311
                              Fax : 70-3841375

Jon WIERINGA   Royal Netherlands Meteorological
                              Institute (KNMI)
                              P.O.Box 201
                              NL-3730 AE De Bilt
                              The Netherlands
                              Tel : 30-206465
                              Fax : 30-210407

Hugh WILLIAMS   ECOTEC Research and Consulting Ltd.
                              28-34 Albert Street
                              Birmingham B4 7UD
                              United Kingdom
                              Tel : 21-6161010
                              Fax : 21-6161099

Wolfgang ZUCKERMANN   EcoPlan International
                              10, rue Joseph Bara
                              F-75006 Paris
                              France
                              Tel : 1-43261323
                              Fax : 1-43260746

SECRETARIAT

Mariette EDELMAN   Department of Parks and
                              Environmental Education
                              Huygenspark 39
                              NL-2515 BA The Hague
                              The Netherlands
                              Tel : 70-3889335
                              Fax : 70-3809656

Hanne HANSEN   European Foundation for the
                                Improvement of Living and
                                Working Conditions
                                Loughlinstown House
                                Shankill, Co. Dublin
                                Ireland
                                Tel : 1-826888
                                Fax : 1-826456

Ann McDONALD   European Foundation for the
                                Improvement of Living and
                                Working Conditions
                                Loughlinstown House
                                Shankill, Co. Dublin
                                Ireland
                                Tel : 1-826888
                                Fax : 1-826456

European Communities — Commission

Cities and the Global Environment:
Proceedings of a European Workshop, The Hague 5-7 December 1990

Luxembourg: Office of Official Publications of the European Communities

1992 – 283p. – 21.0 x 29.7cm

ISBN 92-826-3247-4

Price (excluding VAT) in Luxembourg: ECU 21.25

Venta y suscripciones • Salg og abonnement • Verkauf und Abonnement • Πωλήσεις και συνδρομές • Sales and subscriptions • Vente et abonnements • Vendita e abbonamenti • Verkoop en abonnementen • Venda e assinaturas

BELGIQUE / BELGIË

**Moniteur belge /
Belgisch Staatsblad**
Rue de Louvain 42 / Leuvenseweg 42
1000 Bruxelles / 1000 Brussel
Tél. (02) 512 00 26
Fax 511 01 84
CCP / Postrekening 000-2005502-27

Autres distributeurs /
Overige verkooppunten

**Librairie européenne/
Europese Boekhandel**
Avenue Albert Jonnart 50 /
Albert Jonnartlaan 50
1200 Bruxelles / 1200 Brussel
Tél. (02) 734 02 81
Fax 735 08 60

Jean De Lannoy
Avenue du Roi 202 /Koningslaan 202
1060 Bruxelles / 1060 Brussel
Tél. (02) 538 51 69
Télex 63220 UNBOOK B
Fax (02) 538 08 41

CREDOC
Rue de la Montagne 34 / Bergstraat 34
Bte 11 / Bus 11
1000 Bruxelles / 1000 Brussel

DANMARK

**J. H. Schultz Information A/S
EF-Publikationer**
Ottiliavej 18
2500 Valby
Tlf. 36 44 22 66
Fax 36 44 01 41
Girokonto 6 00 08 86

BR DEUTSCHLAND

Bundesanzeiger Verlag
Breite Straße
Postfach 10 80 06
5000 Köln 1
Tel. (02 21) 20 29-0
Telex ANZEIGER BONN 8 882 595
Fax 20 29 278

GREECE/ΕΛΛΑΔΑ

G.C. Eleftheroudakis SA
International Bookstore
Nikis Street 4
10563 Athens
Tel. (01) 322 63 23
Telex 219410 ELEF
Fax 323 98 21

ESPAÑA

Boletín Oficial del Estado
Trafalgar, 27
28010 Madrid
Tel. (91) 44 82 135

Mundi-Prensa Libros, S.A.
Castelló, 37
28001 Madrid
Tel. (91) 431 33 99 (Libros)
     431 32 22 (Suscripciones)
     435 36 37 (Dirección)
Télex 49370-MPLI-E
Fax (91) 575 39 98

Sucursal:

Librería Internacional AEDOS
Consejo de Ciento, 391
08009 Barcelona
Tel. (93) 301 86 15
Fax (93) 317 01 41

**Llibreria de la Generalitat
de Catalunya**
Rambla dels Estudis, 118 (Palau Moja)
08002 Barcelona
Tel. (93) 302 68 35
     302 64 62
Fax (93) 302 12 99

FRANCE

**Journal officiel
Service des publications
des Communautés européennes**
26, rue Desaix
75727 Paris Cedex 15
Tél. (1) 40 58 75 00
Fax (1) 40 58 75 74

IRELAND

Government Supplies Agency
4-5 Harcourt Road
Dublin 2
Tel. (1) 61 31 11
Fax (1) 78 06 45

ITALIA

Licosa Spa
Via Duca di Calabria, 1/1
Casella postale 552
50125 Firenze
Tel. (055) 64 54 15
Fax 64 12 57
Telex 570466 LICOSA I
CCP 343 509

GRAND-DUCHÉ DE LUXEMBOURG

Messageries Paul Kraus
11, rue Christophe Plantin
2339 Luxembourg
Tél. 499 88 88
Télex 2515
Fax 499 88 84 44
CCP 49242-63

NEDERLAND

SDU Overheidsinformatie
Externe Fondsen
Postbus 20014
2500 EA 's-Gravenhage
Tel. (070) 37 89 911
Fax (070) 34 75 778

PORTUGAL

Imprensa Nacional
Casa da Moeda, EP
Rua D. Francisco Manuel de Melo, 5
1092 Lisboa Codex
Tel. (01) 69 34 14

**Distribuidora de Livros
Bertrand, Ld.ª**
Grupo Bertrand, SA
Rua das Terras dos Vales, 4-A
Apartado 37
2700 Amadora Codex
Tel. (01) 49 59 050
Telex 15798 BERDIS
Fax 49 60 255

UNITED KINGDOM

HMSO Books (PC 16)
HMSO Publications Centre
51 Nine Elms Lane
London SW8 5DR
Tel. (071) 873 2000
Fax GP3 873 8463
Telex 29 71 138

ÖSTERREICH

**Manz'sche Verlags-
und Universitätsbuchhandlung**
Kohlmarkt 16
1014 Wien
Tel. (0222) 531 61-0
Telex 11 25 00 BOX A
Fax (0222) 531 61-39

SUOMI

Akateeminen Kirjakauppa
Keskuskatu 1
PO Box 128
00101 Helsinki
Tel. (0) 121 41
Fax (0) 121 44 41

NORGE

Narvesen information center
Bertrand Narvesens vei 2
PO Box 6125 Etterstad
0602 Oslo 6
Tel. (2) 57 33 00
Telex 79668 NIC N
Fax (2) 68 19 01

SVERIGE

BTJ
Box 200
22100 Lund
Tel. (046) 18 00 00
Fax (046) 18 01 25

SCHWEIZ / SUISSE / SVIZZERA

OSEC
Stampfenbachstraße 85
8035 Zürich
Tel. (01) 365 54 49
Fax (01) 365 54 11

CESKOSLOVENSKO

NIS
Havelkova 22
13000 Praha 3
Tel. (02) 235 84 46
Fax 42-2-264775

MAGYARORSZÁG

Euro-Info-Service
Budapest I. Kir.
Attila út 93
1012 Budapest
Tel. (1) 56 82 11
Telex (22) 4717 AGINF H-61
Fax (1) 17 59 031

POLSKA

Business Foundation
ul. Krucza 38/42
00-512 Warszawa
Tel. (22) 21 99 93, 628-28-82
International Fax&Phone
    (0-39) 12-00-77

JUGOSLAVIJA

Privredni Vjesnik
Bulevar Lenjina 171/XIV
11070 Beograd
Tel. (11) 123 23 40

CYPRUS

Cyprus Chamber of Commerce and Industry
Chamber Building
38 Grivas Dhigenis Ave
3 Deligiorgis Street
PO Box 1455
Nicosia
Tel. (2) 449500/462312
Fax (2) 458630

TÜRKIYE

**Pres Gazete Kitap Dergi
Pazarlama Dağıtım Ticaret ve sanayi
AŞ**
Narlibahçe Sokak N. 15
Istanbul-Cağaloğlu
Tel. (1) 520 92 96 - 528 55 66
Fax 520 64 57
Telex 23822 DSVO-TR

CANADA

Renouf Publishing Co. Ltd
Mail orders — Head Office:
1294 Algoma Road
Ottawa, Ontario K1B 3W8
Tel. (613) 741 43 33
Fax (613) 741 54 39
Telex 0534783

Ottawa Store:
61 Sparks Street
Tel. (613) 238 89 85

Toronto Store:
211 Yonge Street
Tel. (416) 363 31 71

UNITED STATES OF AMERICA

UNIPUB
4611-F Assembly Drive
Lanham, MD 20706-4391
Tel. Toll Free (800) 274 4888
Fax (301) 459 0056

AUSTRALIA

Hunter Publications
58A Gipps Street
Collingwood
Victoria 3066

JAPAN

Kinokuniya Company Ltd
17-7 Shinjuku 3-Chome
Shinjuku-ku
Tokyo 160-91
Tel. (03) 3439-0121

Journal Department
PO Box 55 Chitose
Tokyo 156
Tel. (03) 3439-0124

AUTRES PAYS
OTHER COUNTRIES
ANDERE LÄNDER

**Office des publications officielles
des Communautés européennes**
2, rue Mercier
2985 Luxembourg
Tél. 49 92 81
Télex PUBOF LU 1324 b
Fax 48 85 73/48 68 17
CC bancaire BIL 8-109/6003/700